Getting to the Point.

In a dozen pairs of shoes

Brian R. Stark

Bloomington, IN   authorHOUSE™   Milton Keynes, UK

AuthorHouse™
1663 Liberty Drive, Suite 200
Bloomington, IN 47403
www.authorhouse.com
Phone: 1-800-839-8640

AuthorHouse™ UK Ltd.
500 Avebury Boulevard
Central Milton Keynes, MK9 2BE
www.authorhouse.co.uk
Phone: 08001974150

First published by AuthorHouse 5/18/2006

ISBN: 1-4259-2939-7 (e)
ISBN: 1-4259-2938-9 (sc)

Printed in the United States of America
Bloomington, Indiana

This book is printed on acid-free paper.

Table of Contents

To Coach Rick Weinheimer,
of the Columbus North Cross-Country program,
who taught me how to run with a dream.

And to Mike Nickels, of Camp Palawopec,
who showed me what happens when you do.

Prologue

No more land, no more running. Bowing in the surf to the small audience of friends and family standing on the beach applauding me, a bittersweet feeling swept over me. I suppose the ocean was cold as I stood there smiling, soaking wet. I hadn't happened to notice the temperature of the saltwater when I dived into it and came up with my arms in the air. Soon there would be cake, champagne, and photographs. The next day I would fly across the country at 500 miles an hour. Barreling over each step I had worked so hard to earn, the aircraft would consume entire states not in days or weeks, but in minutes. Until then, I was content to stand in the surf at this frothy finish line that marked the end of a very long journey.

Introduction

One doesn't usually wake up in the morning and decide to run across a continent. Usually there is a reason, albeit not a very good one. You could say that college got me into this mess. While struggling with grades, I decided I needed an incentive to graduate. Of all the things to choose to look forward to upon graduation, mine would be to hike the entire 2100-mile Appalachian Trail from Maine to Georgia. I found a tall color map of the Trail and put it on the wall of my dorm room each year in college. Whenever I did poorly on a test, or I had eight hours left to start and finish a term paper, I would look at that map of the AT and remember my incentive.

Classes were hard for me. Only after retaking the SAT and applying a second time was I finally accepted into Hanover College in southern Indiana. Four years later, I not only graduated, but was chosen to give the commencement speech. A week later I began my five-month "stroll" of the Appalachians.

The AT showed me a wonderful time. During the southbound hike, I won a contest by eating an entire half-gallon of chocolate marshmallow ice cream in 14 minutes flat. Afterwards, I couldn't feel my gums for three days.

I stepped on a Rattlesnake in Pennsylvania.

I met a man in Massachusetts who chose to hike nude every Tuesday. Unfortunately for me, it was Tuesday when I met him.

I was pulled over by a New York State Trooper who asked, "Where's your car?"

"I don't have a car," I said.

"Well, where's their car," pointing to my hiking friends.

"They don't have a car either," I replied. He grudgingly let me go, unaware of our 14-state walk.

I saw five bears. I got to meet folk singers Arlo Guthrie and Pete Seeger.

I carried a small banjo tied to my backpack for 1,000 miles, until I broke it in two when I fell out of a tree.

I hiked 50 miles in one day in Virginia.

My pack weight went from 55 pounds down to 18, as I learned to make do with less.

Living in "the long green tunnel" for almost half a year, with only one goal each morning - to walk, was an addictive lifestyle.

Every week or two I would venture back into civilization and eat five plates of food at a buffet bar, followed by a pint of Ben & Jerry's Ice Cream, then some king-sized candy and a six-pack of soft drinks back at the motel. Yes, that was the life. Despite my in-town splurging and because of my 18- to 20-mile days, I still lost 12 pounds during the hike. As long as I arrived at my determined destination each day, I felt satisfied.

It's no wonder, then, that two years later I had thoughts of returning to that lifestyle. I considered the AT again, northbound perhaps, but realized that the world is too big to limit yourself to one path when there are thousands to choose from. Having grown up in Indiana, I had a good perspective of the midwest. My family had vacationed in Florida and I had hiked in all of our neighboring states. But I had not yet seen the plains, the Rocky Mountains, the deserts, or the west coast. In short, land west of the Mississippi River was foreign to me. The thought of exploring this territory on my own, under my own power, was exciting.

I knew that I wanted to start on the east coast and head west. Not only did I want to start in a familiar area, I wanted to retrace the path of the settlers as they made their arduous way across America. I would be seeing the land the way they did, observing the world through their eyes, as long as you pencil in an occasional Quickie Mart and roadside motel on the horizon.

While at Hanover, I met a couple hiking a newly designated path across the country, the American Discovery Trail (ADT), which just happens to lie right across my college's campus. That meeting had planted a seed and while planning my run, I began to research the feasibility of running cross-country on the ADT.

The American Hiking Society and *Backpacker Magazine* developed the idea for the ADT in 1989. At the time, there were three major trails in the United States: the Appalachian Trail, the Pacific Crest Trail, and the Continental Divide Trail. Although each of those three trails offered a vastly different experience from the others, they all ran north - south, along the major mountain ranges, isolated from each other. No trail existed that spanned the country from east to west, somewhat against the grain of the natural topography.

By crossing the land between the Atlantic and Pacific Oceans, the ADT was designed to connect other major trails and, upon completion, create an interstate system for pedestrians. The ADT sounded like my best bet for a grand tour of America.

There were a few problems with traveling the ADT at the time, however. First of all, the trail was not finished, so locating the path would be tricky. Second, since the trail was not completely established, maps had not yet been published, so even knowing where the trail was supposed to be became difficult. Last, very few people had heard of the ADT, so if I got lost and knocked on a door asking where the trail was, the reply would probably be, "What trail?"

Although these challenges meant that by choosing to follow the ADT, I would be on a difficult path, they also meant I would be the first to travel it by foot from one coast to the other. Also, because of these challenges, I was to be treated to a historical, scenic, and adventurous view of America.

The ADT was designed to accommodate all forms of self-travel, although there are a few places where local trail restrictions apply. Much of the ADT can be bicycled or ridden on horseback, but the one mode permitted everywhere is on foot.

To best determine where the trail should go, in 1990 a scouting team of three people was hired to drive, bike, and hike the ADT. As the team worked its way from one region to the next, they met with local trail enthusiasts who suggested existing trails they could use, and those sections ultimately became the ADT. Starting at Cape Henlopen State Park in Lewes, Delaware, the route roughly parallels Highway 50 across the country to its western terminus, in Point Reyes National Seashore, 50 miles north of San Francisco, California. Where possible, the trail uses local existing trails then scenic backroads to connect each trail section when needed.

I spent a year compiling 500 maps of the route of the ADT. I made decisions about support. Since I would be covering more ground running than hiking, I could afford to carry limited supplies, gambling that I could reach some kind of town most days for food and perhaps lodging. Still, I needed to carry basic shelter, some snacks, maps and water and I finally managed to fit everything into a 10-pound hip pack that I hoped to be able to run with.

There might also have been a subconscious reason to run: When I was in 8ᵗʰ grade, my father and brother spent a week running across Florida from the Gulf Coast to the Atlantic. They trained all winter, getting accustomed to running with fanny packs for long distances. The six-day father-and-son trek across the Sunshine State was lauded throughout my childhood as nothing short of heroic. I had always been jealous of their fame and perhaps always wished to be included when the conversation turned to running feats. So what did I end up doing? Did I pick a wider state to run across, or perhaps a region of states? No, I had to run across the entire country to outdo a performance I'd envied since junior high.

Typical transcontinental crossings employ extensive vehicle support with handlers, equipment, pre-arranged lodging, and services. All this support costs a great deal of money or sponsorship, neither of which I had. I had managed to save $10,000 since graduating from college by living in a primitive log cabin and running to work. By my estimates, I had saved enough to cover my own expenses but not those of handlers, vehicles, and extra support.

Lack of money aside, I loved the thought of crossing the continent solo. With a vehicle following you every step of the way, the temptation to quit – which I was sure I would experience – would be compounded by the temptation of simply getting into the car behind you and throwing it all in. If there is no support vehicle, the motivation to get to the next town is all it takes to keep going. With no more food than a few cheese crackers, a candy bar, and a meager water supply in my possession at any given time, the greatest incentive to keep going was the hope of finding a buffet bar in the next town.

Deciding how to be self-supported came from knowing what to expect. Prior to my run, only a handful of people had completed the ADT: the Scouting Team in 1989, and Bill and Laurie Foot, a couple who had biked and hiked the route in 1997. Another man, Reese Lukei, has traveled portions of the ADT for years.

I spoke with all of them prior to leaving home, and they gave me some much-needed specifics. I would cross at least two snow-covered mountain passes in Colorado, "which means you'll be running in snow-shoes, but you know, you have to be adaptable," Reese said in a phone interview. The most common distance to civilization is roughly 30 miles, and the longest stretches without food or water are found in Nevada along the abandoned Pony Express Route. Those distances of desolation can be several hundred miles long. I figured I could run up to 30 miles per day with the food and water that I would be carrying, but going beyond that seemed risky.

More than anything I wanted to avoid running while wearing a backpack with shoulder straps. I decided to go with an oversized 1200 cubic inch hip pack made by Mountainsmith. It was just big enough for my essential items. When all of the straps were tightened down in the proper order, there was very little swaying of the pack as I ran. To get used to the feeling of the extra ten pounds around my waist, I ran to work with my pack. I worked as a substitute teacher at the time, so I stowed my teaching clothes and breakfast in the pack and ran to and from school each day. Running was very awkward early on, but I soon found that the added weight felt natural, much as I had adapted to my backpack on the AT. On that trek, after a 20-mile day through the mountains with a 40-pound backpack, walking around the shelter at night without it I felt unbalanced and strange. All of us in the shelter would wobble around at night, walking to the spring or outhouse with a little too much sway in our stride, all the while saying, "Oh, wow, whoops."

My experiences and preparations for my run across the country had been thorough. Would they be enough? I was soon to find out.

Chapter 1
In the Beginning...

On Sunday, March 8, 1998, I took a step away from the Atlantic Ocean and began a 5,000-mile solo trail run towards California. My brother Eric spent two days driving me from my Indiana home to Cape Henlopen, Delaware to begin my effort of getting to Point Reyes following the newly designed American Discovery Trail. His shuttle service has become a tradition of dropping me off far from home just to see if I can return under my own power.

Three years earlier, as a college graduation present to me, Eric drove me for 28 hours into central Maine so I could begin my 2,100-mile hike of the Appalachian Trail. This time I had a larger crowd.

My Aunt and Uncle from Maryland joined us along with a local trail official and we were freezing in a howling wind and blowing sleet as we awaited my pre-determined start time of 10 am. Packing up in the morning at the motel, I needed to plan where I would finish my first day of running. A town would make a nice destination because it would offer food and perhaps a place to stay. The first town beyond the coast was Milton, Delaware. I decided to call the bed and breakfast in Milton. The man said there was no vacancy in town. Even though I carried a small shelter, the cold and rain convinced me to push ahead to the next known services along my route, Redden State Forest, which only offered primitive camping.

The forecast was cold rain for two days accompanied by a chilling wind. The temperature outside was 46 degrees with overcast skies, 20 mile per hour winds, and rain.

1

We arrived at the coast several minutes early but because it was so frigidly cold outside everyone waited in their warm cars with the engines running and heaters on high.

A few minutes prior to 10 a.m. I left the car for the last time and headed towards the beach. The small group walked up and over a sand dune protecting the parking lot from the wind coming off of the ocean. Passing an old war bunker and official ADT plaque marking the eastern terminus of the ADT the now unhindered wind was whipping us viscously, blowing everyone's hats off without warning. The ocean pounded the beach with five- and six-foot waves. My brother, in true older brother form, was laughing at my misery as I shivered in my new tissue-thin nylon shorts. He did say that he would leave his cell phone on during the drive home in case I wanted to give up and have him come get me. A mad flurry of shaky photographs, a toe in the water, and I was running up a dune in the cold rain of Delaware, headed for California.

This day was the first of what would be 238 days, and five of us were there to be a part of it. Even with heart-felt support, supporters can get cold, and that's probably why they got into their cars so quickly, said a hasty, "good luck," through barely cracked windows, and drove off.

Fifty yards later a television truck pulled up to me. The cameraman got out in the driving rain and asked me a few questions while filming at the same time. When he left I was totally alone. Being around friends and family supportively watching me had been a good feeling, but when they were gone, I felt the solitude all the more due to the cold, driving rain as I ran 500 miles from home and 5000 miles toward my finish line.

That feeling of isolation sunk in deeper throughout the day. What on Earth am I doing out here in the rain? Am I crazy? My hips hurt from the overloaded pack. My legs felt funny because in a fit of last-minute preparations, I hadn't run the entire previous week.

As I made my way slowly across my first of 13 states in the beginning hours of an 8-month journey, I entertained thoughts of quitting. My brother couldn't be more than a half-hour away, I thought. He could turn around and get me. Everyone would understand. It's cold out here!

But who quits on the first day? I had told all of my friends and all of my family that I was going to run across the United States of America. My hometown newspaper had written a front page article on me, and I had 12 pairs of shoes and 500 maps waiting to be shipped to selected Post Offices across the nation addressed to, "Brian Stark, Transcontinental Runner, Care of General Delivery." Trail volunteers who had spoken with me over the phone during my planning months were expecting my arrival in the coming seasons as well. I will at least get through one day and see from there, I decided.

A series of confusing back roads flanked by rural neighborhoods filled with trailer homes and flat farmland brought me to Milton, my planned overnight stop for an easy first day. Unfortunately, due to the unavailability of lodgings, Milton was now just my lunch stop after a rainy 13 miles.

I walked into the first diner I saw and stood at the door just inside waiting to be seated for a long time. I was dripping wet, disheveled, and perhaps a little scary looking, which is probably why the waitress ignored me for so long. Is this how it is going to be for eight months, I wondered? Dripping with water, smelly, and standing at a "Please Wait to be Seated" sign in a restaurant? Yes.

Finally, a server approached and asked me to sit in another room. The waitress said she'd be closing in an hour and the grill was already closed but she did agree to serve me an omelet. It wasn't really what I had in mind but at least it warmed me up some. I finished with two cups of hot chocolate for dessert and let myself out the door. I ran through the small town until I came to a large unmarked road where I went inside a gas station to ask directions.

"Where are you trying to get?" the cashier asked me, which later became a standard question that really has no good answer.

"Well, California, but right now, just out of this town." That sent a rush of chatter between the hot dog chefs and register girls.

Even after one of them straightened me out they were still telling customers walking in, "Do you see that guy over there? He is running to California!"

Though only eight more miles, the rainy afternoon seemed to stretch into forever on my way to Redden State Forest. Even more depressing was knowing all it offered was primitive camping. I had a sleeping bag and a small tent, but the last thing on my mind after 21 miles in the rain on my first day was to sleep outside on the ground in a puddle.

At 4:30 I finally turned onto a driveway at the Forest, tired and soaking wet. I knocked on a home near the entrance. It was the park manager's home, and Lloyd Simmons came to the door. I didn't know what to expect. A miracle perhaps?

Picture a wet, stray (talking) puppy looking up at you from your front step. "Excuse me," I began, "but I'm running across the United States to California. This is my first day, and I am looking for a dry place to camp out tonight. Would you happen to have a barn or a garage that I could sleep in?"

He smilingly responded, "I think we can set you up a place." He then directed me into his pick-up truck, and we drove down a long gravel road into the woods behind his home. As we entered the thick stand of pine trees and headed down the narrow dirt road into the dark forest, I started to wonder if I'd made a wise choice. The way he started talking I thought he was putting me up in a barn, which would have been fine with me, but he continued down the road past several barns until we arrived at an immense lodge, an immaculate, huge wood and stone building with many rooms and a newly remodeled kitchen. There was even a fire still going in the fireplace from a group earlier that day. I had the entire place to myself.

I sat down next to the smoldering embers admiring the immense fireplace. As the warmth seeped into my sore muscles, I was overcome with emotion from the first day and cried. I cried because I was tired. I cried because I was stressed out. But mostly, I cried because I knew, sitting in front of that glowing fire safe from the cold rain outside, that there was nothing the remaining 4,779 miles could throw at me to make me stop this trek. That's when Lloyd returned with a knock on the huge wooden door. He said he was going up to the house and wanted to invite me over for a spaghetti dinner and to see if I was on the evening news! With three bagels and two candy bars to my name, I readily agreed.

We watched the news in his living room. There I was, running down the road in the rain, entertaining thoughts of calling my brother's cell phone from the next phone booth. I was glad I stuck out the day seeing how things had turned out.

We had a perfect spaghetti dinner. We talked about my run, Lloyd and his wife, Sally, talked about his upcoming retirement and their planned move to the Chesapeake Bay area. It had been a fairy-tale ending to a challenging first day, all due to two wonderful people who took me in for the night. The weather forecast said it would be in the 60s then drop down to the 30s by mid-week.

The morning of day number two, Lloyd came by, knocking on the lodge door at 6 a.m. "There's a tornado warning for this area until noon. I'd suggest you stay here and wait for the weather to clear." It was very nice of him to allow me to wait out the storm in the lodge. I slept some more, wrote in my journal and swept and mopped the lodge floor to try and repay some of the generosity I'd been given.

Several hours later it seemed that the weather was improving, and I decided my time had come to press on. Had the Simmons not taken me in that night, I surely believe the trip would have ended at the first pay phone. During dinner that night, I was explaining to them how thankful I was for their generous hospitality and that I felt they had "saved" me.

Lloyd just smiled and said, "You need those little surprises every once in awhile, but you can't come to expect them or they won't happen." He spoke as if he had many of his own experiences from which to speak, and his words stayed with me every time I was in need of a friendly stranger and was wondering if another nice couple's lives were about to be interrupted by my knock at their door.

I was tired and sore the second day. My attitude had been refreshed at the lodge but my body was still adjusting to the act of running large miles with an overstuffed hip-pack. To train for this trip I had used what I learned from my hike of the Appalachian Trail. It is not necessary to be in peak shape at the start of such a long trip, as it is at the starting line of a race. During the race, you can punish yourself as much as you need to meet your goal. Afterwards, you can recover as long as you want. On a very long pedestrian trip, however, being in top physical shape at the start is among the least of your worries. So long as you are healthy and aptly prepared, the physical conditioning will come with time.

It is more important to start slowly in a journey like this, trying to enjoy the beginning as much as possible and getting into a routine that you realistically could see yourself doing day after day for many months. With a very long trip such as mine, I not only had to assume what my body could do over the course of a day, but also assume what it might be able to do on a repeated basis. If my body got tired during the eight-month run, it was more important to take a day or even two off to recover rather than push myself and risk injury, thus ending the trip. This has been my basic approach to running, and it proved quite successful during my transcontinental run.

The second day I finally left the security and comfort of the lodge and proceeded westward. One day down and already a great story. I tried to imagine the tales I would have before this run would be over.

Would I survive an animal attack? Would I get hurt, lost, or injured? How much national television coverage would be at the finish if I made it? Would I meet a guy named Louis who had spent time in a federal prison but now was a multi-millionaire and decided to furnish me with a support staff and a deluxe recreational vehicle? All morning I daydreamed about such things. To work out the stiffness in my back, hips, and legs, I interspersed walking segments in my running until I worked my way to Bridgeville, Delaware.

The town has the ironic slogan, "Welcome to Bridgeville. If you lived here, you'd be home now." I couldn't imagine a funnier sign to be reading on the second day of a 5,000-mile run. The first order of business was to find a place to sleep. If the chance arose for affordable lodging, I would opt for it. Otherwise, I was prepared to camp.

I checked in town for a motel to no luck. I was told there were two bed & breakfasts. The informative person in the Chamber of Commerce gave me directions to the first home. This was the first time I realized that most people do not know much about their own town.

They generally don't know how to give directions, "I can't tell you how to get there; I just go," they tell me as they laugh at their inability to name the street that is 12 yards from their house. They don't know what services they have in town either.

"A motel? I just don't know if there is one any more. There used to be one."

Lastly, the only person they know who to ask is not available, "Well, you know who you should ask is Leroy. He could tell you anything you need to know. His great-granddaddy settled this town, but he's gone to Florida for awhile. You could call him but I don't have his number, and, I'm not sure, but he might be dead."

I tried to remember the person's directions. Most people don't seem to understand that being new to their town I didn't have a clue as to the layout, landmarks, or streets they were describing. At least in a car, you usually arrive in town on a main road, near the town's services. But arriving on the ADT, you might pop out from a trail, a dirt road, or even a driveway, thereby preventing any orientation to the community. I walked ten houses down the main street and found the bed & breakfast I had been directed to. Instead of a, "Vacancy" sign in the window, I was greeted by a fading, "For Sale." I then went on to the second bed & breakfast.

I found it and the owner invited me in. This is also where my theory began that certain people will tell you the most horrific event that has happened to them within five minutes of meeting you. First, upon complimenting her on her many fine furnishings, she told me about the major fire which had started in the attic. A previous owner or perhaps a guest had left a kerosene lamp burning in the attic window, and it caught fire because it was next to a pile of dirty laundry. By the tone in her voice, it sounded as though the laundry's being dirty caused the fire rather than that the clothes were too close to the lamp. Next, she told me that she was a guardian for a grandson who would be home soon.

"He is 12 years old and last year he found his father dead. He had killed himself. And his father had found his father dead, and his father found his father dead." Then she asked, "So, would you like a room?" We settled on a price and, another first, I asked for the "Transcontinental Runner Discount." This typically came to be an additional ten percent off whatever discounts were already being offered (AAA, AARP, or Travel Clubs).

I was granted my discount and treated myself to a pizza dinner followed by a hot bath as I looked over my maps for the next day. There was a hikers' lean-to shelter 29 miles away in another state forest. I didn't expect it would be wise to try to reach it in one day, but I decided I would see how the next day went.

Chapter 2
The Rain, The Cold, and Me

The cold wind howled as I ducked behind a drainage pipe on the side of the road to put on all 13 items of clothing I had with me. I emerged from behind the drainage pipe, bundled in three layers of tissue-thin nylon, and headed west along a quiet two-lane highway. I was even more sore than the previous day. Though I had occasionally trained at home wearing my 10-pound hip pack, I hadn't experienced running with it day after day until now. By mid-day though I felt better and decided to focus on reaching the backpackers' shelter 29 miles away. The challenge and excitement of trying to reach my destination consumed me. It wasn't until near the end of the day that I realized I had completely neglected to plan for what I would need at the secluded shelter – namely, food. At my last opportunity, I stopped in a small grocery store and bought a snack bag of party mix and a banana. I added these to my earlier purchases of a candy bar and two granola bars – ah, dinner! Water wasn't even a consideration at the time.

Arriving at the shelter just before dusk, the temperature quickly plummeted. I soon realized my gross error. The shelter was a typical backpackers' retreat: a three-sided structure with a wooden sleeping platform. The fourth side was open. Even though the shelter was built with its back to the prevailing wind, a constant stiff breeze managed to billow in through the open side. My portable shelter consisted only of a thin sleeping bag and a bivy sack (a cocoon-like tent). I kept all 13 pieces of damp clothing on and crawled into my sleeping bag and cocoon. My thirst was growing exponentially, and I only had 12 ounces of water left when I should have been consuming a gallon after such a long day. I ate my party mix and candy bar and took a sip of water for dinner.

Some time in the afternoon I had crossed out of Delaware and into Maryland, finishing my first state. Though Delaware is only 45 miles wide, I was proud of myself for crossing it and already being in Maryland. If I quit or died now, at least I would know that I made it across one state. My celebratory dinner this night hardly felt like a feast. I was learning great lessons early on. Focusing on the details would be just as important as focusing on the larger goal. From now on, I would make sure I had enough food and water when I camped out.

After my snack, I arranged my pack as a pillow and was able to doze off for three hours. I awoke at 11:00 p.m. shivering, hungry, dehydrated, and nowhere near dawn. There would be no more sleep that night. The coldest night in my 26 years taught me that my untested tent-sack was so waterproof that it kept moisture in as well as out, and my clothes were now soaked with sweat. To make the situation worse, I had chosen not to carry a ground pad, and my butt was freezing from direct contact with the cold platform. (Poor planning for an Eagle Scout.) To minimize numbing from the cold floor, I systematically rolled onto different body parts, as if I were in a rotisserie set on chill. I decided that as long as I was going to be damp with sweat, I might as well use my clothing as a pad. I took off my thin nylon shorts and placed them under my hip, hoping even a micro-layer of fabric would improve insulation. Unfortunately there was no remedy for the freezing temperatures and I lay shivering throughout the night.

Nothing could take my mind off the time. I tried not to look at my watch more than twice an hour. Sometimes, when I had used every trick in the book to distract myself, I would look at my watch to find that 40 blessed minutes had gone by. At other times, what seemed like just as long had really only been a few minutes. Originally, I planned to sleep until 8 a.m., allowing for the sun to rise and the air to warm. But the longer the night went on, the colder I got and the earlier I decided to pack up. By 3:45, I flicked on my lightweight headlamp and began madly stuffing my soaked bag into my pack in the dark howling wind.

I was so desperate to run and generate warmth that I neglected to account for how much colder the full force of the wind would be once I left the shelter. By the time I had taken three steps away from the shelter I was pummeled by gale-force, icy winds. It was as if the wind was screaming, "HOW DARE YOU CHALLENGE ME FOUR HOURS BEFORE YOU HAVE THE HELP OF MY ARCH-ENEMY, THE SUN?" Spinning around, I instinctively jumped back into the shelter and numbly unzipped my pack to retreat to my sleeping bag. That's when I saw the wet sleeping bag staring back at me from inside my pack. "Go ahead," I imagined it taunting me, "Pull me out, I'm cold *and* wet now." When I began thinking about crawling back into that wet sack and shivering on the wood floor, I knew I had no choice but to keep moving.

I started running and quickly found myself surrounded by farm fields, with only one object blocking the wind- a very thirsty, extremely tired, six-foot tall man half shuffling in the dark. To lighten the mood of my painful situation, I began a loud commentary on how I was doing. I imagined a float from Macy's Thanksgiving Day Parade, sponsored by the NFL and gone horribly off course, driving slowly along side me with Jack Arute and Keith Jackson on board.

"I don't know, Keith, *I* don't think this guy has it in him."

"*Whoa, Nelly*! Did you get a look at that wind gust? Let's take another look at that, he *really* got knocked with that one!"

I continued this drama all morning until the sun rose. The wind had been blowing directly into me for four hours, and at one point I got so cold that I turned around to block the wind with my back. This felt much better, so I ran backwards for half a mile. While running backwards, I noticed the first light of sunrise coming up over the vast farmland horizon. It was truly beautiful. The sunrise was brilliant purple, red and yellow upon swirls of clouds. A photograph was needed to capture this incredible night and morning. I took out my camera and a small plastic tripod.

Because there was nothing to set the tripod on, I set it on the road. The height of the tripod was only a few inches, so I had to lie down to frame the picture. Lo and behold! While lying on the pavement, I noticed the blacktop was still warm from the day before! If I had known that during the night, I would have slept on it! I lay on the road face down for several minutes, enjoying the heat radiating up through my numb body, until a pick-up truck came around a bend out of the darkness and I had to roll out of its path.

Once I started running again, my hands got so cold I resorted to sticking them down my pants to keep them warm, even though I was already wearing two pairs of mittens and had stuffed my clenched fists into plastic bags I'd found on the side of the road. When a car would get close, I would pull my hands out for a few seconds, until I got tired of worrying what others thought and just kept them in my pants full-time.

I was shuffling down the road with my headlamp still attached to my head long past sun-up, a bandana tied bandit-style over my face, and my hands in plastic bags down my pants, when a rusted brown Chevette came up from behind and slowed down next to me.

"Do you need any help?" the driver asked with concern. I turned my head to look at him. Either he thought I shook my head "no," or he got a good look at this unexpected creature sporting three layers of clothes and two hats, with his hands down his pants, and decided to rescind his Good Samaritan offer, because he hastily drove off before I could get a word out.

I was soon within a few miles of Queenstown, Maryland. The thought of hot food consumed me. A precise breakfast order went through my head: "A 16-ounce hot chocolate, water-*no ice*- egg platter, and toast." I found a small diner in town and stuffed myself with three plates of food, jumbo home fries and an entire quart of orange juice, all while slowly thawing in a corner booth. During my meal I enjoyed eavesdropping on the locals as they commented about the record cold temperatures they were having and how they had "braved" the wind as they walked the ten feet to their cars.

Later that day at a Comfort Inn, I recovered in a hot tub, watched HBO, ordered a pizza, and chugged mugs of hot chocolate, compliments of the desk staff. Going from one extreme to another – freezing for 16 hours to the comforts of the average business traveler – seemed like a dual lifestyle, but bridging the two were my feet. They took me from one to the other and I tried to imagine what the next 235 days – and nights - would hold.

Chapter 3
Capitol Steps

The first obstacle on the ADT heading west is the Chesapeake Bay. Most people in their cars use the Chesapeake Bay Bridge to cross this obstacle of water, but there is no pedestrian lane across the bridge, so even the bridge itself has become an obstacle for trail users. In fact, pedestrians are only allowed on the bridge one day a year when it is closed to vehicles. The bridge is one of three locations on the ADT where the traveler, ironically, cannot walk. Since I wasn't lucky enough to be there on pedestrian day, I checked my notes. A taxi shuttle could be arranged to cross the bridge but I didn't feel like going to such extremes. I stood on the entrance ramp to the bridge and stuck my thumb out in front of a sign that read, "No stopping, standing, or parking." I wondered who would pull over for me in such a place. Traffic was heavy and I figured someone would eventually stop for me. It was fun trying to imagine who it would be.

From previous hitchhiking attempts to get from trail to town, I've developed a sense of patient assurance. You gain knowledge that, depending on where you are trying to hitch and what you look like, if you wait long enough, someone is bound to give you a ride. After 20 minutes, an older man in a black Datsun pick-up truck pulled over. When he heard about my mission to run across America he said, "I heartily agree with your perspective." I enjoyed his companionable affirmation during my short ride across the bridge and thanked him as I got out on the other side of the bridge.

For the next several nights I had arranged lodging with friends and relatives so I was looking forward to low-mileage days and plenty of company. I entered Annapolis city limits and ran by the Naval Academy.

My body felt better now as it was starting to adjust to the mileage. Inside the city, the ADT joins the WB&A trail, or Washington, Baltimore, and Annapolis. The WB&A was a rail road track that is now abandoned and has joined the ranks of thousands of other rail road projects whose corridors have been turned into biking and hiking trails by removing the tracks and laying down asphalt or cinders. Former First Lady Hillary Clinton named the WB&A Trail on the list of *Trails 2000*, a program intended to build new long-distance trails for urban recreation near cities. This particular section has not been worked on however, and it was only a mile of overgrown railroad bed.

Upon leaving that section, my map showed the trail turning onto Admiral Drive. My cousin, Jamie, was living on Admiral Drive but I had no idea that his apartment would come into view when I crested the next hill. Seeing his home was the first connection I had with anything I had experienced before the start of the run. Months earlier, Lydia, my girlfriend, and I had driven there in 12 hours by car from Indiana and now I was arriving from the opposite direction on foot! After hellos and a shower I borrowed some clothes while my laundry was being washed. I enjoyed eating in public in "normal" attire. While on my own, choices for dining wear boiled down to "formal"- tights, or "casual"- nylon shorts. We went to dinner where we sampled fresh seafood at a restaurant on the water.

The next day's section of trail went through Bowie, Maryland, a town that has designed a complete urban trail system for pedestrians to commute to work on trails. There are bike overpasses, landscaped sidewalks, and several city parks to pass through. At one point in the city, a section of the trail was under construction and I was standing in a neighborhood intersection trying to decide which way to go. I was in the middle of my "where-the-hell-now" meditation, which is where I just stand in place and look around, sniff the wind, and maybe stare at a map. Just then a black Fiero pulled up in front of me and parked in the middle of the intersection. The driver had a dark beard and mustache, slightly balding and sported a pair of those dark-as-night fold-up style sunglasses that all Fiero drivers are required to wear. Picture every composite police sketch you've ever seen of a suspect, "wanted for questioning" and put him in a tinted Fiero. This is what had just pulled up to me. I asked if he knew where the pedestrian trail went from that point and he just pointed down a nearby street without a word spoken. Perhaps he was in the middle of an FBI sting operation. I'll never know, but he was correct in his direction. I decided I could press on that day for Greenbelt, Maryland, which I had been told offered several hotels. To get there, I passed through the United States Agricultural

Center and Testing Fields. The area is so sensitive that the government reportedly closes the roads at 6 PM. I did not want to get locked in so I tried to keep making miles as it was nearing dusk. I exited the area and entered a small residential neighborhood. Someone must know where a nearby hotel is, I thought, so I asked the first person I saw who was walking up to his car. This turned out to be a mistake.

Upon hearing my question, the local guide pulled out a key chain of over 100 keys and started to open his car. "Wow, with that many keys, you must be a school teacher," I remarked. "Actually, it's just an obsessive compulsive disorder," he replied. This affliction became evident over the next 12 minutes as I was in a hurry to get a quick "Fiero finger point" to the nearest lodging but my new friend entered into considerable elaboration as only an obsessive compulsive person could. "Another way you could go," the sun had now set and the temperature dropping, "is up this street here and left onto this, you know, some people like to go that way but I don't like to go that way." "Uh huh," I replied quickly, "so turn right and keep going straight? OK, thanks." "Now, for eating establishments," he continued, "a lot of people go to this... T.G.I. Friday's. Now I don't care for that place but you might want to go there. To get there, you need to..." "Ok, thanks, I really need to get going." It was going to be at least four miles to this area and it was already getting dark. The best comment, and one which I still enjoy, was his final parting which he yelled with importance as I was running away, "And remember, it's not a city, it's a 'historical district'!" I made it to a Mariott well past dark where I spoiled myself for a night.

A new theory developed the next day. I call it "The Gimme Theory." Anytime I approach strangers and ask them for directions with a map or trail route in my hand, they automatically snatch it from my grasp, as if to say, "Give me that thing, you never could read maps." What they don't know until they have grabbed it from my hand is that since the ADT is so new, the only "maps" I have are brief notes to "Turn left at Jct of MD 648." One time in Maryland, I asked a phone service repairman to come out of a hole and give me directions. "Duckettown Road? Buddy, you are *hell and gone* from Duckettown Road! Let me see that thing," taking my map from me. Actually, I was right on track, Duckettown Road was only a mile further but he was thinking of the other end of Duckettown on the opposite side of town.

Another theory that I began testing is that men, by and large, will wave back to me from their vehicles and women will not. When waving to women, they seem to stare at me, as if trying to figure out if they know me or not. A passing motorist has to earn a wave from me. From inside a car, waving is not such a big deal, but when in the act of running, it alters the movement of the body and adds to fatigue when repeated thousands of times. Therefore, the effort it takes to raise my hand, shake it a little and look for a response is only going to be spent if the driver is likely to appreciate it. If a car pulls over completely to the other lane to give me room, they earn a wave. If they wave first, they get a response. However, if they just blow by me, they get nothing. Country roads are exponentially better for waving than city roads, I found.

Some waves I received are the simple one hand in the air. Other waves are more unique. Over the course of the transcontinental run, or transcon, I received every form of waving imaginable: two fingers off the wheel, one finger off the wheel, salute, thumbs up, arm out the window, the great Kansas Chief Salute, double wave from both passengers, but my favorite greeting of all has to be from motorcyclists. When passed by a large pack of motorcycles, inevitably, the leader and usually the tail-end biker will give me "fists up," which I liked to think is the secret sign of, "you're one of us, guy, keep going." Of course, my assumption could have been mistaken and really meant, "Woohoo, at the next rest stop we'll turn around and eat him."

In the Marriott elevator the next morning on my way to breakfast the man next to me said, "I see you have the same motivation as me this morning." "What's that," I asked? "To exercise." I was just wearing my work clothes. "Want to join me for an easy 5000-miler?" I wanted to ask him. Later that night I had arrangements to stay with a colleague in Washington D.C. The ADT follows the Bear Creek Bike Path, a corridor of forest that takes the traveler through Rock Creek Park and the heart of the city while concealing the urban landscape.

In order to get onto the bike path, however, the ADT uses a series of seemingly random neighborhood streets. Running down one such street, I noticed a woman whom I assumed was a prostitute getting out of a car. I normally don't make such assumptions except that it was mid-morning, she was dressed in a very skimpy and frilly outfit and was folding several dollar bills, putting them in her pocket, saying, "thank you," to the driver. Next, as I was running past her, she yelled down the street with a high-pitched air of interrogation, "Where you going with that little pack?" "California," I replied over my shoulder, without stopping. "With just that little pack?" she said louder now as I was getting further away. "Yep." "Where do you sleep," she continued. "On the ground." "Where do you eat?" "Wherever." "Well, how do you know where to go?" I had a map in my hand and just held it up saying, "Maps," with a chuckle. Just then, my map indicated that the ADT turned again on another street and turning right, she yelled, as I was now 75 yards away, "Hey! That's not the way to California!" as if there is one neighborhood side street in downtown Washington D.C. that a person would have to take to get across the nation.

Doc, my college friend and host for the night lived on Connecticut Avenue. After looking at my one-dimensional map, the plan was easy. I would run along the bike path in Rock Creek Park until I got to Connecticut Avenue then turn right and find his house. All went well until I arrived at Connecticut, perched 80 feet above me on an overpass. My options were to continue until I found an "off-ramp" that would take me up to the road on the bluff or scale the steep cliff from where I was. Never being a fan of adding unnecessary miles, I opted to scale the cliffs. Once at the top, I was instantly time-warped again into another dimension. For the last several days I had been on back roads and bike paths, running along rural areas and farms. Now, with only a 100-yard climb, I was instantly transported into the middle of the nation's capitol with stoplights, taxis, graffiti, and noise. I felt like an alien in a strange land.

Shrugging off my disorientation, I ran down Connecticut Avenue for several miles before I found my friend's home. Doc had told me on the phone that he didn't have much space but was willing to offer me a place to spend the night. When I arrived I saw that all of the windows were boarded over and a large sheet of plywood had replaced the front door. There was a note tacked to the front plywood. It said, "Brian, come around to the back of the house." I went down and found my friend. He wasn't kidding. His room, a basement bedroom in a large home, held a futon in the couch position, a computer, small desk, television, and stereo. There was no room for anything else. I found out why the doors and windows were boarded over.

A few months earlier, the family that lived upstairs had a large fire that burned much of their home. Doc's small room in the corner of the basement was the only room not affected in the fire so they agreed to let him continue to rent the room even though the house was no longer heated. That night, I slept on a smoke-damaged couch in the chilly basement living room and would have had a nice view of the city out the picture framed window if it hadn't been covered over by particle board.

I had partnered with the American Hiking Society (AHS) to raise awareness for trails during my run and since they are based near Washington, they happily agreed to meet me and try to hold a press conference when I got to town. In the meantime Doc and I toured the National Art Museum and the Air and Space Museum. That night, I met AHS staffers for dinner and another free lodging.

Monday morning there was talk that Vice President Al Gore might be at the press conference but soon after I was informed that there is a good chance no press will show up. Opting to carpool, the entire staff and I, seven of us, piled into a station wagon and drove to the Washington Monument for a photo session. Some pictures were taken of David Lillard, then president of AHS and me, with the Monument in the background. The photo op accomplished, I thanked them for their help, set off from the Monument, and two miles later, joined the C & O Canal Towpath.

Chapter 4
Canal Mule

From Georgetown to Cumberland, Maryland, the ADT follows the Chesapeake and Ohio Canal Towpath for 184.5-miles. The C&O Canal towpath is the actual footpath mule walked while pulling boats up and down the canal paralleling the Potomac River. The C&O is one of my favorite sections of the entire ADT. Inside the canal are 74 lift locks once used to raise and lower boats as they floated up and down the canal. The project was abandoned in 1924 when massive flooding wiped out the canal operation. The National Park Service has taken the canal corridor under its wing and has developed it for use by weekend bikers, hikers and equestrians. There are campgrounds with outhouses and water pumps, historical markers, and developed sites of interest. Biking the entire canal trail is a popular weekend getaway for many D.C. area trail enthusiasts. The Canal now serves as an excellent recreation trail and portions of the actual canal have been restored for summer boat rides. I found loads of interesting information in the many historical markers dotted along its path. Each marker tells something different of life on the canal.

With the Potomac River on the left and the Chesapeake and Ohio Canal on the right, the trail in Maryland is surrounded by water for 184 miles.

I learned that both the C&O Canal and the Baltimore and Annapolis (B&A) Railroad broke ground for construction on the same day. There was a grand race to see who could finish their project first and thus control the shipping industry from the Chesapeake Bay east to the Ohio River. While running along that trail, I thought back to life at that time. Did the railroad workers ever get thirsty and ask the canal workers for water? Would the canal workers ever ask to ship goods in on the completed tracks? It must have been an interesting time.

To build the canal locks, stonemasons would carve individual blocks out of the surrounding hillsides, drag them to the lock, install them in place, and then carve their initials in the face of stone. By doing so, they could prove to the lock manager that they were the ones who placed this stone and, thus, could be paid accordingly. Even 100 years later, one can still sit on the edge of the now abandoned locks and study the worn emblems of the stonemasons. Some were double "XXs," others were a series of tic-tac-toe lines. A few, and what I guessed to be the artisans of the group, were ornate triple "Ss" or even the shape of an actual padlock.

The canal company hired families to live in small lock keepers houses next to the locks. At any time of day or night, a boatman might come along and need the canal operator to open and close the lock gates for him while the boat was raised or lowered to continue on to the next section. As I ran down the towpath, I enjoyed the scenery of forest around me. I was amazed by the immense solitude, so close to the nation's capitol. And then I found out why things were so quiet.

When I planned my trip, there were two obstacles of primary consideration that had to be crossed in the right season. I wanted to get over the Rocky Mountains of Colorado after the snow had melted from the previous winter (sometimes as late as July), but needed to be over the Sierra Nevada of California before the seasonal snow began falling as early as September. Other considerations were crossing the deserts of Utah and Nevada in relatively cool seasons, and making sure that wherever I ended up during the hottest point of the year, I would be near water.

This seasonal planning enabled me to traverse the landmarks of the nation without much difficulty; however, it did cause certain inconveniences early on in the trip. To allow for an ample traveling season, I wanted to start as early in the spring as possible. March seemed the earliest date that I could afford to subject myself to outdoor temperatures. Earlier than that and I would have risked severe winter conditions for sure. There were also drawbacks to starting as early as I did. Many parks, campgrounds, and outdoor attractions remain closed until late spring. While on the C&O Canal in March, none of the water taps in the campgrounds had been turned on. Luckily, a few of the concession stands along the canal opened for the season just as I came through, offering a pleasant splurge of sugar and preservatives. Despite the limited services, I was relieved to have at least a few days of trouble-free route finding. Unless I swam the Potomac River on the left, or waded the murky canal on the right, running straight for a week on the two track gravel path would lead me to Cumberland, Maryland.

The further I ran from Georgetown, the less maintained the Canal and towpath became. One particular day, while trotting along at my comfortable six miles per hour, I read a sign that said, "Caution, towpath not maintained. Do not continue if River is high. Bikers prohibited from continuing. Use detour on River Roads." Mentioning bikers and not hikers, I decided that the sign implied that hikers were welcome to continue. The smooth layer of gravel that usually tops the path soon disappeared and I found the towpath becoming a narrow muddy trail. This was clearly not the original path used by horses and mules. Instead of a steady straight path parallel to the canal, this trail meandered through thickets and tall trees. At times the canal was over 80 yards away on another side of a ridge. Additionally, the Potomac River seemed to be edging closer and closer to the trail I was on. Finally, I found myself at water's edge staring at a sheer rock face. There was no piece of flat land on which to continue. Apparently, the river was high and I had not noticed it.

The trail must have been under the surface of the water. With everything in the world important to me for this trip attached to my body by a single plastic two-inch buckle around my waist, I dearly did not want to take a fall into the muddy green river. My camera and down sleeping bag would be hardest hit if I fell in.

I decided that there was enough of a narrow ledge to sidestep and rock-climb my way across the rock face hoping to reach the continuation of the trail beyond this immense boulder. I carefully placed each step and made sure I had a good handhold before taking the next step. At times when I had stepped onto a miniscule nub of rock that I did not think would hold my weight, I would lament, "There's no way I can go any further." Somehow, though, each time I found another nub to stand on. All the while the Potomac River was flowing swiftly, just inches below, daring me to continue. I finally came not to the end of the boulder but the beginning of a literal smooth vertical slab of rock with not so much as even a nub to hang on. Turning back, I slowly made it back to the muddy trail. If there's anything I really hate, it's retreating in defeat. I really didn't want to have to go a half-mile back to the detour sign and decided maybe there was some other way I could get around this rock. I found, behind overgrown prickly vines, an abandoned wooden log staircase. The first five steps had completely rotted away and I had to scale the decomposing creaky framework. At the top and perched over the river I found myself on the edge of an overgrown power-line swath. I ran down the swath and came into a small settlement of houses with signs warning, "NO TRESSPASSING." I entered one such yard covered in mud, sweat, and trail grime from my adventurous morning and knocked on the door. An older man came out, chuckled at my story, and kindly told me how to get back on the towpath. No detour for me, but doing so would probably have saved me over an hour.

Three days and 60 challenging miles along the canal, I arrived at the white blazes denoting the Appalachian Trail. The 2100-mile Appalachian Trail (or, "AT" as hikers call it) is headquartered in Harper's Ferry, West Virginia. The AT is co-aligned with the C&O Canal and the ADT for just two miles. More than most any other point on the route, I was looking forward to running the section of the AT I had hiked three years earlier. The double white blazes on a cement post along the trail were the first sign I saw indicating I was once again in "the long green tunnel."

I thought back to three years ago when I stood here the first time. I had only hiked half of the AT at that point, didn't have a clue as to my future, or even the rest of the southbound hike. Now, I was running east-to-west and crossing the same dirt, this time bound for California.

I stopped at Harper's Ferry, a historical town noted for being the site where John Brown, the Abolitionist, was finally captured after trying to capture the Government Arsenal in 1859. I jogged up the historic, narrow, winding stone steps to the Appalachian Trail Conference Office to revisit old memories. It was too early in the season to be meeting through-hikers (those attempting to hike the entire AT in one trip) but I signed the hikers' guest book and volunteered a few hours of time stuffing envelopes with trail information to be mailed to the ever-growing number of trail enthusiasts. Hopefully, with time, the ADT and other trails will divert some of the impact from overuse off the long-standing AT.

The staff at ATC invited me to a pizza lunch and we talked trail stories and what all the trail legends are up to these days. We talked about Wanderin' Jack, a compulsive smoker who has hiked the trail some nine times. Once, while hiking with him far from any town, Jack ran out of cigarettes. Several hours later, I watched him roll up chewing tobacco in a business card and smoke it. "It's really not too bad!" he said with a thick Boston accent. Then there is the paranoid schizophrenic whose parents support him as he tries to hike his way to normalcy. One year on the trail he claimed to be a Navy Seal and would jump out from behind trees with his stick-rifle and shout, "Navy Seal! How many miles have you hiked today?" If you weren't planning on walking at least 16 miles that day, he would "shoot" you with his stick. The year I hiked the AT he claimed to be Amish because he didn't have a stove, car or other conveniences.

After lunch, they took a picture of me for their hiker's registry and I continued down the trail. Near milepost 130 along the canal I found my first tool of the trip, a pair of vise grip pliers. One of the books I had found about transconing was by James Shapiro, titled, "Meditations from the Breakdown Lane." In his book, Shapiro refers to finding hundreds of tools on the side of the road but not having any use for them, leaving them where they were. I love tools and decided while reading his book that if I ever found anything of interest or use during my run, I would carry it until it served its purpose. Just past mile 140 on the canal I arrived at the town of Little Orleans. There are two buildings in downtown Little Orleans: a garage and a tavern. There is a tradition in the tavern that anyone who wants to plan for their financial future can sign a dollar bill and tack it up on the ceiling of the bar. That way, if you ever go broke, you can always return to get your dollar. The owner, appropriately named "Bill", has hundreds of bills up on the ceiling; mostly one-dollar bills but there are also fives, tens and a few twenties. He says that people have left $100 bills but that he keeps those in his "safe." I was glad to get to the tavern by dusk as it was getting cold at night again and I didn't want to camp in a closed campground without any drinking water. After a country fried steak dinner, I inquired about a sign I had seen posted outside, "Apartment for rent." I hoped that I could rent it for just one night. Bill said that the owner was a friend of his and that he would call for me.

Soon I learned that yes, I could rent it and the owner was willing to come pick me up and take me there, as it was six miles away. Upon arriving, I saw that the rental was the upstairs of a home and he was already renting to a family on the first floor. We climbed the outside staircase and walked into what I knew immediately was a mistake. It sure beat a cold, wooden, outdoor platform in Delaware but to pay for such accommodations was sickening. "Ok, here's your bedroom (four beds with piles of sheets on them). Over there's the kitchen (as if I have anything to cook). The bathroom is over there (an empty bedroom that had been amateurishly converted into a bathroom with a plastic shower stall, dilapidated sink unit, a toilet built on a pedestal to solve a plumbing miscalculation, and exposed plastic piping everywhere. "Alright, that'll be $40."

I said, "How about the heat, it's pretty cold in here,". "Oh, right." He tried to light the gas heater to no success, then yelled out the window to a tennant down below to turn on a gas line. A voice came from below, "It's already on." "Well, it shouldn't get too cold tonight," he said, "You'll be alright. Let's make it $35." "No heat?" I said. "That's why I came here! How about $20." He agreed and as he was leaving I asked, "Now, you can pick me up in the morning right?" "NO! I got to be at work at 4 in the morning. Good night." I was on my own.

But things have a way of working themselves out because the next morning I got a windy ride into town in the back of a pick-up truck.

The last great site on the canal was the Paw Paw tunnel. Built between 1836 and 1850, up to 3000 workers dug the 3,118-foot long tunnel with black gunpowder and lined the finished product with six layers of brick. One great story about life on the canal involves this tunnel.

In the late 19th century, two boats came from opposite directions and met in the middle of the tunnel. The tunnel had only been designed to be wide enough for one boat at a time. This meant that if two boats met inside the tunnel, one of the boatmen had to be kind enough to back up a quarter-mile to let the other boat pass. On this particular occasion, neither boatman offered to back up and they sat in the tunnel for three days. It was customary for the entire boatman's family to live on the boat with him and help him. The feud was holding up other traffic and the man in charge of the tunnel finally had enough and built a fire on the towpath inside the tunnel and smoked the boatmen out. I stood in the middle of the tunnel and tried to imagine each boatmen, having sat on his boat for three days in the cold, dark, and damp tunnel, with his wife and kids, choking on smoke and wondering if he could wait longer than the other boatman to give in. It must have been quite a sight. In their own way, those two men were as stubborn about backing down from a challenge as I often was on my present day adventure – but at least no one was trying to smoke me out, yet!

Chapter 5
Strange Food, Stranger Lodging

I had completed 314.8 miles in 17 days averaging 18.5 miles per day including days off. The beginning had been just about the pace I had imagined. I prepared to cross into West Virginia, my third state. The only thing in my way was the Potomac River. Crossing it meant I would have to pay a toll to the nation's only privately operated toll bridge, built in 1937.

West Virginia offers tunnels, trestles, and thought-provoking road signs.

When you approach the bridge, a toll master shoves a broom handle nailed to a pork and beans can out a toll booth window, where you are expected to deposit 50 cents to cross. I was looking forward to the encounter but was told earlier that since the bridge was a low water bridge, it was actually underwater the day before I arrived. With no other way to cross the river, I decided to check things out for myself. Luckily that morning, the river had receded six inches and I was able to cross, practically jogging on water.

I had been told by other travelers in West Virginia to expect to get lost a lot while in the state. The roads seem to have no rhyme or reason, as I quickly confirmed. I knew that camping would be inevitable in the next few days as I would be crossing the Dolly Sods Wilderness, a huge mountain range in the Monongahela National Forest. I had been hiking in the Dolly Sods nine years earlier and knew there to be neither shelter nor houses in the Forest. I decided to try and find some foam material to help me stay warm at night while camping. I found a carpet warehouse in my first town of Green Spring, West Virginia. They offered me a piece of carpet foam, which they graciously custom cut to my body shape as I lay on the warehouse floor. West Virginia hospitality! Despite the additional weight of the foam, I knew that the weight would be worth it as I would have more restful sleeping while on the mountain.

My map said to take Route 19 into Fort Ashby, West Virginia. I stopped at a house and asked a woman if she could direct me to the road. "I've never heard of 19," came the reply. Undeterred, I made my own way into Fort Ashby and passed a fort built under the command of George Washington, one of the few still standing.

I had a late lunch buffet at the only restaurant in town. While asking directions for the correct way out of town, the staff caught wind of my trip. The owner's daughter came over and got my autograph. The cook showed me where to go, after a debate between staff with comments such as, "Oh! I know where they're taking him! They're taking him up by ol' Johnson's place where we had that picnic last year. Yeah, that way is hard to follow." "No, he's not going that way! He needs to go up over the water treatment plant and get on that road. That's where they're taking him." It became routine that directions referenced "they" as the source, as if there was some great omniscient power directing my course like master puppeteers. In the meantime, the waitress made me a complimentary club sandwich and put it in a large carryout foam container, which was nearly equal in size to my hip pack. I wore the pack and carried the sandwich as I ran to the edge of a water treatment plant. The additional insulation from my foam pad kept me dry and comfortable through the chilly night and I ate my toasted frost-covered sandwich as a late night snack.

Having learned hard lessons about leaving a sleeping bag in frigid temperatures, I forced myself to stay in my bag until 7 AM, when the sun finally burned the thick frost off of my bag. Finally, at 7:30, I quickly packed up my things as workers pulling into the parking lot gave me curious glances as I lay behind their Employee of the Month parking space. A few of them – with puzzled looks on their faces – stood and watched me crawl out of my sleeping bag buried in the tall weeds and beat a hasty exit.

A morning just isn't right in West Virginia if you don't get lost right off the bat. I stopped in a food store to ask directions and learned two things from the owner. First, I was completely off course. Second, he was the father of ten sons and five daughters. We chatted while I ate an endless array of never-go-bad breakfast foods as he described a scenic alternate route that would take me into Keyser. I made it into town where the local librarian responded to my question about lodging in the area.

"Well, if you are in a bad way," she began with a kind voice, "we can contact some of the local organizations to help you out." From the way I looked and smelled after a couple of 25-mile days, and having camped out at a water treatment plant, I cannot blame her for taking me to be a homeless person.

The next morning my maps indicated I needed to get to the very small town of Scherr. The route also listed me going through the lost communities of Ridgeville, Antioch, and the Nancy Hanks Memorial (Abraham Lincoln's mother). These were not "towns" as most people know them. Often times, a town like Ridgeville would end up being two houses at a fork in the road. On occasion, water can be found in these rural areas but purchasing food was out of the question. The road map I had been given was confusing to read. I told people I was to follow "Road 9 and 3." In my map, this was written as "9/3." The people I was speaking with thought I was trying to say, "93," which just happens to be a major highway in the area and leads right into Scherr, bypassing a scenic section of hills and small communities. Of course, this is not the route that I was interested in. After having run 11 miles out of town on "93" I asked a road crewman if the present road was going to take me through Antioch. He told me it wasn't. As if I wasn't dealing with enough, I had arranged for a newspaper interview at the Nancy Hanks memorial at 11:30 AM. When I found out that I was on the wrong road heading *away* from my interview, I got upset, turned around and started running faster than I should have to make my appointment. To get back on track, I had to double back and run the same three-mile stretch of road that I had just come down. If there ever was a damnable offense to transcontinental running, or "doing a transcon", it has to be running a section of road that you don't have to run, and further, to turn around and run it again. I made it 25 minutes late to my appointment only to find out no reporters were waiting for me.

Based on past experiences of getting information from others, if I had explained first that I was trying to get to Scherr by going through all of my noted landmarks, I am confident of the response I would have received.

(I heard some variation of the following statement hundreds of times on my trip.)

"Oh, I see, they've got you going in circles! That way doesn't make sense! Ridgeville's way over this way and Scherr is on the other side."

With a hectic beginning to the day and an intense sun burning my thighs, I finally made it to the famed town of Scherr. The one town store was still open when I arrived after completing my 27-mile hectic but scenic day of mountains, gurgling streams, and quaint settlements. Even though it was only a small country store and everyone all day long had been saying to me, "Where are you staying tonight? Scherr? There's nothin' in Scherr. A small store, but they don't have anything to eat." It was a haven to me. Non-pedestrians don't realize that when you don't have food, any place that does is a good place to eat. Yes, the store in Scherr is small, but I managed to gorge myself to the point of pain on only $15. I bought a loaf of bread, a large pack of ham slices, a large bag of sour cream and onion potato chips, a tube of potato crisps, two packs of cream-filled cakes, a half-gallon of orange juice and three 20-ounce bottles of soft drinks. Plus, the woman in the store gave me a tube of sausage and a slice of cake free!

After my meal, I scanned the area for a place to stay. I was not going to sleep in a comfortable bed this night. However, the folks in the store suggested that I camp in the nearby two-room schoolhouse. It had most of its windows still intact, the floor was clean and solid, and there were even two outhouses out back, one for boys and one for girls I assumed. I used the girls', not because I felt the need to break the rules but because the boys' toilet seat had already been eaten by termites and was home to a number of other weeble-wobbles. I slept well but woke up several times as I had the previous several nights. Perhaps it was my body adjusting to the exercise, or maybe it was the four sodas, quart of orange juice and half-gallon of water I had begun drinking each night before bedtime.

Seeking refuge in an abandoned one-room schoolhouse.

Chapter 6
Déjà vu

March 27 was the day of the big climb up into the Dolly Sods Wilderness, a steep ascent into a primitive wilderness area. It was also one of the biggest surprises of the trip. The town of Scherr sits on the edge of the mountain that is host to the Monongahela National Forest. That meant that as soon as I left town I was climbing uphill for four hours. Just prior to my ascent, I passed a second food store and decided to stock up for dinner that night. It was going to be my most remote night of the trip so far and I didn't know if I would even be able to get clean water once on the mountain. I bought two 20-ounce bottles of water, four candy bars, and two packs of crackers. This I added to my remaining half loaf of bread, summer sausage, squished pack of fig bars, and an oatmeal cookie. All of this food combined with the extra weight of my carpet foam made my pack over 14 pounds. It's still not much weight for an eight-month trip across the nation, but compared to ten pounds, it was a big adjustment, especially when all of that weight was being carried by a wide belt around my waist as I spent all day going straight up a mountain. At the beginning of the ascent, a car came along, slowed down, and a man said, "I'm going up the mountain if you want a ride." "Thanks, but you see, that would be cheating." He replied with, "Oh, so you're going to hike it, are you?" And hike it I did.

On the way to the top I checked my map several times and noticed, "Bear Rocks," the name of a trailhead that I would be arriving at later in the day on top of the mountain. It sounded familiar but I couldn't remember why. Up the mountain I went, along the single lane dirt road switch backing slowly uphill from left to right for hours. When the forest

turned to solid pine trees and exposed rocks, I knew I was getting close to
the summit. Finally, I broke through the trees and saw Bear Rocks and
instantly knew why I had remembered the name.

Ten years ago, when I was 17, as a summer camp counselor at Camp
Palawopec in Brown County, Indiana I led a co-ed hiking and whitewater-
rafting trip to West Virginia. I had done a significant amount of camping
and hiking but was still fairly new to organizing a two-week trip for eight
people. On that fateful trip, we simply packed our bags full of food and
gear, got in a van, and headed for the Mountains of West Virginia. It
all sounded good until we got to the mountains and realized that by not
having a route picked out before hand, we were clueless where to begin our
hike. I remember asking a few storeowners where some nearby trails were
and after being pointed in the right direction, we drove to a trail, parked
the van, and just started hiking. No map. No route. No plan. Just an
area hiking guide and a trail that started in a parking lot. As one might
imagine, it wasn't long before we got lost.

We hiked for four days -- bushwhacking some, hiking on old trails,
and studying our book, trying to guess where we might be. Finally, we
met a computer programmer deep in the woods who thought he had found
a virtual screen-saver in the nook of two rushing streams - until a pack of
eight wandering campers rebooted his hard drive. He pointed us towards
a nearby hiking trail which led us to the same forest road we had driven
on to get into this wilderness area. The only problem now was that we
were on the *complete opposite side* of the wilderness. We would either have
to hike 17 miles along this road back to our van, or send one person to get
the van and pick everyone else up.

I was the self-appointed rescuer and, rather than hiking back to the
van, figured I could run there much faster. One of the girls in the group
had a decent sized hip pack which I borrowed and filled with a few water
bottles and snacks and started my run. At that point in my running career
17 miles was a challenging day of running, but the excitement of "saving"
the group (after I had gotten them lost) propelled me.

During that several hour run, I passed picnickers, families out
harvesting ripe blackberries, and hikers. Being surrounded by others
enjoying the day felt affirming and I naively assumed running across the
country would be no different. Wouldn't it be great, I imagined at the
time, to run across the country with nothing but a hip pack? It was a fun
daydream at the time, but I quickly forgot all about the idea once I reached
the van. After I picked up the stranded campers, who were greatly relieved
to see that I had made it, the trip continued without a hitch as we rafted
with a professional rafting company for the final three days.

Ten years later, during my transcon, I was in total shock to realize that I had arrived at the exact same spot while wearing my large hip-pack and running across the country! I had arrived at the inception point of the idea to even do this trip and the recollection didn't hit me until I was standing in the parking space where the van had been. It would have been neat to share this moment with others, but the forest service had closed the area with gates near the mountain top due to heavy snow. In some ways, being alone made it even more special, however. As I reflected on the incident, I realized that few could have shared that emotion with me even if they had been in the pine trees with me.

Still in disbelief, I continued on and had to traverse large patches of deep snowdrifts across the road. I was trying to get to a campground several miles away. The snowdrifts were many feet thick and partially melted from the sun the day before. As I would step onto a pile, sometimes one leg would break through the crust and sink up to my knee, scraping my shin and calf in the process. Other times, the snow would support my weight. It seemed that each step was different so that I would almost always be walking with one foot at the other leg's knee level. It was very slow going.

I arrived at the campground but, since the roads were closed, the place was empty. First, I sat at a lonely picnic table and had a late lunch. The climb up the mountain had taken its toll, and I knew that my remaining 20 ounces of water was not going to be enough for the night and next day. The campground had hand pumps for water but the handles had been removed for the winter. I decided it might still be possible to draw water out of the pumps.

At first, I stood close to one of the massive four-foot tall pumps and tried to lift the steel casing on top that draws the water up the pipe. By the size and magnitude of the pump, I figured the handles to be at least three feet long. I was now trying to do the action that usually takes the power of a three-foot steel lever. I couldn't move the casing more than a few inches. Still determined, I managed to stand *on* the pump, with my feet precariously balanced on the lip of the spout. Now, with a bit more leverage, and several feet off the ground, I bent down and tried pulling the casing up towards me. With all my might, I was able to force it up but it took at least a dozen times before I was able to draw any water out of the pump.

I tried imagining what I must have looked like perched there. A lonely dirty runner on top of the biggest mountain chain on the East Coast, clad in grimy nylon running clothes, legs scraped up from snow abrasions, shoes muddy from melting snow and dirt, perched atop a steel pipe pulling up on a casing while my face turned purple from the resistance. All my efforts were worthless however as I couldn't even catch the water coming out below while perched above. From my days living in a log cabin in Indiana, I knew that it might be a long time before the water ran clean. So far, it had only choked up black, lumpy pump phlegm. My hands were cramped from grasping the casing, my arms worn out from pulling up, and my feet were sore from trying to hang on to the lip of the pump. I gave up.

Just before dusk, as I was wandering around the campsite, I found a spring, about fifteen yards behind the pump, clear, cold, rushing, and right at the source. I laughed in disbelief at the turn of events, and the wasted effort when an unlimited supply was just yards away. Little experiences like this began to accumulate and give me the confidence that in hard times, an easier solution could often be found. As a result, the trail experience became less problematic and I learned to deal with challenges in new ways.

My last objective of the day was to find a comfortable place to sleep. The ground was saturated from the melting snow. I was planning on sleeping on one of the picnic tables when I saw two cinder block outhouses nearby. They were designed to accommodate a wheelchair and thus had plenty of floor space. At first, the thought of sleeping in a public restroom seemed crude, but, given the options, I decided it was the best choice. Outside, I pulled up some tall grass, folded it over, made a mini-broom and swept out my mountain chalet. Due to the cold temperatures and the campground being closed for several months, the outhouse didn't smell a bit. There were bars to hang my clothes on, five rolls of toilet paper, a skylight, a toilet just a foot away -- and all heated by natural gas! What else could one ask for?

I slept for 12 hours that night, my best night yet.

Unbeknownst to me, Lu Schrader, the West Virginia coordinator for the ADT, had arranged to have a friend drive a hot dinner up the mountain to me as a surprise. Alas, the locked gates, deep snowdrifts, and being hidden in the restroom of a closed campground would have surely prevented anyone from finding me that night.

Throughout the next day I followed hiking trails towards the Canaan Valley Resort. I encountered my first stream crossing. It was easy enough, only a few inches deep and about 15 feet wide. The second, however, took considerable concentration. At several times on the second crossing I found myself thigh deep in a rushing cold snow melt and had to retreat to get a branch to steady myself to keep from being swept away. That was some very cold snowmelt! Once across, and soaking wet, I had to resume traversing the snow piles which now completed the "tar and feather" process of wet shoes now caked with snow. On the occasions when my legs would plunge into a snow pile, a clump of icy snow would fall into my shoes and it would take the body heat of my feet to painstakingly melt the ice as I plodded on.

At the edge of the wilderness I heard voices. Straying 50 yards off the trail I walked onto a ski slope full of people in sweaters and snow pants downhill skiing! It was nearly 70 degrees with blue skies, and most of the ground was mud but here was a perfectly maintained ski slope with hoards of families making their leisurely way down the hill. I set up my tripod in the snow and took a self-portrait just as a family skiied past, likely wondering what a muddy guy in running clothes was doing standing in the middle of their ski run.

Leaving the wilderness after a long downhill, I emerged onto a country road. A car soon approached and a young man rolled down the window asking, "Are you the person running across the country?" I told him I was, surprised to be recognized, and he told me that he and his family had just seen an article about me in the Keyser newspaper. They asked if I had a copy of the article and I told them I didn't but that my mother would enjoy reading about me. I gave them her address and they thoughtfully sent the article to her. Throughout the journey I continued to ask motorists who recognized me to send copies of stories from papers all over the country to my mother. Thanks to their generosity, I now have a bulging scrapbook as a memoir of my trip.

I was looking forward to another night of pampering after my trek over the mountain. Again, the dual lifestyle of my trip became evident as I registered for a room while standing in my grubby outfit in the resort lobby. There were unique insights into this form of traveling, however.

First, the experience of living as simply as possible, I was carrying only those things that I needed on a daily basis. How many people can say they possess only what they need? Second, my objectives were clear. Each day I set out with one goal in mind: get to the next town 25-35 miles away. If I made it, I succeeded. Third, exercising as I was, my body could afford to eat anything and as much of it as possible.

Then I had the dual lifestyles of camping out versus motels. If I was in a very small town that had only a gas station, such as a few nights in West Virginia, Ohio, and Kansas, I likely would expect to sleep on a picnic table in a city park. One night I slept on a picnic table in a park in Kansas. During the night a woman walked by with her dog and, realizing there was a silhouette of a figure lying on a table, increased her pace out of concern. This feeling of homelessness was the worst drawback to traveling solo across the country. People simply did not know I was running from one coast to the other and the reason I was sleeping in their park in their town was not because I had dependencies or was scheming a bank heist. I was sleeping in their park because their town was the right distance between two other towns and, in order for me to continue, I had no choice but to stop there. Additionally, and even more importantly, by staying in a town overnight, I could get both a dinner and a breakfast before leaving -- even if the gas station selections were only white bread, American cheese, soft drinks, and candy bars, as many times they were.

Other nights, when choices were many, I might opt for a reasonable motel room. And then there were the deserved nights, the times when I had just come out of the woods after sleeping in an outhouse on a snow-covered mountain, and I would decide to treat myself to a nice room and a big meal. Having saved the resources to splurge from time to time continued to renew my vigor.

Grateful for a brief return to civilization, with room key in hand I went into the lodge and took a hot shower, scrubbed the mud off my shoes, washed my clothes with the room shampoo, and watched HBO. At such times, after reflecting on the incredible occurrences such as Bear Rocks, the ski slope, and the stream crossing, after the shower, dinner, and journal writing, these are the times when it would be really nice to have company, someone to share the day's events with in conversation. "Remember that? Could you believe how cold that stream was? Remember the look on that kid's face on the ski slope when he went by?" But instead, my conversations were with waitresses who took the tone of, "What are you, biking or something?"

"Yes, something like that." If they pressed for more information, I would explain my trip and what I was doing, then wait to see if they had just registered anything I had said. Usually, it was an unimpressed, "Oh."

When I was finally able to clarify to a few that, yes, I was actually running –on foot – across the continent, they confessed that they originally thought I was driving, as some people apparently confuse hauling a big rig with the term "running."

It was only two more days until my first of 12 mail drops. I was getting excited to see what awaited me in the mail. I was also ready for a new pair of shoes, as the current ones were worn out from two and a half states of freezing cold, muddy water, and 400 miles in 22 days.

Chapter 7
Candlelight Breakfast

I had camped out the night prior to my arrival in Hendricks, West Virginia. There was no spring nearby to provide much-needed water and I came into town early the next morning on fumes. Luckily, it was downhill into town and I arrived at the post office in mid-morning. As I walked into the lobby, Glen, the postmaster, knew immediately who I was. After three weeks of staring at a stack of packages addressed to Brian Stark, Transcontinental Runner, Care Of: General Delivery, there must not have been much doubt in his mind when I walked in the door. I asked if I could have some water and he replied, "Of course! I bet you also want your packages as well!" He handed me a large pile of boxes and mail and said, "Wait, there's more." When I finally had the collection in my arms, I looked down at my hip pack. My morning's bounty easily tripled the amount in my pack. What on earth was I going to do with all this stuff, I wondered? Luckily, most of it was food, which could serve as breakfast. The rest was mail and articles from friends and relatives. I was getting ready to walk outside and sit on the curb for an hour going through all the mail when Glen invited me into his office saying, "You can read it in here if you like. We'll set you up a place."

He let me drink as much cold clean water as I wanted, and even gave me a chilled Tropicana Twister Juice from his lunch! After the previous evening's meager dinner of crackers, candy bars, and 8 ounces of water, his juice really hit the spot! Then he cleared off his desk and let me sit in his chair to read my mail. I shared the home-baked lemon bars and cookies with him and read aloud excerpts from mail. "Dear Brian, Welcome to West Virginia! How are your feet?" Another was written on the back of a list of actual forest service complaints, "Too many rocks in the mountains,' 'Too many spider webs and bugs. Please spray the wilderness to rid the area of these pests,' 'The places where trails do not exist are not well marked,' and my favorite, 'Too many trees, couldn't see the scenery."

In the hour that I was in the office, only one customer came in and I am not even sure that was for postal reasons, more likely to confirm a fishing date. On that Christmas-like morning I opened three boxes of food and nine letters! It was a touch with the world I had left. Most everyone just wanted to say, "Good luck. Keep going."

Once read, I mailed the letters home, to be kept as mementos. I ate about half of the food I had been given but could not finish the sweets, so I carried as much as I could run with and packaged up the rest, mailing it ahead to Parkersburg, where I could eat it later. Glen helped me tape all the various boxes and send them off again. When I asked if he needed money for the tape, he replied, "Oh no, it's all part of the service."

Wonderful experiences such as this confirm my belief that small town post offices are the place to be. From my experiences, large city post offices are more prone to lose your mail due to the large volume they handle. If they lose your mail, no one would ever remember reading your name on a package and they have to charge for every supply. In small town post offices, however, the service is exceptional, the attention is personal, and the experience is always wonderful. I knew this from my mail drops while hiking on the Appalachian Trail three years before, so when I set out to plan this run, I intentionally picked small town post offices whenever possible to use as my shipping locations.

The next morning, the temperature was rising as I left town and I slowly began to melt into the pavement. It was the hottest day of the trip thus far. The route for the day was along farm roads and the baking sun beat down on me all day. Entering an appropriately named area called Valley Furnace, I was near dehydration and exhaustion. Several hours of steamy running down the hot blacktop road brought me to a small community park with a spigot, picnic shelters and tables. I mixed several energy drink packets that Lydia had mailed me with the cold spring water and drank a gallon of needed fluid and electrolytes. After a short afternoon nap on a picnic table and dreading my return to the hot road, I decided to press on solely in the hopes that the upcoming town of Philipi would have a motel and a restaurant.

It wasn't long before my hopes were dashed, as the only commercial structures I found in Philipi were two gas stations, a church, and a phone booth. I went into one of the gas stations. It was typical of the others I had experienced during the past month: wooden, creaky floorboards and dusty coolers half-filled with cold meats and egg burritos packaged ages ago. A standard glass case displayed a few expensive fishing reels under several layers of packaging tape where a previous angler leaned too hard. Two locals were sitting in the only seats when I entered. "What can I do for ya?" the owner asked.

"What do you have for dinner?" He simply threw his head in the direction of several display racks of chips, sugar cakes, and sodas. "We also have a cooler of microwave sandwiches over there if you like," he said. I was still too hot to eat having just come out of the "Furnace," so I bought a few cold drinks and sat outside.

It was late afternoon. The only food in town was behind me in frozen containers. Also, from where I was on the edge of town, there was no shelter to sleep in. I used a payphone to call Lu Schrader, West Virginia trail coordinator, for advice. He said that there wasn't much in the way of services around that part of the trail and wished me luck. I was on the edge of saying, "Look, I'm really hot, this town has more dust than people. What do you say we rustle up a contact and get me picked up for the night?" But I didn't say that. I simply said that it was rather warm, that I was in a small town, and that I was pretty much still on schedule. After all, Lu, like all of the other state coordinators, is a volunteer with many other things to do than rescue hot and weary runners from the middle of nowhere.

After hanging up, I scanned the town again for options. There were the gas stations; I had already checked them out. The phone booth had done me no good. The only other option was to approach the church across the street. There was a house in the side yard of the church, which I correctly assumed to be the manse. After knocking on the door, a very nice couple came out and invited me to sleep in the new fellowship hall under construction. The woman also said that she would bring me a dinner. The fellowship hall was well underway but by no means yet completed. The walls and roof were in place and the cement floor was new. One of the church members on his way into choir practice saw me setting up camp on the concrete floor and said, "Let us know if that roof works!" My hostess brought out two hoagie sandwiches, two soft drinks, and two bananas. It was the perfect meal. Once again, I had judged a situation from the layout of my despair and had been shamefully proven wrong about my prejudices.

Several hours earlier, being hot, covered in sweaty dust, worn out and hungry, I had wanted to be at any other place in the world but this dumpy little town. Now, with a dinner in my belly, a dry ground to sleep on, and restrooms at my disposal, I was a new man and humbled by the turn of events. It would not be the last time that I learned this lesson, however.

The new roof did work and a good thing too, because at 7 a.m. two workmen from the church came in saying, "Up and at 'em, time to get to work!" It was pouring rain. I ran over to the gas station for a delicious microwave breakfast and eagerly headed out the door, ready for a refreshingly soggy 25 miles.

Several miles out of town and having turned onto a small one-lane road, I stopped at Lou's Country Store and Bakery. Lou was out front sweeping off the porch and we chatted some while I stood out of the rain for a few minutes. When I told her of my trip she said, "Well, if you're running all that way, you'd better come in here and get some food." By her tone and openness, I felt as if I were going to camp out in my friend's backyard and she was going to send me off with some snacks for the night. She gave me a large bottle of apple juice, several homemade pizza loafs, and a bag of fresh bread rolls. I carried those rolls for over a week, savoring them as midday snacks, the home baked goods being a welcome respite to the endless junk food I was consuming.

This particular section in West Virginia was confusing because all of it is on rural back roads that are not marked. The roads are only listed by numbers on maps yet are known only by common names to the locals. And some don't even know the road's name, just whose house it takes you to, which didn't do me much good. The confusing route coupled with the large amount of hills in the state made my pace very inconsistent.

The best way to judge distance besides major road crossings is to have an established pace. I could run six miles per hour, which translated to running ten-minute miles. By using my watch, I could tell that ten miles had gone by if it had been 100 minutes, or one hour and 40 minutes. If I got lost and had to backtrack, then that would add to the time. If I stopped to ask directions for ten minutes, then I had to subtract that time from my watch. While running, even at such a slow pace, it is surprisingly difficult to keep an eye on all the landmarks around and not miss an important sign or turn. Also, while running uphill, my pace was much slower, and while running downhill it was faster. For all these reasons, I started realizing that in West Virginia, I was having a very hard time judging distances and therefore began to walk.

My walking pace was an established three miles per hour. If I knew exactly where I was and could determine that a possibly confusing junction might be coming up, I would start walking and use my strict 20 minutes per mile measure versus my inconsistent 10 minutes per mile run. In this way, I would not say, "turn south onto route 8/3 in 1.4 miles, but would rather look at my watch and say, "Ok, it's 1 PM, take a left at 1:28. By perfecting this method through the state, I could often get to my junction within 20 seconds of my predicted time. Later in the run, when my running pace became just as established, I could do the same but over a prediction of 20 and 30 miles with an error of less than two minutes.

The next day I joined the 74-mile long North Bend Rail Trail (NBRT). The NBRT is an abandoned railroad corridor that boasts 35 train trestles and ten train tunnels. The trail has been designed very well for bikers, hikers, and equestrians and passes through quaint West Virginia towns, some now catering to travelers while others continue to hang on to their mining days.

I had an appointment to meet a reporter and photographer at one of the train tunnels. As I came within a few miles of the tunnel, I noticed a McDonald's Restaurant in a small town beside the rail trail. I decided I had enough time for a quick milkshake before the interview. I had been carrying several McDonald's gift certificates someone had mailed me and was eager to use them. Upon entering, I was not able to hold myself back and quickly found myself seated in front of a large chocolate milkshake, two cheeseburgers, a large order of fries and an apple pie. It was the perfect 2210-calorie snack to finish the afternoon. My pit stop splurge cost me some time however and I arrived 15 minutes late for my interview at the tunnel.

Luckily, I saw the reporters had waited for me as I made out two figures standing in the cool dark entrance of the tunnel. I threw up my arms in a greeting from a hundred yards away. They took lots of pictures of me at the tunnel entrance. (Most of the tunnels are less than a quarter mile long but one is over a half-mile.)

At the end of the day, I had been told that a room was waiting for me at the Salem-Teikyo University Campus in Salem, West Virginia. When I arrived however, I learned that the arrangement had fallen through and I was once again left on my own to find lodging for the night. Since I was on the campus of a university I knew that the chance of an extra bed in one of the dorm rooms was good. After talking with a coach and a resident assistant I was given the key to an empty dorm room for the night. I ate dinner in the cafeteria and enjoyed the small college atmosphere – reminding me of my own college experience at Hanover in southern Indiana. With continued luck, the trail would lead me to my alma mater in another month.

Six years earlier in 1992, while a freshman at Hanover, I was behind my dormitory waterproofing the inside of my new backpacking tent. I heard a rustling outside and looking out the small door noticed a pair of tan well-shaped female legs. Crawling out of the tent as any college student would, I met Brittany, who was hiking across the country on the

ADT with her friend Bhaskar. They had started in Delaware and had set a leisurely pace across the country. I had dinner with them and they told me of the ADT, the first account I had heard of it.

I remember that day well. Also on that day, actor Woody Harrelson, a famous graduate of Hanover, was visiting campus. Many students were crowded in the dining room to meet him while he ate. Not wanting to be overcrowded, I chose to eat outside behind the cafeteria. When I walked out onto the dining room patio, I saw Bhaskar and Brittany huddled under the eave of the building out of the drizzling rain, eating their lunches in peace and solitude. How ironic, I thought. Here are three celebrities. Woody, whom everyone knows from his days on the television show Cheers and the movies in which he has starred. And there is also this lonely couple that have walked 600 miles from the East Coast. At the time, no one knew of their fame and I felt fortunate to have joined them in the rain outside. I asked them many questions about their trip. Later in the year, I learned that Brittany eventually made it as far as Kansas City while Bhaskar continued alone, making his own route across the west and into California.

Ever since that meeting, whenever I ran across a school campus or into a small town, I thought of how I felt when I first met Bhaskar and Brittany. Would others see in me the same outgoing spirit I saw in them? I still remember the way Bhaskar told me of the numerous maps they were using to cross the country and imagine that my tales of map woes were received with the same reaction.

When I ate dinner at the Salem-Teikyo University campus dining room, I hoped for the same interaction with students as Bhaskar and Brittany had had with me. Alas, because of spring break, the campus was nearly deserted and I ate alone.

After leaving town the next morning, with rain still sheeting down, I came across the small town of Smithburg. That was lucky for me, as I had left campus without breakfast. Inside a small country store attached to the local post office, I ate a Star Crunch, a Zebra Cookie, a pack of peanut butter crackers, and two bottles of apple juice while the nice lady told me about her four children and how her son had seen three people murdered.

Rural dining - Note the dinner and breakfast selections on the menu.

I didn't know that another town, West Union, was only three miles away. But I overate anyway and stopped a half-hour later for a more substantial lunch of meatloaf, mashed potatoes, waffle fries, and a milkshake.

I made it to Pennsboro that evening after trying unsuccessfully to take a picture of myself in a long tunnel using my camera, timer, and tripod. It's very difficult to set up a mini-tripod in a pitch-dark tunnel. First of all, I couldn't see through the viewfinder to frame my picture. Once I thought I had framed it and pushed the button, I didn't know where to stand because I couldn't see where the camera was. Additionally, kneeling on the jagged soot-covered ballast in the tunnel while looking through a pitch-dark frame was really painful on the knees. However, I hoped that years later the treasured pictures would be worth the effort.

The trail coordinator had told me that a bed and breakfast in Pennsboro was willing to take me in for the night so my spirits had been up solely in the knowledge that I had a nice bed waiting for me at the end of the day. It is hard to describe the relief this gives a person when they do not have to be concerned with finding a place to sleep for the night. The last thing I wanted to do at the end of a 30-mile day was eat a bag of chips and sleep on a mouse-infested barn floor. I entered the outskirts of a town and asked a woman walking her dog, "Excuse me, Ma'am? Could you tell me if this is Pennsboro?" That sort of question was always good for a laugh. "It sure is!" she said with a smile. Down the road a little further, I trotted up the steps of the immaculate Rose Hill Inn Bed & Breakfast perched atop a perfectly manicured lawn overlooking the town. As I reached for the door, it opened before me and a man said, "Hi! You must be Brian!"

Innkeepers John Shaffer and his wife took great care of me, putting me up in the best room in the house, and offering to do my laundry. "How long has it been since you washed your clothes?" I had to think. When I was in a hotel room I would rinse my clothes with the hotel soap but it had been awhile since the clothes had been agitated and scrubbed. I recalled staying with my aunt and uncle just outside Washington D.C. on the C&O Canal. "Poolsville, Maryland," I remembered finally. "Let's do some laundry," John replied.

Before entering the Bed & Breakfast business, my host had attended culinary school. Being a bona fide chef, he put out quite a spread for me as I was the only guest that night. When I awoke the next morning, I walked into the dining room to find a full table of food laid out just for me. There were stacks of pancakes, a selection of cold cereal, a fruit salad, bagels, muffins, a carafe of orange juice, tea, and milk. Standing beside the table with chef's hat and double-breasted white overcoat in place, cloth napkin draped over his arm, lighting the candles on the table, as is custom at his breakfasts, my host had impressed the largest of appetites. I ate to the point of maximum intake, barely putting a dent in the items offered. I had just enough time to waddle over to the Pennsboro glass factory before a reporter and his friend came over to run with me for the day.

The Pennsboro Glass Factory is a small operation but the quaintness of the factory puts no limitation on the mountainous piles of glass at their disposal. As I stood 20 feet outside of the Quonset hut style kilns, I studied the enormous piles of colored glass around me. One pile was 20 feet wide, entirely composed of thousands of broken beer mugs with "Slim Jim Racing" painted on the side. Another pile was even bigger, totally made up of dark purple shattered vases. Others were soft pink ballerinas with broken necks and legs. Another pile was hundreds of broken red ornamental China plates.

As I was glancing around at the piles near and far, my eyes peered down to what I was standing on. Directly underfoot, mixed in with dirt and gravel, were hundreds of thousands of marbles. I picked up one. It was oblong. I picked up another. It was double jointed. A third was shaped like a comma, and the rest were also unique shapes. Apparently, I was told, the marbles have to come out of the fire in uniform shape. Some orders ask for flat marbles but they all have to be flat to make the order correct. I assumed that whenever the order came out wrong, they simply dumped the bad marbles out in the front yard. Perhaps they melted the marbles at a later date to try again. I picked up a few hundred, which I carried with me and gave to people who helped me along the way for the next several states.

Mike and Kent showed up to run with me. Mike is a reporter for a local newspaper and since all three of us were eager to get on the road, we did as fast an interview as possible. He started with a few basic questions but realized it would take too long to do a formal interview so he just said, "Look, you know what I need to ask, so why don't you just give me the answers." He was right. By this time I had given so many interviews on the same subject that I knew exactly what he wanted to know and the order I needed to tell it to him. I simply started listing the pertinent answers. "Brian Stark, 26, Nashville, Indiana, substitute teacher, renovated log cabins, summer camp director, Camp Palawopec, that's P-A-L-A-..., hiked all of AT in '95. Started March 8, hopes to be done by mid Oct. Utah and Nevada will be hardest, 110 miles without food or water. Slept in outhouse in Dolly Sods." We kept going for a few more minutes, and then we started our run. It was fun giving an interview that way.

Running down the rail trail with my two companions, they told me they were training for a marathon and after they finished running 12 miles with me they were going to turn around and run back to the bed and breakfast.

We talked easily as we ran down the trail. We talked about arguments they get into while on training runs together. Sometimes their arguments get so intense that they end up yelling at each other as they run along the serene trails and back roads of their beautiful state.

At one point, we were running through a long train tunnel. Even with all the changes that go into converting a rail trail, when you are running through a half-mile long narrow pitch-dark tunnel, you easily find yourself wondering, "What would I do if a train came around the corner?" Not just a train, in fact, but anything out of the ordinary. Tripping on a stray brick, stepping on a snake, or having someone jump out at you are any of a number of things that go through your head as you keep telling yourself that nothing will happen. On an impulse, I took out my one toy, a ½ ounce harmonica. Without Mike or Rick knowing it, I placed it against my lips and blew hard in a simulated train whistle tone. Even though it was dark, I could feel them jump sideways with a startled cry.

Fortune was with me again that night as the North Bend State Park Lodge offered to put me up in a room for free. Only one more full day left in West Virginia! That night I was finally able to meet and thank Lu and his wife Midge for all of their work to get me across their state in one piece. They drove quite a distance to meet me for dinner at the lodge dining room.

I enjoyed learning more about the politics of the ADT from Lu, as he has been with it since the beginning.

The next morning was the last full day in West Virginia. I was eager to get to Parkersburg. If I could make the 32 miles into town by 5 PM, I would get the second box of food sent ahead from Hendricks. I encouraged myself to make my running segments longer and even got them up to an hour without stopping. Sure enough, with mounting excitement, I arrived at the outskirts of Parkersburg at 4:45 PM. As is always the case when you are in a hurry, and especially when you need directions, the person giving them will be moving in slow motion.

"Can you tell me the fastest way to get to the post office?" I asked while jogging in place.

"Well, that's a ways from here you know."

"Yes," I replied.

"Ok, if you go down this here road, you're going to come to a junction. Now that junction is a little tricky because several boys have been taking the signs down but you'll know which way to go when you see my cousin's house. It's the one with a big Silver Maple in the front yard. You won't actually go past his house but if you do, you'll know you're on the right track." Visions of the postmaster locking the front door were going through my mind.

As soon as I felt I had enough information to head into town, I thanked the man and tore away, running much faster than I had on any part of the trip thus far. It was at least 3 miles farther to the post office and I arrived at 5:20 p.m. I decided that there might still be someone inside and went up to the building anyway, overjoyed and also oddly depressed to learn that it was going to be open until 6, so the frantic run had been unnecessary.

I got my box and checked into the Blenderhassett Hotel, definitely one of the best hotels I visited in the entire country. With some negotiating, I was able to get a special rate. My room was enormous, with a giant living room, separate bedroom, two televisions, a phone in the bathroom, and one of the best meals in a hotel dining room of the entire trip.

That night, I was feeling starved for a movie in a theatre. I had been catching old HBO movies in my room, as I lay on my bed, eating a pint or at times a quart of Ben & Jerry's Mint Cookie, or Cookie Dough Ice Cream, waiting for my running clothes to dry after washing them in the sink. I craved company. I needed to be in a theater. Across the street from the hotel was a cinema and, after reading the marquee and not seeing anything to my liking, I decided to go anyway, just to sit near other people in the dark and feel normal once again. The nearby munching of popcorn.

The toddler asking obvious questions throughout. The young couple on a first date. These were things I was familiar with and now longed for.

I walked across the street, wearing my "Sunday Best" of tights, long sleeve shirt, and rain jacket, and went into the theater. I bought a ticket to see "Sphere", starring Dustin Hoffman. Once my eyes adjusted to the darkness, I eagerly scanned the seats for that all-familiar crowd of couples, friends, and single people sharing an evening at the movies. But my eyes landed on no filled seat! The theater was empty, and I watched the film alone.

Chapter 8
Wet Nights

The last several days of warm West Virginia hospitality had spoiled me for what was to come in much of eastern Ohio. In Ohio, the ADT joins the Buckeye Trail (BT), a 1,200-mile hiking trail that circles the state. By joining the BT in southeastern Ohio, the ADT is able to traverse the southern half of the state on rugged hiking trails and back roads.

Stepping off the bridge spanning the Ohio River, I entered the town of Belpre, Ohio. Passing a beauty salon on the trail, I decided to stop for a haircut. My sweaty disposition was a sharp contrast to the ladies having their hair set and highlighted, but I entertained the beauty stylist with stories from the road as locks of my hair fell to the floor.

Fifteen miles later, relieved to have actually found one of the now-familiar but seldom actually seen ADT logo stickers on the back of a stop sign, I arrived at the very small town of Vincent. The only service being a country store. I chose a tube of Pringles, two bags of Doritos, two packs of Captain's Wafers with cheese, a quart of orange juice, and a four-pack of pudding. It was like Thanksgiving on the covered porch of that small country store.

As I was finishing my meal and watching a drizzling rain begin to fall, I pondered my options. It was only 4 p.m. To stay in this little town that early in the day without a place to sleep seemed pointless. I looked at my precious map, which I took great pains to keep dry and legible. I would literally be lost without it.

The next town was Chesterhill, now 18 miles away. Did I have it in me? I had run 15 miles already, and I was tired from my post office sprint the previous evening. I felt sure I wouldn't make it, but some instinct told me to press on anyway. There comes a time when you have to trust fate to take care of you. I decided on that day, in the rain, in front of a country store in Vincent, Ohio to let fate take its course.

Clipping my hip pack snug around my waist, I headed out of town and jogged along the country roads, happily winding my way north and west through warm soft rain with no particular destination in mind. Eight miles later, I needed a bathroom. I continued on, sure that some solution would present itself. As would happen time and again, just when I thought I could go no further in my "urgent" condition, I came across an outhouse in the middle of nowhere, this time next to a covered wooden bridge under construction. It is amazing how often instances like this worked out with a happy ending. Hikers call these moments "Trail Magic."

*   *   *

Some stories of Trail Magic are harder to believe than others. One of my favorites involves a friend of mine who was hiking near me on the AT. Everyone on the AT has a trail name. His was Six-Iron because he carried a six-iron golf club as a walking stick, using its head as a handle. Starting in Maine and hiking to Georgia, Six Iron and I began with the longest and most remote portion of the entire trail, a wilderness stretch of 100 miles without any food or services. Early in that section, Six Iron lost his walking stick. While in Monson, Maine, the first stopping point for southbound hikers, a pair of hikers found a nine-iron golf club to replace the club he had lost.

Also in the wilderness, another hiker, Forrest Hamster, lost his left hiking boot on a narrow footbridge while crossing one of the many treacherous bogs. He simply described the incident as slipping off the bridge, plunging his leg into the black murky water, and when he pulled his leg out, there was only an oil-black sock where his boot used to be.

That same day, still in the wilderness, another hiker found a replacement left boot and gave it to Hamster. Hamster is the type of person who remains content no matter the circumstance, and he wore the ill-fitting unmatched boot for the next 200 miles. In both cases, Trail Magic provided the hikers' needs.

I had my own share of Trail Magic on the AT. Once while crossing Virginia, I was hiking late into the night trying to make it to the next town. I had long since eaten all my food when I came across a group from an outdoor school for kids at risk. They had just finished their dinner. The kids and their leaders had cooked more food than they could eat and were preparing to bury ten pounds of the excess in huge pits they had dug in the ground. As I walked into camp they offered me the leftover food before it was given an improper burial. I ate five plates of piping hot stew, potatoes, and cobbler that night, much to the amazement of the school group.

The same thing happened while hiking in Maryland. I was in a similar predicament: my hunger had out-talked my intention to spread out my rations until my next food box, and I was again hiking big, hungry miles to get to town early. Even my flashlight batteries were dead, and I was running through the sunset trying to make the next shelter before dark. Arriving just past dusk, I found a man who was only out for an overnight. Oddly enough, he had decided to bring a week's worth of food with him in his large backpack. When he heard of my sorry plight, he gladly gave me all his food, and the next morning he even drove me into town for a hot breakfast.

Trail Magic was also an integral part of my run on the ADT. In fact, due to the nature of my run and the fact that I was alone, I believe I was the lucky recipient of even more Trail Magic than on my AT hike.

*   *   *

As darkness neared, I began looking for a place to camp. Chesterhill was just out of reach for the day's mileage. I felt so good. I didn't want to stop. I wanted to run all night, and I might have, except that two and a half hours after sunset, the raindrops got fat and hard. During the day, the light rain had been a fun way to keep cool and added some excitement. Now, however, in the pitch dark with no idea where I was or where I would find shelter, the rain took on a different persona. My skin turned cold, I could only see a few feet in front of me from my tiny penlight. I felt like I was encased in a leaky black tunnel with no end in sight. I stopped in my tracks and asked myself, "Now what?" Throughout the day, I had eagerly awaited my fate. I had run 26 miles in the rain after an equally hard day in West Virginia, and now I was paying the price for it.

"NOW WHAT?" I asked aloud this time, unhappy that fate did not appear to be taking care of me after all. Just then, I looked to my right and saw that I was directly in front of a farmhouse with a single light on in the window. I peered into the home from the edge of the yard, trying to size up the family I was about to introduce myself to. I couldn't make out any figures inside. I summoned my courage, walked up to the door and knocked.

There was a quiet pause of stillness in the house. "Who could it be at this hour?" they must have been thinking. No car had pulled up. No headlights in the windows. The door slowly opened and cautiously exposed a large figure that, to my relief, wasn't holding a shotgun. Dripping wet, I repeated my now familiar greeting. "Excuse me, sir, my name's Brian and I'm running to California from Delaware and found myself in front of your farmhouse when it started raining. Do you have a barn or a shed that I could sleep in for the night?"

I figured his response was either going to be in the realm of, "Sorry, sure wish I could help ya," or "I don't see why not." Luckily for me, he was agreeable and gave me an enthusiastic, "Sure!" then escorted me over to his barn. He showed me a ladder to the hayloft where I arranged some bales into a bed and laid out my tent sack and sleeping bag. He showed me a spigot where I got some water. Then I settled in for a cozy night in the hayloft, safe from the storm under a pinging tin roof.

Sleeping in that loft is one of my best memories of the trip - being warm, dry, comfortable, tucked away, and writing in my journal by flashlight. A cow in its stall serenaded me with an occasional "moo" throughout the night. Someone came out at 6 a.m. to feed the chickens. I slept until 7 a.m., content in my nest. When I finally got up, it was still raining and I once again resigned myself to the inevitable soaking process. Luckily, Chesterhill was only seven miles away, and it made for a nice pre-breakfast warm-up.

Pete and Marjorie Shaw had opened the Village Restaurant in Chesterhill for business just days before I walked through the door. The inside of the establishment was quite small, only a few tables, with two of them joined together and occupied by a familiar sight. Of my several theories developed during my run, one is of the group of coffee shop locals. In every town, in every small coffee shop and restaurant I entered, there was a group of older men, sitting together, telling jokes, drinking coffee, and usually stealing glances at me. This shop was no different. I tried to avoid direct eye contact as I made my waterlogged way towards the restroom to change into my only dry outfit. I hung my wet clothes on a coat rack while I ate.

As I was finishing a delicious omelet, large orange juice, and wheat toast when Pete, the owner, came over to my table. He leaned over and asked in a hushed tone with a smile, "Are ya walkin' far?"

"'Bout 4,800 miles," I said with a smile.

"I think that's great," he responded. Then he brought over my check and laying it on the table said, "If you'll autograph your bill, I'll take care of your breakfast for you." I gladly signed it and learned his story as we continued to chat.

Pete was a coal miner who was looking for a better life. He was spending his vacations from the mine building his dream of owning a restaurant. This was exactly what I had set out to do. I wanted to meet the people in the small towns of America, and hear their stories. The past few days had fulfilled and surpassed that wish for me. The running was the means of transportation, but ultimately it was a very small part of the trip. It was the people who really provided the richest experiences.

Chesterhill was also noteworthy, as this was where I joined the Buckeye Trail, a 1,200-mile hiking trail encircling the state. Downtown, I spotted the telltale sky blue blazes, two inch by six inch rectangles painted on telephone poles, trees, and posts, marking a massive route around Ohio.

Portions of perfection, a rare stretch of grassy trail in Ohio.

I was in a good mood. I was to be picked up by Tessa, a college friend who was now attending Ohio University. We had made arrangements to meet at Burr Oak State Park, which would make for a 32-mile day. Following the blue blazes, the BT was on dirt country roads most of the way. These were quite challenging, as it had been raining for several days. Much of Ohio was sopping wet, as was I, and the dirt roads had the consistency of peanut butter. I had expected West Virginia to be hilly, but not Ohio. Having run across both states, I would now judge southern Ohio to be the hillier of the two.

Granted, there were routes I could have taken across the state where I would have seen very few hills, but along the ADT, I was subjected to a repeated barrage of them. Often a road would climb straight up a ridge, only to cross it and plummet down the other side, make a sharp bend, and go straight back up the hill I had just come down. This, coupled with the amount of saturation in the ground, made for very slow going. It was the first time that I had ever sunk three inches into a road and slid back a foot with each step. Often, these roads included a stream crossing. There were no bridges on these primitive roads, and it was simply a matter of having to go right through the stream to continue on the trail.

After each stream crossing, the water in my shoes only attracted more mud to clump on my feet until there was four pounds of mud clinging to each foot as I tried to jog-slide my way up a steep hill to the next ridge.

As I ran through a small subdivision just prior to entering Burr Oak State Park, a large dog started following me. I've had dogs follow me before but when I am running in a strange area, I always command the dog to "stay," so he doesn't get lost. This dog was sneaky. When I first noticed him running behind me, I yelled, "Go home!" He simply cowered a little and waited for me to resume running. "Stay!" I hollered. He just looked at me. At one point, I ran back to him and bluff-charged him. As soon as he saw me coming, he stepped off the trail a few feet and started sniffing the bushes, as if he wasn't really following me. Finally, I gave up trying to get rid of him and let him do what he wanted.

I had to run all the way around the lake, a nine-mile trail along the very edge of the water, and the dog constantly stayed 15 yards behind. I finally arrived at a ranger station, where I asked two park rangers to try to contain him and drive him back to his neighborhood. They brought out a large metal pole with a loop cable on the end. We all learned very quickly that this dog had seen those before, as he got very nervous when he saw it. I tried holding him while they roped him, and he tried to bite me. I thought for sure he'd go home then, but when I gave up again and ran on, he was still behind me. My last comment to the dog was, "Buddy, you really don't want to follow me where I'm going."

Chapter 9
Bad Cheese

I finally arrived at the meeting spot minutes before Tessa and her friend, Chad, got out of their car to greet me. They took me to Athens and I waved goodbye to my canine friend. The rangers said they would send someone later to check if the dog was still in the area.

We arrived on the campus of Ohio University for a welcome day off. On the drive there my friends talked enthusiastically about trying to set up newspaper interviews for me.

The next day, Chad and Tessa had done a good job. In the space of a few hours, I gave interviews to reporters of three newspapers and had my picture taken for each. I also spoke to a senior writing course. The course was "Autobiographical Quest" and they were studying the characters in Huckleberry Finn. After a discussion of the book, I spoke to the class and showed them the contents of my pack and shared a few stories. Though not floating on a homemade raft, my modern day quest to see America seemed like an updated version of Mark Twain's book, if Huck Finn had worn Nike's.

After my presentation the instructor asked me what sorts of issues I was dealing with along the way. It wasn't a question I'd ever been asked and though I denied having any issues at the time, I later realized what the challenge of the journey was, and it had nothing to do with running. The feeling of being an outsider in every community I ran through was one of the most difficult issues to live with daily. People would look at me when I entered a restaurant, covered in sweat and dirt, eating two meals, a milkshake and dessert. That feeling of isolation was the most difficult part for me. In the end, I feel one lesson from the journey was to always foster compassion, that one can't really know another's needs based purely on assumption or appearance. Just as it would have been impractical for me to explain my trip to everyone who gave me a questioning glance, I try to remember that long after the trip had concluded there are still people with needs and I may never learn their story, but my kindness is owed to them.

The next morning, Chad and Tessa drove me back to Burr Oak Lake where I was relieved to see my canine friend had either gone home or had decided to follow his own trail to California. After several miles I came upon a family of four out for a hike in the rain. Three young kids and a dad were covered in mud and were complaining to their father in the lead.

"Excuse me, sir," said the father to me. "But would you happen to have a candy bar?"

"Do I have a candy bar?" I was taken a little off guard that he was asking if I had one, as people usually offered me the food. "Well, yes, actually I do."

"Oh, good," he said. "You see, my daughter is diabetic and she needs some sugar right now."

"Oh, I see," I said hesitantly. It was going to be a long day with no guarantee of a place to stop for lunch. I needed all the food I had, which was not much. "Well," pulling off my pack, "I have a King Size Snickers Bar, two packs of cheese crackers, and a brownie."

I selfishly didn't want to give away any of my food but under the circumstances the young girl needed a snack more than I. The girl looked over my array of food and, deciding the giant Snickers was too much sugar, opted for the brownie. Then the father asked me how much farther it was up the trail to the park lodge. I quickly deduced that this man was not prepared for his excursion.

"Let's see," I began. "You can continue along this trail that will take you 24 miles around the lake back to the lodge. Or you can continue following these light blue blazes for 1197 miles around the entire state of Ohio until you reach your lodge. Or you can turn back now and do the same three miles you just hiked."

"Ok, kids, turn around," the father said, already reversing course without pausing.

"Aw Dad, you mean we have to go all the way back the way we came?" cried his kids, who had just spent a full morning in the rain trudging through the mud. The last I heard of their fading voices was the father responding to the complaints, "You heard him, what do you want to do? Hike even further?"

That day the trail took me through chest deep thickets of poison ivy and despite a long hot shower to try and wash off the plant's oils, I had several rashes starting to spread. By day's end I had reached the small community of Shawnee, Ohio. There is a great main street in Shawnee with large storefronts and a city park in the middle of town, but business has not been good lately and most stores are vacant. I entered the only restaurant still open and ordered the Fish Special.

After quickly cleaning my plate, and still feeling famished, the waitress came over and asked in waitress-monotone without looking up from her order pad, "Would you like some dessert with that?"

I replied in a quiet voice, not wanting to be heard by the three other people in the quaint dining room, "Actually, you know, I think I'll have another one of those specials."

For the first time, my server looked up from her receipt pad, paused as she stared at me for a moment as if trying to figure out if I was serious. I ate the second meal just as quickly as the first and sat at the table scanning my map for any possible lodging nearby for the night. The waitress had brought my check some time earlier and, when I didn't stand up to pay, she came over, looked straight into my eyes, and gently asked,

"Would you like some dessert too?"

"Yes, please," I said gratefully.

Even though there were no official accommodations in town, I felt that a sheltered place to sleep could be found if I searched hard enough. Outside the restaurant I asked a man mowing his yard if he knew of a church in town. He directed me to the home of one of the church employees. I found him standing in a garden. I introduced myself and described my dilemma. He considered letting me sleep in the church's new fellowship trailer but the key to the trailer was out of town with the minister. Instead, he offered to drive me ten miles to a motel and restaurant and even pick me up the next morning!

That night I enjoyed a scalding hot shower to relieve the patches of poison ivy that had developed on my hands, back, and sides. The hot water trick is a personal remedy of mine that goes against doctor's advice but works well for me as the hot water first intensifies the itching, then relieves it without having to scratch. Also, the running water helps wash away the oils that would otherwise spread. I called my family that night, talking to Lydia, my mom, and dad. My dad's only comment to the barrage of stories I told him was, "I hope you're writing all of this down."

I passed a good number of dogs that day. They ranged from tiny yappy dogs who chased at my heels to ones who couldn't be bothered. One, a St. Bernard, was lying in his yard. As I passed, he looked lazily my way, inhaled with a mild weariness, paused for showmanship, then let out with one resounding, "Wooooooof!" and lowered his head. As if to say, "There, I did it. You know where I am if you need me."

Later in the day as I was running along a section through the woods, the trail markers became obscure and I had to slow down to keep from getting lost. Whenever I lost the trail, my first remedy was to retrace my steps to the last marker. Then I would proceed very slowly looking for any blazes, side trails or other evidence of a direction I had not noticed before. This section was particularly confusing and I searched for more than 20 minutes to find the continuation of my trail. I tried backing up. I tried searching for depressions in the ground from the feet of others over the years. Finally, I resorted to inspecting every tree for any evidence of a blaze and found one fleck of paint, about the size of a fingernail trimming, almost obscured by a crack in the tree trunk. At that moment, that fleck of dried paint was the continuation of the 5000-mile thread I was trying to hang on to from one ocean to another.

Unfortunately, the direction that thread led me in was headed straight across a flooded valley, dammed up by a colony of beavers. Now that I focused my attention on an area that at first seemed unlikely for the trail, I could clearly see the next blaze on the other side of the small lake and upon inspection, even saw a blaze on a tree in the middle of the lake! Not wanting to wade through deep black muck for fifty yards, I went upstream to the beaver dam and crossed half of the body of water on the amazingly strong twig structure. I still had 20 yards of water to cross once the dam ended. Picking an area that seemed to be the shallowest, I stepped off the dam and onto the streambed, only to immediately sink up to my knees in sodden compost and mud. Fears of becoming trapped in that stream miles from help flashed through my mind, but I decided that if I kept moving, I could lessen the sinking of my body. I quickly shuffled across the streambed, only sinking up to my calves with each step. Some later asked what I would have done had I become stuck in that muck. It's hard to say what may have happened, but I recall many similar instances on the trip where failure was simply not an option. To even entertain the thought seemed to invite that other outcomes were possible.

Lydia's aunt and uncle lived in nearby Granville, Ohio, and had agreed to pick me up to be their guest for Easter. Despite my dirty appearance, they took me in where I cleaned up, washed my shoes, and wore my Sunday best outfit to the Easter service followed by an all-church brunch.

"Hello, I'd like to introduce you to our niece's friend, Brian. He is running across the United States," my hosts would say.

"Oh, really? Nice to meet you. Have a sugar cookie."

I felt a little out of place wearing my tights and T-Shirt in the Sunday crowd, but I appreciated the hospitality and the chance to share a holiday with relatives of my girlfriend.

*   *   *

Everyone has heard unusual tales of courtship. Lydia's and mine surely could compete with the best of them. Try to keep up and you will be astounded by this tale. I had grown up in Indiana while Lydia's family moved around a lot while she was growing up. She attended junior high school in Evansville, Indiana and that's where our story starts. There she met, Leslie, who is still her best friend. When Leslie grew up she chose to attend nearby Hanover College where we were in the same graduating class. In our freshman year, Lydia came to visit her junior high school pal on campus. I met Lydia during that visit and we had a fun weekend, eating in the dining hall together and going for walks around campus. That was the last I heard of Lydia for some time, although Leslie played quite the matchmaker. She would mention, "Lydia asked about you on the phone last night. I think she really likes you."

Four years later, in my senior year at Hanover, I received a mysterious postcard. It was from Lydia, saying that she was having a contest with her roommate and they were trying to see how many postcards they could get from different states. Then she apologized for writing, hoping that I hadn't forgotten her and said that she still remembered the good time she'd had on her visit to Hanover.

I thought the card was cute and wrote her back. For the next three years we wrote each other off and on and, gradually, our letter writing increased. Our letters soon led to phone calls and one night on the phone I suggested we get together for a visit. She was in graduate school at Duke University, and I offered to drive to see her in North Carolina. We hit it off right away.

A month later, she flew to visit me for Valentine's Day. During lunch, where she met my dad, a bizarre story unfolded. It started with a conversation about Lydia's family roots. Her mother's side of the family was originally from Elkhart, Indiana. Upon hearing that, my father perked up and said,

"I grew up in Elkhart!" Then my dad asked what her mother's maiden name was.

"Koehler," Lydia said with expectation.

My dad then asked, "Didn't Mr. Koehler sell Electrolux vacuum cleaners?"

"Yes!" Lydia said, "He was my grandfather!"

"And I seem to remember that they had a daughter, Sue," my dad continued, foggily recalling his past.

"Yes, yes! She's my aunt!" Lydia exclaimed. (I had just spent Easter with "Aunt Sue" in Ohio.) Now things were getting really spooky.

"We were friends in high school," my dad said. That was too much. Then we met my grandmother and things really got spooky. Lydia's grandparents, it turned out, had been best friends with my grandparents *63 years earlier*. They double dated at the high school prom, went on double dates all through school and they stood up in each other's weddings! Later, my grandmother produced scrapbook photo albums of both sets of our grandparents at different stages in their lives.

The plot continued to thicken as we later learned that Lydia's father's side of the family had connections to me, as well. Growing up, her father's Sunday school teacher was the landlord of a log cabin I had been living in prior to my run! With cosmic connections like this taking place over a 70-year span, it's hard to imagine our future wasn't laid out in the stars.

*   *   *

After the church service and a nice Easter meal with Lydia's relatives, I caught up on my chores for the day, writing in my journal and doing laundry. While washing my socks that night, I noticed a small hole forming on one of the big toes. It was the second pair I had gone through. I was using socks made by Wigwam Mills. I had chosen the model, "3000-mile socks" to run in. The socks were guaranteed by the manufacturer to last that many miles. It was a large claim that I doubted any sock could live up to. However, I imagined that the sock company had faith that no one in his right mind would actually run 3000 miles in a single pair of socks, much less keep track of the mileage. The company was apparently not aware of my plans to run 4800-miles, the equivalent of, in their calibration, one and a half pair of socks.

After the second pair of socks wore out in only 300 miles, I called the company and was put in touch with the customer service department. A representative on the phone told me to launder the socks and mail them to the company, where their analysts could determine what had gone wrong and decide whether or not to send me a replacement pair. I informed them that I was running every day and could not mail them my only pair of socks. I was patched through to someone with more authority and was promised a shipment of three pairs of socks to my next post office address.

Those three pairs lasted the remainder of the trip. I attribute this to the better running conditions of the plains and west, where mud was less prevalent, so it didn't have the same corrosive factor on fabric as in West Virginia and Ohio.

The next day I was in for a real treat. I entered Hocking Hills Recreation Area with its famous Ash Cave, Old Man's Cave, and nice park facilities. Old Man's Cave is an area developed during the days of the Civilian Conservation Corps, or CCC. There are elaborate stone steps carved out of the hillsides, stone-lined tunnels leading through giant boulders, and picturesque waterfalls along the trail, all nestled in a lush canyon.

My map showed that the park offered a dining room on the west side of the park, located just off the trail. According to my contour line-free map, I could stay on the trail until I saw the lodge on my right. My guidebook, however, recommended taking an access road some distance around to the lodge, but I decided the trail would be faster. When I neared the area of the lodge, I realized why the guidebook had suggested using the access road.

Standing in the pit of the narrow gorge, I could see the edge of the lodge facility, perched on top of the gorge wall, more than 300 feet above the valley floor. My choices were to run several miles back up the trail, then run several more miles along a road to the lodge, or try and climb the bluff. Premonitions of headlines claiming, "Transcon Runner Falls to His Death Trying to Save 3 Miles." After searching the bluffs, I found a path that was reasonably safe to climb and ascended the steep hillside. There were areas that were clearly difficult, but at no time was I in grave danger. I quickly envisioned a humorous moment about to take place as I neared the top. The very point I had chosen to climb to turned out to be an observation deck at the end of a walkway. When I saw the wooden platform railing, I pictured a couple having a romantic moment sitting on the edge of the bluff taking in the sunset, just as a muddy runner grasped the railing in front of them and climbed over the top. Fortunately (and a little disappointedly I might add), there were no honeymooners on the deck.

I arrived at dinnertime and enjoyed a fine meal before setting out to find a place to sleep. There were family cabins for rent at a cost of over $100 per night. I called veteran ADT Trekkers, Bill and Laurie Foot to ask if they knew of an inexpensive place in the area to sleep. They could not think of any. I saw meeting rooms in the basement of the lodge, which were vacant now that the lodge was closing for the night. I spoke with an employee while putting on my best face and genuine friendliest composure, but after making a few phone calls she told me it was against park rules for anyone to spend the night in the lodge. She offered to have me driven to a nearby hotel, but I decided that I had not yet been beaten.

Outside, I searched the property around the lodge. In the backyard was a very large swimming pool. It was equipped for wheelchairs and I decided to sleep under a wide aluminum ramp going into the pool. The weather forecast for the night had predicted heavy rain, so I knew I should be under some kind of protection.

I laid out my sleeping bag and ground cloth under a portion of the ramp on the pool deck, choosing a section of the ramp as low as possible to keep blowing rain from hitting me. I lay down in my new shelter, and the storm arrived five minutes later. At first there was only thunder. Then, with a crack, there was instant lightening and heavy rain. It was then that I realized how foolish I was for laying under a massive metal object in a lightening storm. More dumb revelations were to follow.

As the rain pounded down, the cement pool deck became saturated. Once the surface was soaked, the rain began forming evil streams, something I had not foreseen. One stream was headed my way, intent on soaking all contents under the ramp. When the stream was only a few inches away, I curled my body to avoid the water headed my way. Soon all was lost, and I was forced to lie on wet pavement with sheets of rain and mist blowing in on me from both sides. I did not sleep much that night and when I awoke, my down sleeping bag was wet, a carnal sin in the world of camping.

At least I was close to breakfast, so I hastily stuffed my belongings into my pack and trotted the 50 yards back to the dining room when it opened.

After breakfast, I once again scaled down the cliff below the observation deck, but this time I had the added concern of wet, slippery ground. I slid-stepped my way back to the valley floor, content with my inexpensive if uncomfortable night.

Several cold stream crossings and muddy stretches had once again built up my hunger. I arrived at Bess' Carry Out Country Store where I bought dinner for the night. A loaf of bread, an eight-pack of American cheese slices, a short pack of smoked ham, and a can of Pringles were my selections. I was starved for company and asked if I could eat my $15 worth of groceries in the store. The cashier replied, "They don't like people eating in here." I went outside and sat on a picnic table. The store had no single serving packets of condiments, and I did not want to buy an entire jar of mayonnaise for my sandwiches, so I had to eat them with cheese only. Anyone who has ever eaten white bread with uncooked American cheese without condiments knows that my dinner experience was far from pleasant. With each bite it became more difficult to continue.

As I struggled with my dinner, a man appeared from a nearby house and walked over to me. The picnic table I was sitting on looked as though it was in his yard, so I swallowed a ball of cheese and doughy bread and braced for a confrontation. Instead he asked, "Are you the guy running all the way across the country?"

Relieved, I told him I was. He said that a contact of mine had called him and told him to be on the lookout for me. My hopes leaped at the thought that he would help me find a place to sleep, but when I cautiously told him I was getting ready to search for a place to stay for the night he just said, "Oh."

Then I asked, "You wouldn't happen to know of a *barn* or a *garage* or a small piece of *carpeted floor* where I could sleep, would you?" (We were no more than twenty yards behind his garage and house.)

He thought for a moment, and said with a small laugh, "No, I sure don't." It looked as though I was on my own once again for lodging.

I choked down the rest of my dinner and went back into the store to buy some more snacks and drinks for the night and next morning. I bought some snack cakes, a soft drink, and some doughnuts for breakfast. It was this last purchase that finally aroused questions from the cashier.

"What are you, biking or something?"

"Actually, I'm running from Delaware to California." The clerk's face was expressionless. A little way down the road I came to the Tar Hollow State Forest, which my map claimed had drinking water. The building was closed and all the outside water taps had been turned off. I found a small barn across the road with a nice clean bed of straw and camped inside for the night, content in my primitive lodging with the occasional sounds of barking dogs announcing my presence through the night.

Chapter 10
Sleepovers

After getting some water the next morning from a nearby house, I made my muddy way over the hillsides of the BT. By mid-afternoon, I had arrived at the outskirts of Londonderry, Ohio. At the edge of town, I was desperately thirsty and stopped at the first house I came to, an older trailer home next to an over-flowing trash pile. The woman at the door took one look at me and, after going inside for a second, came out with a tall glass of ice water and an ice cold Pepsi with sweat beads dripping down the sides. It just goes to prove that you can't judge people by their yards.

Bill and Laurie Foot ADT biker-hikers had connected me with Mike and Connie Snyder in town. Connie is the local postmaster and she had offered to take me in for the night. Inside the post office I met Connie and wrote postcards while she closed up the office for the evening. We drove home and I was treated to a shower, laundry, and a gigantic dinner.

The next morning, Connie treated me to a huge breakfast and a great lunch to go. In the evening, I met my great aunt and uncle from the area and we had a good dinner at a local restaurant. Being in their 80's, they were amazed when I got up for my eighth plate at the salad bar. "I wish I had your appetite," my Great Aunt Mildred said. "I wish I had his legs!" my Great Uncle Glenn replied when he marveled at hearing of my daily mileage. We then got into an interesting discussion of the state of the world based on his recent rather grim experience of the sale and subsequent destruction of his much-loved tree farm. In a voice suited for a commentary at a Washington D.C. museum, Great Uncle Glen said, "People these days seem to be caught up in a frenzy called, 'progress.' It seems to throw things so out of focus that I'm not even sure what progress is anymore!" I said something in agreement as a reply and we both smiled, sharing a moment of converging philosophies. They saw me off with a bag of Hershey Kisses and a loaf of homemade bread.

Connie's assistance wasn't over yet, however. It turned out being friends with a postmaster was a valuable asset. She had friends and relatives scattered all the way along the ADT and she prepared to connect me with them.

First, I stayed in the home of Dan, Connie's brother. Dan owns a construction company and his wife takes pride in feeding the entire crew of workers a brunch every week.

Dan and his wife fed me a great dinner of mashed potatoes, chicken, ribs, green beans with baked beans, corn, salad, and potato casserole. Their daughters made up a bed for me in their basement. They had recently built their home themselves and I marveled at the finished product as Dan and I played guitars on the living room couch.

Dan dropped me off the next morning saying, "If you need any help between here and Cincy don't hesitate to call!"

Connie's magic continued as I made it to her sister's house in Ripley where she and her husband took great care of me. With each passing of relative and acquaintance however, my invitations became a little sketchier. Initially, I had been nearly adopted by Connie and Mike, but ten days later, I would call a number I had been given, explain my trip and how I got their phone number, and hear a hesitant pause on the other end of the line. "Oh? Um, ok, I guess."

It was a very long day of running on Texas Sheet Cake-like muddy trails. At one point a vast number of trees had blown down across the trail. Most were massive – too low to the ground to crawl under and too much effort to climb over. There were over 25 such trees in this section. I had an incentive to get over them, however. My mother was driving in from her home in Columbus, Indiana to Sinking Spring, Ohio to meet me for the night. It was to be a 32-mile day. Several of the stream crossings were near waist-deep in very cold, muddy water. I finally arrived at the access road into Sinking Spring. My mom said she would meet me on the main street in town between 5 and 6 p.m. It was now 5 p.m. and town was just three miles down the very road I was standing on. However, the official ADT crosses the road and meanders through yet another forest for seven miles before reaching the town limits.

I decided to let fate decide what I should do. Should I run in on the road, and skip seven miles of the ADT only to be driven back out here the next morning and have to run back into town? Should I run the official trail and be late in my arrival? I even thought about hitching in to meet her, as I was tired, soaking wet, muddy, and hungry. I stuck my thumb out for 3 minutes and when two cars didn't stop for me I decided to keep going. I ran the official trail into town, making me a half-hour late but my mother was waiting for me, right in "downtown" Sinking Spring. I came over the crest of a hill and saw her car, driver's door ajar, arm waving out the window, white fluffy West Highland Terrier, "Daisy," yipping and yapping at the soggy guy she didn't recognize anymore. After a long hug she presented me with an oatmeal-raisin-chocolate-chip cake, Gatorade, pretzels, and peanuts. After such a challenging day, her snacks were a welcome treat.

We drove to Chillicothe, Ohio to find a motel and chose one with an indoor pool and Jacuzzi. After dinner, I sat in the motel's hot tub with two young girls and a gawky young man. The man was trying unsuccessfully to convince the girls that he was a "hustler" in a large nearby city and had been hired by more than 800 women for his services. He tried to appear unfazed when they refused to believe his stories of being in high demand, but he certainly did not woo any women that night. I remained quietly amused as my muscles melted in the soothing hot water.

It's hard to sit in a hot tub with other people and pretend not to be paying any attention to what they are saying. In the few hotels I found with a hot tub, I looked forward to meeting other hotel guests, but the rare occasions I found myself soaking with strangers never resulted in anything more than a mumbled greeting.

Later the next day, in the solid drizzle, I stopped at Serpent Mound State Historic Park for lunch and a break from the rain. Serpent Mound is a giant earthen snake built on a hilltop and is believed by most to be a Native American structure. A museum next to the mound is filled with theories of the site. Most believe it is a depiction of a snake eating an egg. The most creative theory is from a scholar who insisted that Serpent Mound is a sign from God that the Garden of Eden was originally located in southern Ohio.

At the end of the day I arrived in Peebles and met Steve, a friend and fellow postmaster of Connie's. Steve is a very nice man who took me to dinner and an evening church service. At the church, I stood in front of the congregation and was introduced. Church members later reminisced with me about a man they remembered who was walking all of the major rivers and preaching the gospel in local churches along the way. "Man, now that man could preach!" they said.

Steve had a friend in the next town of Wamsley whom he thoughtfully had made arrangements for me to stay with the next night.

As I entered town and jogged up to the house I had been directed to, I read and re-read my notes to make sure that there wasn't some kind of mistake. A brick chimney lay in the yard like some elevated walkway inviting me in. The outside clapboard siding displayed more bleached gray bare wood than the white coating it wore so many years ago. The yard was a collection of interesting and potentially useful appliances, furniture, and the usual collection of aluminum cans. During the miles of mud, streams, and cheese cracker lunches, I often daydreamed about a family with royal heritage awaiting my arrival at day's end. Fantasies of palatial estates with butlers, silk sheets, and Olympic-sized Jacuzzis with accomplished conversationalists filled my mind. I had a feeling this was going to be different sort of lodging in Wamsley. I found the Bell's, my host family, working in the back yard.

The father was replacing siding on the back porch and his wife, two daughters, and a son were looking on from the lawn. I explained who I was and they said that the person Steve had spoken to couldn't take me in after all and that person had called this family who agreed to be the latest participants in this customized underground railroad.

The Bell family home gets its water from a pitcher-pump on the back porch. Hilarious family tales soon came out as each person went around and told his or her funniest memory of growing up in the most primitive home on the block. Stories were told about using the outhouse in the middle of winter and of how one time the city water ran out and the family graciously helped their needy neighbors by rationing out water from their own well.

Inside, the home assumes a more intimate level of maintenance. Heavy curtains fill interior doorways and Duct Tape remedies worn spots in the linoleum. Due to poor insulation, and the fact that their primary heating source fell off the house some time ago, the family now spends $200 per month to heat their home with kerosene heaters. Mr. Bell informed me that the home has been falling down for 18 years.

In the living room, the television was surrounded by the most impressive private collection of videotapes I have ever seen. There were over 500 new videos! When I asked how they acquired so many videotapes, they explained that they believed it was better to buy a movie for $15 - $20 and watch it over and over, than to rent one for $3 and only be able to watch it once. I calculated they would need to have 3000 movie nights or, *one every night for eight years*, to get their money's worth. But the funniest of all were the true tales of courtship and how this family began.

Mr. and Mrs. Bell were married at the ages of 16 and 15 respectively. At 16, Mr. Bell was just beginning a career as a gravedigger. The teenager and his friends would regularly engage in "car swapping" after work. The only problem with this unusual hobby is that while Mr. Bell was at work in the ditches, Mrs. Bell needed to go to the store to buy diapers and groceries for their young children. As she explained, she was pregnant for the first six years of her marriage. At that time, the driving age in Ohio was 18 and 15-year-old Mrs. Bell was not legally allowed to drive. The police understood the situation and generally looked the other way. However, as the Bell's owned a different car each night, it was hard for the local police to recognize just which car the young mother was in on any given day.

To add to the situation, I was told by Mrs. Bell that, "Back then when we lived in the hills, you didn't go anywhere without shoving a wire hanger down in your boot, because you just know that you're going to lose your muffler when you go to town on them holler roads. And being pregnant you're tryin' to fit under the car after you've set somewhere for an hour so you can let the muffler cool down so you can touch it, and then you try and crawl under there with a bowling ball attached to you, it's tough!"

They served me a great dinner and that night I had another unique bedroom. The Bells were the local Sunday School teachers and had a key to the church. I slept in the Sunday School room with a newly renovated restroom located across the hall. Just before I said my goodnights, we watched "The First Wife's Club," – on video of course.

A country home serves up simple generosity.

Chapter 11
Trashvertizing

The next day I was running down a nice section of new trail deep in the woods, following carsonite posts with the shiny new ADT stickers, when the trail suddenly ended. A trail relocation had not been finished, and I arrived at a road crossing seven miles away from the older version of the now abandoned trail. Fortunately, I met a park ranger who gave me a ride to his office where a congregation of rangers and I poured over forest maps before coming to the conclusion that I was lost. Rejoining the abandoned trail, I hitched a ride off the route at the end of the day into the nearby town of Manchester, Ohio.

I entered the office of the only motel in town, where I noticed a Boy Scouts of America sticker on the door. Attempting to get the best price, I asked, "Do cross-country running Eagle Scouts get extra discounts?" He took one look at me, smiled and charged me the bargain rate of $19.90.

The next morning on my way out of town I stopped for a breakfast of French Toast. I was even hungrier than normal and requested a double order. It wasn't more than three minutes before those slices were gone. Since my appetite was not dented, I asked for two more orders. By now my hunger was in full swing and it didn't want to have to wait for the next plate to be prepared so I asked for two doughnuts while I was waiting for my next two orders. By the time I had finished my two doughnuts, two large orange juices, and four orders of French Toast, the kitchen staff had emerged from the back room and was staring at me in awe. Unfortunately, I couldn't stick around to sign menus, I was excited to get to the Counterfeit House, an attraction I had been looking forward to for 500 miles.

As I made my way back up the hill from Manchester to rejoin the route, I noticed a Reese's Cup candy bar wrapper on the side of the road. Perhaps it was my "meager" breakfast, or my body anticipating high caloric need during the day's run. Whatever the reason, the instant I saw that wrapper I knew that I had to have a Reese's Cup right there and then. At the top of the hill there was a small gas station, and I bought not one but two packages of the peanut butter and chocolate delights. Sitting there on the steps of that gas station at 8:15 a.m. eating my 500-calorie snack, I coined a new phrase, "Trashvertizing." My new definition would read as follows, "trash•ver•tize (trash'ver'tiz'), v. 1. The practice of secret agents in the candy bar industry who place their product in highly visible and appealing locations such as ditches and gutters where passersby will see them and be tempted to purchase said candy bar at next opportunity."

Arriving at the Counterfeit House a few miles later I noticed that the house itself looked in disrepair. There was no "open" sign or other evidence that visitors were welcome. I approached a trailer in the side yard of the house and knocked on the door. An older woman came to the door but, upon seeing someone she didn't recognize, locked the storm door and waited to hear what I wanted. I explained that I was running across the country and had been looking forward to touring the Counterfeit House for 500 miles. Unimpressed, she simply said, "Well, it's closed. The roof leaks and it's not open to the public." I was heartbroken. What mysterious things were inside that home just a few yards away? Perhaps this woman was getting back into action and used her, "Sorry, closed" speech to cover the printing operation going on in the shadows of the old home.

When I pressed her for a few stories about the old days she finally sized me up through the screen and gave in to storytelling as she unlatched the door and came outside. As we sat down on the porch swing she slowly warmed up to me and told me about this amazing site and her connection to it.

Oliver Tompkins built the "Counterfeit House" in 1840. Mr. Tompkins designed the home for the purpose of making counterfeit 50-cent pieces and $500 bills. Just why he chose to make only those two denominations is unclear. The doors to the home had special locks designed so that even when locked, "authorized" people could enter by turning the knob a certain way. Several slots were carved away above interior doors. These slots were where the counterfeit money was stored in bags and then replaced with real money when an exchange took place. In the attic, there is a small window in which Mr. Tompkins placed two lights. One was green and the other red. From the advantageous position of the home on a high bluff, the building can be seen from the Ohio River over one and a half miles away.

Boat captains who knew of Mr. Tompkins' business could look up the hillside and if the green light was on, it meant that the coast was clear and that they could come up to buy money. If the red light was on, however, it meant trouble and to stay away. For additional security, seven chimneys were erected in the home. Of the seven, only two were actually used as such. The other five were false double chimneys that had stairways built inside them. Through an elaborate system of ducts, the two real chimneys sent flumes of smoke out the five fake chimneys. From inside the fake chimney, and hidden behind a plume of smoke, Mr. Tompkins could see who was coming up the hill.

In the back of the home was the actual counterfeiting room. It was built with no doors or windows. The only access to the room was through a trap door in the ceiling and a trap door in the floor. The floor trap led to an escape tunnel that went over one hundred yards underground "big enough for a man and a horse," to a nearby cliff, as a grainy photocopied brochure stated.

As legend has it, Mr. Tompkins' sister, Ann, tried to pass one of his phony $500 bills in Cincinnati and that exchange led police to follow her to her brother's home. When the police were closing in, it is believed Mr. Tompkins and his daughter escaped through the tunnel and blew it up on their way out. To end the police chase that lasted for several years, Ann returned to the Counterfeit House with a coffin that she said contained the remains of her deceased father. A mock funeral was held in the home. It is rumored that Mr. Tompkins watched the funeral from one of his chimney lookouts.

Though I never got to go inside, my new friend made the history of the house come alive with her stories. I did notice, however, that she seemed tired of her connection with the home. She had lived in it for a number of years with her husband who is now in a nursing home. She obviously felt pain and loneliness but said that she just got to the point where she couldn't take care of him any longer. She said that later in the day she was going to mow the yard. I couldn't imagine that she still took care of the daily chores and I offered to do it for her but she declined. When I asked why she was no longer giving tours of the home, she explained that over the years the Counterfeit House has suffered neglect and the roof needs to be replaced.

With such an unusual home like this and its historical significance, I asked whether she had spoken to the local historical society or the chamber of commerce to get help with the building's restoration. That was apparently the wrong thing to say as she replied, "Oh, those people don't want to help me. They don't want to give me anything for the house." She went on to say that the roof is leaking so badly it needs to be replaced before the entire inside is ruined. That would cost $5,000 alone. I thought surely there was some kind of grant or foundation nearby that would be willing to fix the roof until the rest of the funds for restoration could be raised.

By this point in her story, she was much friendlier and even offered me food. Grabbing my arm she asked," Can I get you a cheese sandwich?" and went inside towards the kitchen before I could answer. "How would you like a can of Turkey Franks? I've got Ice Cream! A Coke?"

Each time she would say something, she would turn around, go inside and get it, and each time that she got something, she reminded herself of something else to offer me. "Here's a Hi-C Juice Box, that will be good. Oh, and here's a Reese's Cup bar, you'll need that!"

I didn't want to tell her about my recent trashvertizing experience, so I took it and enjoyed my third one of the morning. We traded addresses and I was exceedingly pleased with my visit to the Counterfeit House, even though I never saw the inside.

It rained on and off during the day but I didn't care. As I ate my home-made lunch out of the rain under the steel beams of a one-lane bridge, I began to fanaticize about moving to Manchester, Ohio after my run and completely renovating the Counterfeit House, giving tours, and telling people how I came to know its history. That dream occupied my thoughts until I arrived in Bentonville, at which point I had decided that I was going to excavate the original tunnel by hand, replace the roof by myself, and mow my new friend's yard twice a week for free for the rest of my life.

That evening, I got a ride off the trail back into Manchester for another night at the cheap motel. After dinner I heard an auctioneer announcing an incredible deal for sale down the street. I traced the voice a few stores down and went in to have a look. Sure enough, an auction company was taking advantage of the people's buying bug and had rented a store, gutted it, and placed a hundred or so folding chairs in one half and had merchandise for bid in the other half on a stage. There were roughly sixty people inside smoking, staring at the items for sale, and buying things that they surely couldn't have lived without. "We got here a Big Wheel Tricycle. The seat's missing but it'll make a good gift. Who'll give me $5?" There were other depressing items such as flimsy plywood wishing wells and questionably operating electric razors, "SOLD! For a dollar and a half!"

My forty-fifth day of running took me along a scenic river road and my map indicated that the last remaining covered bridge in the Ohio Highway system was coming up. Sounded neat, I thought. The maps I was using were so outdated, however, that when I arrived at the bridge, the road had been rerouted and the only remaining remnant of it was the cement abutments.

In the next town of Neel, which had two houses, my country road petered out into a cow pasture. Looking hard, I could still make out the original lane, which was now just a deep swath of grass between two fences. About a quarter mile down the "lane" I came to a very old bridge over a stream crossing. This one, like the last, had long been worn away and someone had placed a thin rotting board across the abutments. The span was about ten feet and the drop was eight feet into mud and water. The board looked of its age. I tried to decide if I should try crossing it. The murk below didn't look good for either wading through from below or falling into from above. I asked myself, "Someone must have used this board at one time, right? If it held them, maybe it will hold me." As I took my first steps, I could hear the fibers flexing and separating. Halfway across, the board was flexing so bad I feared it would simply bow until I was gently lowered into the muck. Perhaps all of the termites locked arms to support me because it held my weight, barely, and I made it across and into Georgetown for the night.

Connie's magic continued once more as I had been invited to stay with her sister, Roenna and husband, Frank in neighboring Bethel.

On the way to their home we passed the home of Steve Newman's parents. In 1983, at the age of 28, Steve decided to circle the earth on foot and walked out the front door of his parents' home. He returned four years later having completed his journey. I recall reading Steve's book, "Worldwalk" and his sketchy beginning. About an hour after he had left home, walking down the same road I was now running, his mother and brothers drove out in their station wagon to see how he was doing. He was not fairing well. In the rush to get out the door and begin his 15,000-mile walk, Steve had forgotten to take his water bottle and was now thirsty. His pack was also too heavy and he was slumped over shuffling down the road under its weight. His brother offered to wear his pack while his mother turned around to go home and get his water bottle. I felt a connection to Steve and his inauspicious beginning, as I recalled my own tentative first hours on my journey. Though I wasn't rounding the planet (yet), I hoped our similar beginnings was reassurance that I would also succeed.

The next morning I picked up the Buckeye Trail and promptly resumed the now almost daily ritual of getting lost. Bill and Laurie Foot compiled the one-year old data book I was using as my main resource for the ADT. It had not been verified for its information other than when Bill and Laurie actually biked and hiked the trail as they wrote it. I was their editor so to speak. For the most part, the data book was an excellent resource and I couldn't have done the trip without it. In addition to listing roads, trails and turns, the data book posts mileage going in both directions, trail towns with zip codes and services offered. It was an indispensable resource but there were a few instances where the trail simply didn't match the description in the book. One instance in particular is a side note in the data book referring to western Ohio. It says, "Bikes can be ridden from here to Cincy." When I had read that ten days earlier, I had become excited to think that the miles would be coming easier, and that the route was going to be on "established" roads for the remainder of Ohio.

Only a circus clown would have tried to ride a bike across that decomposed toothpick over the abandoned stream crossing and waist deep weeds! Several miles of traipsing along a muddy trail that I didn't need to be on and bushwhacking through a vast barren prickly field, I finally came out at a private horse camp. Several people were around cleaning up the camp for the coming riding season. When I approached two women cleaning up a picnic, they straightened me out with my directions and then offered me their leftover picnic feast. I was hungrier than one of their pack animals and gorged on fried chicken, coleslaw, beans, rolls, chips, a slice of pie, and a Coke. All I had asked for was directions and some water but I left with much more.

Only a few hours later I arrived in Batavia. Ohio has a food store chain called UDF or United Dairy Farmers. Their motto should have been, "We keep Brian Stark going" as they offer 40-ounce milkshakes! In addition to my quart-plus sized ice cream Styrofoam vat, I also succumbed to Ding Dongs and a bag of Doritos. It was a Thanksgiving meal that made me proud to be a pilgrim.

Later in the afternoon I passed a young woman running on the road. It had been some time since I had seen anyone else outside, much less running. "Hello!" I greeted her enthusiastically. She just looked at me blankly. A few miles later I was stopped by a man in his car.

"Are you a hasher?" he asked, referring to the international running club, the Hash House Harriers, with the self-titled motto: A drinking club with a running problem.

It turned out a local club was having an event and a few of the runners had gotten off course. I told him about the straggling woman behind me and he drove off.

I arrived in the next town with no idea as to where any motels were so I approached the first shop I saw, an antique store. The owners, Shirley and Stan, were very accommodating and spent 20 minutes on the phone trying to get a good deal on a nearby hotel for me. The cheapest was over $60. They talked between themselves and soon offered to take me home with them for the night. I had known them for perhaps 25 minutes when I climbed into their backseat to go home with them. They served a delicious dinner on a 500-year-old table once used in a sewing factory. In fact, antique needles and pins can still be found in the cracks of the wood.

Back in town after breakfast all of the shopkeepers were getting ready for a street fair. I helped Shirley and Stan set up some antiques on the sidewalk and then they suggested that I go next door to their neighbor's shop and help her, as she couldn't lift heavy objects. At first I was obliged to help, but soon I felt that I was in for more than I had bargained for.

It started out simply enough. I moved a cement lion onto a tabletop. The lion weighed 100 pounds.

Having done that, I moved a patio set to the front walk. Then I was handed cleaning products to wipe off the furniture.

Next, I moved a child's picnic table and finally she said she had just one last thing. Actually, it was two things, but since they were identical, I suppose they counted as one.

She said that she had two urns upstairs in storage and she would like to have them downstairs on display. When she said urns I pictured the small vases that you put loved one's ashes in. "No problem!" I said.

"Really?" she asked, impressed. "Great!" When I went up the stairs, I learned a little more about antiques. These urns were not the dainty ash capsules that I had envisioned. They were solid black cast iron flowerpots, the kind that adorn long windy tree-lined driveways. They weighed 200 pounds each and were far too heavy for one person. I decided I would at least try to lift them; after all, it was downhill to the first floor.

I tried picking one up. Nothing happened. It felt as though it were bolted to the city sewer pipes. I tried squatting and bear hugging the hunk of metal. It barely lifted off the ground. "If I can do this, I will be the hero of the day," I thought, trying to rouse my reserves. With all my might, blood filling my head like a balloon, veins popping out of veins, I got it in the air and knew it would only be a few seconds before this massive beast decided to drop on its own. Then came the steep and narrow attic steps leading back downstairs. By this time the street fair had already started and the store was quickly flooding with shoppers. If this urn toppled out of my grasp and crushed a colony of grandmothers it would not bode well for iron sales that day.

Browsers in the store saw me coming and made way for the huffing beet-red nylon shorts tanned Samaritan lugging God knows what down the attic steps. "Where... do.... you... want this..." I gasped.

"Oh, um, how about... well... I don't know, over there I guess."

I set it down and she said, "Great, that's one!" I was done at this point, but I didn't want the urns to think they had beaten me. Back up the stairs I went, trying to imagine how I could possibly bring down the second pot and still get in a full day of running. With untamed no-nonsense bestiality, I brought down the second urn and set it on a table just as my arms were giving out and locking in place. I am sure that those urns are still for sale sitting right where I left them – cash and *carry*.

The shopkeeper must have felt bad for asking me to move so many items so she wrote a check to the American Hiking Society on my behalf. Fundraising really is hard work, I thought.

I thanked the shopkeepers and began my final approach into Cincinnati, weary arms and all.

Chapter 12
Porkopolis

Running the local Little Miami River Trail, I passed bikers, walkers and horse riders as I made my way into Eden Park in Cincinnati. The feeling I got from running through Cincinnati was much better than that of Washington D.C. The city was much cleaner, the people seemed more open and I did not have the hint of fear that I did in the nation's capitol.

Beth, a relative, picked me up for a few days. She was principal at the Seven Hills Lotspeich School and I gave presentations to the students for two days while in town. The first morning Beth had left early and had left instructions for me to uncover a Jeep in their backyard and drive it to school. It was the first time I had driven a vehicle in 57 days and, to be truthful, I was hoping to remain a strict pedestrian for eight months. The Jeep was fun to drive, however, and I quickly readjusted myself with modern travel.

During my presentation to students in the fourth grade, I talked about the three essentials to life: food, water, and shelter, and then proceeded to explain how I maintained all three during my run. I also used a pull-down map to describe the states I had run across so far and those yet to cross to get to the Pacific. Soon after, a barrage of questions came from the students.

"What if you break your leg?" one asked.

"Well, hopefully I will not be too far from a house and I can get help."

"But what if the house is 200 miles away?"

"Well, I hope that does not happen." Other questions followed.

"What's been your most difficult thing?" ""What's been your favorite part?" They were all excellent questions, particularly coming from a fourth grade class. I was very impressed. I had come from a town just a week ago where adults were outbidding each other to buy broken tricycles at a Friday night auction to the sharpest collection of students I had ever met.

I emphasized to the kids the importance of setting goals and planning what things they might like to accomplish when they get older. Later that afternoon, a teacher told me she overheard two students agreeing that, when they got older, they were going to buy hip packs and run across America together.

The next day I ran across the city and into Bicentennial Park, passing the statue of the Flying Pigs dedicating "Porkopolis," Cincinnati's nickname for once being the leading pork exporter. The park is beautiful with colorful playgrounds and a clean atmosphere. There were business people sitting on massive concrete steps overlooking the Ohio River, eating their lunch while chatting away on cell phones.

Nearby was a bronze plaque marking the ADT coming through the city: "960 miles to Delaware, 3700 miles to California." A nearby couple offered to take my picture as I sat on the wall over the plaque. Even if the mileage had grown a little over the years, it was nice to see such a substantial trail marker. At best, signage along the ADT consists of a series of decals and vinyl emblems strategically placed on the backs of stop signs and tacked into posts.

Passing River Front Stadium I got onto the Roebling Suspension Bridge (designed by the same architect known for the Golden Gate Bridge, also on the ADT) for my eight-mile jaunt across Kentucky and my second trip across the Ohio River. Once across the bridge, I entered the city of Covington, Kentucky and proceeded west to Devou Park for some reputed spectacular views of downtown Cincinnati.

Running through Covington, I took a wrong turn and ended up in neighborhoods where my fair skin and skimpy nylon running shorts definitely qualified me for a minority population. I finally got back on track and started ascending a large hill as I entered the park. As I did so, I came upon a larger man who was also running up the hill. It did not take long to catch up to him. "Hi!" I said, always glad to see others out on the road.

"Gasp... hi, ...gasp," he said.

"Can you tell me how to get to these great views in the park?" I asked in normal controlled breathing.

"Yeah...gasp,... you go, up...gasp...well... gasp... just follow me..."

"Ok," I said. I loved this. I was getting snooty, but 960 miles of mud and Fritos will do that to you. Just then a car came towards us and the man dropped back behind me.

"Say," he began, "how much...gasp... weight...gasp... do you have.. in that pack?"

"Oh, I don't know, maybe ten pounds," I said.

"And you.. run.. with that?"

"Sure." After I mentioned where I was ultimately running to, he dropped back to a shuffle, saying, "You'd better go on without me." The views were spectacular.

Done with Kentucky in less than two hours, I was ready to cross back into Ohio for my third crossing of the river. To get back into Ohio, the ADT traveler must take the Anderson Ferry. Cars are $2.75, bikes are 50 cents and pedestrians are a quarter. I got two dimes and a nickel out and boarded my ship. Leaning against one of the tug railings, and standing next to a double line of parked cars, I enjoyed the second section of trail where transportation is a requirement.

The next morning I arrived in North Bend, Ohio, the site of my second mail stop of the trip. In addition to my new pair of shoes, I also received two boxes of food and 12 letters. Everyone in the Post Office was happy to see that I had made it that far and likely more so that I was finally collecting all of my mail that had demanded so much of their limited shelf space for several weeks. Also included in my batch of goodies was a package from the folks at Wigwam Mills. My three replacement pairs of socks had arrived, and it was time to treat my feet in style.

A few miles later I crossed into Indiana. "Back home again," I thought. I had just come 980 miles from the east coast to my home state - on foot - in 52 days. It was a very good feeling to see all of the Indiana license plates again. Birds seemed to be chirping me on, restaurants seemed more frequent, and a young boy shouted a greeting from a passing school bus. "Hey you, get out of our..." I believe he had wanted to say "town" but as I was on a country road miles from anywhere, it wouldn't have been appropriate. So he began again, "Hey, get out of our..." This time I believe he was going to say, "state" which would also have been inaccurate as it was my state as well. What he really had meant to say, I imagined, was "get out of our 'unincorporated community.'" It could have been a lot worse, but that little kid on a big yellow school bus was the only one on the entire trip who yelled something even remotely offensive to me.

Inside the city of Lawrenceburg, Indiana I got a room at a hotel. The woman at the desk asked me for my license plate number and when I told her I arrived there on foot, she said, "Well, since you don't have a car, I guess you will have to *walk* three doors around the building and up the flight of stairs," a statement I found more confusing than derisive (how would my having a car affect my negotiation of the stairs?) My first night back in my home state had started as quite a welcome home party.

Just west of Aurora I left a section along busy Highway 50 where cars and trucks were whizzing by me with no shoulder. The trail route turned onto Laughery Creek Road, and the now familiar serenity of back road America was mine again. Just as things were getting quiet in the country I heard a, "yipp, yapp, yapp, bark!" Three puppies had picked up my scent and decided to tag along to California. I tried yelling at them. I chased them. I commanded them to stay, but they just kept following me.

It had been raining for the past several days and the runoff had made its way to the nearby streams. One such stream brazenly spilled across the road I had been running on. Rather than build a bridge over these usually low creeks, folks seemed to be content to let the stream flow over the road. With the additional rain from the past few days, this small stream, which would usually only moisten your ankles, was now a raging river with a very strong current. A deep drop off on the downstream side of the road churned with frothy yellowish water.

I was standing on the bank of the stream with three puppies now questioning whether they picked the right jogger to follow and we were trying to figure out if I could make it across the stream when a farmer came out of a house behind me wearing denim overalls. As he got closer, I could tell he was getting on in years. He had white hair, his thin six-foot frame walked with a careful balance. There were no full introductions and no formalities.

All he said was, "Sonny, my name's Junior, and I wouldn't try it." He then turned around and started to walk back up to his house. I stopped him to ask why he wouldn't try it. He stood with his back towards me for a moment, then turned around and said, "You only go around once in this crazy life and it's not worth chancing it on something like that. No sir! Don't go on trying that." Now that made me a little mad. Certainly I did not want to get hurt, but I had crossed a number of fast-flowing stream crossings in the past two months and had suffered no more than some mud and cold legs. True, none of them had been this swift nor with nearly the same drop off but I had been in the drink before. I asked if cars came by very often thinking perhaps I could get a ride across the water.

"The only guy who comes through here is my neighbor, drives a dump truck by here once a day and he already came by this morning, won't be anyone else till tomorrow."

I took out my map and studied what other options I had for getting around this wall of water. The only way to get around this stream safely was to take a branch road an extra 11 miles where it would rejoin the ADT on the other side. I was battling with what to do. It was hard deciding whether the old man knew what he was talking about. His parting words to me before turning and going back to his house were, "It's just not worth chancing."

I might well have tried it had it not been for a bad water accident I had experienced a few years earlier. I was leading a canoe trip of camp staff in my hometown in Columbus, Indiana. We were going to canoe past our normal take-out point to see if the water was safe to take kids farther down the river to where the next take-out point would be. The one obstacle on the trip and, granted, the excitement of the whole reason for doing this, was to canoe over the falls which are the remnants of a low head dam. I had been told rumors that former staffers used to canoe over them but no one could remember for sure if it was true. As we approached the dam and its five-foot drop we beached our canoes and climbed a nearby lookout tower in a city park for a better view.

From atop the park's tower we could see that the dam was actually split into two routes by a huge block of cement in the middle of the river. It appeared that the right side was flowing faster and might prove a better ride than the shallower left side. Back in the river I asked a few people if they thought we should put on our life jackets. Being staff, most decided the precaution unnecessary and I was the only one to put one on. My reasoning for wearing one was more for purposes of floating fun than safety. Few people realize that from the water's edge, downstream dams and waterfalls are invisible. Because the water falls to a lower height than the water you are on, it appears that the river is simply one continuous path of calm water stretching far into the horizon. I had driven over a bridge looking down at this waterfall all of my life, however, and I knew what was coming.

As we neared the falls, the noise of the falling water increased and we could make out mist rising from the frothing turbulence. Several whoops and hollers went through the group, as my canoe was the first over the falls. There was a tremendous amount of scraping from the fiberglass canoe as we went over the cement dam but we made it in one piece. The other three canoes followed and only the last one came close to tipping but righted itself just before being swamped. We had made it. We had so much fun going over it in canoes that a few others suggested that we play in the falls. We beached our canoes and walked upstream to the base of the falls we had just come over. It was surprisingly shallow and we climbed up onto the top of the dam. One of my friends, John, and I started walking across the top of the dam and over to the left, unexplored side. He was standing ahead of me and we were looking down at the rush of water gushing past our feet. We were contemplating riding the flume on our backs and just as we were asking each other whether or not we should go for it, John started slipping in slow motion on the thick bed of moss covering the downstream side of the dam. As he slipped slowly down the embankment, he turned around to reach for me and as I grabbed him, we both fell down and into the churning water. As soon as we slipped off the dam, I realized we were in trouble. The left side, unlike the right side of the dam, was much, much deeper, at least ten feet perhaps more as we never touched bottom. The perfect undertow and turbulence generated by the low head dam grabbed our feet and yanked us down underwater without warning. The way a dam current works is that the water is forced down at the edge of the dam. Once being forced down, the water, and any other object trapped in it is washed in a cycle underwater and downstream for a few feet, back to the surface, upstream to the dam, and back underwater.

The moments that we were coming up for air were not long enough to get a good breath. I luckily still had my lifejacket on. John did not and he was coming up less often than I. In a state of panic, John grabbed my neck, just as we all had been taught a drowning person would do. He was trying to use me to stay afloat. This made me go under water more often. To keep him from drowning me I swam away from him. By using the floatation from my lifejacket I was able to break out of the cycle of the current and helplessly watch from the edge of the falls as John continued to go through the cycle. The rest of the group had been watching us from atop the cement block in the middle of the river and at first had thought our screams were from delight. When I was out of the current and was screaming for John, they realized the severity of the situation but could do nothing to help.

All I remember was shouting "John!" and watching my Teva sandals float downstream and away from me as the Velcro had been torn apart in the turbulence. Finally, and amazingly, John surfaced a few feet away from me out of the current of the dam, and I helped his near limp body swim to shore.

Apparently, as we fought the current, it only helped in keeping us in its cycle. John later said that he remembered losing strength and when he finally reached exhaustion, the dam eventually washed him out.

We had both been spared from a stupid mistake that almost cost us not only our lives but also everyone else's on that trip. Ever since then, I have had a keen respect for water and the power it can possess. Remembering the horror of that day made me rethink trying this stream crossing more than anything.

A few minutes later, Junior came back outside one last time. After walking across his yard in silence, he came right up to me and finally said, "I've got an old John Deere Tractor in the barn. I suppose we could both climb up onto it and try and ride it across the creek." I thanked him for his offer but the thought of ruining his tractor not to mention both of us drowning in this stream just cemented my final decision to run the extra mileage. As I turned back to begin the long detour, Junior commanded, "Now wait a minute. What about those dogs? You've got to take them back home." The last thing on my mind now was adding any unnecessary mileage to an already 41-mile day. How's a dog to learn that some runners shouldn't be followed? Junior wouldn't budge however and we stood there trying to figure out what to do with the dogs until a car came out of a nearby driveway and stopped to look at the unlikely situation. I knew this car was my only hope and both Junior and I eventually talked the driver into taking the puppies up the road for me.

As happened over and over on my run, times of tribulation ended up turning into jubilation. As I was making my way along the detour, I passed a man working in his workshop. I told him of my trouble crossing the swollen stream and meeting Junior, which gave him a knowing laugh, and he offered to take me in for the night and drive me around to the other side of the stream the next morning. That night his family fed me pizza as I shared stories of life on the road.

Chapter 13
Alma Mater

The next day I was about to receive the surprise of my life. After a soggy fourteen miles in the rain I arrived at Canaan, Indiana, the meeting place where my mother would be arriving again in a few hours.

Traveling on foot, I enjoyed seeing every single object on the side of the road. Broken reflectors, a lug nut from a blown tire, and a doll's head were some of the joys of sightseeing that day at six miles per hour. Seeing such minute details of the country, it is easy to see why I was surprised to learn that I had run through the entire town of Canaan without even knowing it. Canaan offers an elementary school, a post office, one public telephone, a restaurant, and a very unique store. After a farmer told me how to get into "downtown," and with several hours to kill, I walked to a nearby elementary school to see if I could speak to some classes.

After meeting with the principal and explaining my offer, I was put in touch with Mr. Mathews, a 5th grade teacher. Upon talking with Mr. Mathews we learned that we had both gone to nearby Hanover College and his father was even the dean of students.

"Oh, my gosh, I know him!" I said with a laugh, "We used to talk quite a lot about my grades!"

The 5th grade students were good listeners and afterwards I went outside to try and find a snack while I waited for my mother to arrive, now just over an hour away. The restaurant in town was closed and the only place left to buy food was reported to be some type of store inside a man's house. I wanted to call my mom and find out how far away she was. The woman in the post office directed me to the pay phone. It was on the edge of town, bolted to a wooden telephone pole on the shoulder of the road. With trucks whizzing by and a light rain falling, I barely heard my mom over the faint connection that she would be there as quickly as possible.

Walking back into "town" and needing something to eat, my postal host now assured me that the house next door was, in fact, a grocery, and after knocking on the door, I entered a living room. If any effort had gone into making the front of this house appear store-like, I couldn't tell. Food inventory in the "store" included a variety of a half-dozen candy bars balanced on a shelf over his couch. In the corner of the room was a refrigerator and inside were cold sodas. I picked out three candy bars and two sodas and paid the man on the couch watching television while sitting under his inventory.

Snacks in hand, I rested on the deck of the closed restaurant and wrote in my journal. I became so cold and wet from the spring drizzle that I took out my bivy sack and climbed inside.

Finally, I saw my mother's car driving up the street. I heard the yipping of her dog, and started moaning to myself. "Oh, no, she brought Daisy again." My whining didn't last long, however. When my mother pulled up on that small street in Canaan, I saw in the passenger seat, Lydia, my girlfriend from Arizona. I was in complete shock. We had not planned to meet until Kansas!

Over the past several weeks Lydia had planned to surprise me on my run. She had bought her plane ticket to Indianapolis and was going to simply drive to wherever I arrived that given day.

After a long hug, we retrieved her rental car hidden a few blocks away and bid my mom farewell while I continued on with Lydia's support.

The next day, Ted Eden, an English professor at Hanover, came out and ran a great 28-mile day with me into Madison. The views were spectacular. After several days of rain, everything was bright, green, and crisp. We ran along a high ridge, trotting along farm bluffs overlooking the Ohio River.

Since home was now only an hour away, several friends and relatives drove down to see me and I enjoyed all of the visitations for a day.

Arriving at the Hanover campus entrance, my family took pictures of my arrival at my alma mater. Running across the familiar campus after having run each street hundreds of times while a student there, my arrival this time felt like the ultimate homecoming and I felt fortunate that my college was becoming a part of my trans-American route. I spoke to a class about my trip and we had dinner with friends Beth and her son Troy Mathers. They had been very supportive. To enable Lydia and me to keep in touch, they sent hundreds of minutes of pre-paid phone cards through the mail, which I then used for all of my long-distance calls.

The last morning on campus, Ted helped me set up a web page for my run. We also set up an e-mail account with a link on the website. This way, people could check my page and I would update it from local public library computers. I could also receive and respond to e-mail from these libraries. (This trail journal is now posted on the ADT website, www. discoverytrail.org) Thanks to Ted's kindness, my batches of mail became a large source of inspiration as friends and strangers cheered me on. Any given day when I checked my mail I would have 20 or more messages from supporters encouraging me.

That day, Lydia had to leave to catch her plane back to Arizona. I was sad to see her go but we told ourselves that we shouldn't be upset since the meeting was a surprise anyway and seeing her was just a bonus.

Sam, a student at Hanover agreed to run with me out of town that morning. The terrain around the Ohio River is totally unique to the rest of southern Indiana. Steep cliffs wherever you turn offer exploration in canyons, dangerous drop-offs, and challenging hiking.

The trees along the river are generally scrawny from the decades of flooding and poor soil quality near the water's edge. There is often a great deal of trash along the shore of the Ohio. At times, it seems that there must be the nation's largest plastic bottle factory just upstream and, for kicks during lunch, they release a few hundred bottles in a factory-wide bottle race from Madison to the Mississippi Delta.

As Sam and I ran along the river, the temperature was quickly rising. I was struggling with the hills while Sam's stride looked fresh and effortless. Then I figured out why. As I left campus that morning, my pack weight suddenly shot up to record levels. Word got out that one of my staple energy foods was chocolate-chip cookies and my grandmother had brought *five dozen* to give to me. My mother had also brought a few dozen, and friends on campus also gave me a bag full. As Sam and I were running along the river, we had to make the steep 300 foot ascent up the valley hillside several times as the road whimsically went up and down the same hill. I was carrying my pack, now laden with seven-dozen cookies and several bottles of water. Sam had nothing but his shoes and shorts! I was feeling embarrassed for breathing so hard up the hills when I already had 1000 miles under my belt, but next to me was a guy who could run a 2:40 marathon with no training and he wasn't carrying 84 cookies and 48 ounces of water. The weight of my treats would be worth it however, as they would soon save my life. Sam turned around just in time to run back to campus for his first class, making for an 18-mile morning run without a drink.

I planned to stop at Lexington for a short 13-mile day. After a light lunch in the only store in town by mid-afternoon, I decided to press on. I arrived next at Pigeon Roost State Historic Site, a monument where 24 settlers were killed during the War of 1812. The site offered a picnic shelter and tables but no water. By 6 p.m. I had arrived at the entrance to Clark State Forest. Thunderstorms had been predicted in the area and I wanted to be prepared.

I had sent home my Gore-Tex bivy sack with my mom and had been sent a large sheet of Tyvek House Wrap by a friend. I had heard of Appalachian Trail hikers using Tyvek for tents, ground cloths, and even sleeping bags and thought it was worth a try. The material is waterproof, quite tear-proof, and a very nice insulator from the wind and cold. In addition to all of this, it is commonly found at construction sites in wet regions and scraps are often free of charge!

To prepare for the coming storm, I laid my Tyvek on a table inside a tiny picnic shelter in the middle of a large field. The shelter was one of the smallest I have seen. It just barely covered the dimensions of the picnic table. Next, I placed my sleeping bag on top of the Tyvek, and once inside, wrapped the Tyvek around me to form a "human burrito." I made sure all of my possessions were either under my head or feet to keep them as dry as possible and to keep animals at bay. Just as I settled into my cocoon, the storm came.

The wind picked up and rain started blowing onto the seats of the picnic table, but so far, none was blowing onto me. Suddenly, I saw a giant flash of light and heard a huge crack! A tree, about a hundred yards away was struck by lightening. It didn't take much common sense to realize that I could very well be the next to illuminate. As I pondered the situation, I realized that I had an endless supply of cookies. I was exhausted, as usual. I was cozy, under my outdoor canopy bed, and I wasn't about to move in the rain just because of a little nearby lightening. After a 33-mile day carrying a diminishing supply of 84 cookies, lightening no longer seemed like such a big deal, and I peacefully slept through the raging storm.

The next morning, things were again pretty and crisp and I joined the 58-mile Knobstone Trail heading south towards Louisville. The trail is notoriously challenging due to its repeated short elevation gain and loss and with the recent rain, it was now also exceedingly muddy. At one point, I almost impaled myself.

While crossing a small stream on a slick log my wet, muddy shoes slipped off the trunk and I found myself falling back-first onto the log. Most of the branches had broken off leaving long sharp daggers in every direction and my back was falling towards them with nothing to stop me.

Visions of the branch daggers puncturing me flashed through my mind. Fortunately, the bulk of my pack, and perhaps all of the cookies, deflected the branches from piercing my back and I bounced off the log, landing in the stream, and thankful that things had not turned out worse.

Running through a park later that day, I saw a lone man inside a rock shelter. There was a fire going in the fireplace. Since it was still drizzling and cool, I decided to warm up with a fireside chat. I learned he was a minister from nearby New Albany.

"On a day with God," he said as I entered the shelter. "If I can't be at peace, how can I expect my congregation to gain peace from me?" He had a good point. Then he asked me if I had built the fire in the fireplace.

"No, I just got here."

"Hmm. That's strange, I didn't build it either," he said. His comment made me wonder if I had decided to stop in and chat with this man or if our meeting had somehow been arranged by another source, as if my good fortune and his quest for peace hadn't met by coincidence.

By 3 p.m. I had finished the 17-mile section of the Knobstone Trail and was gearing up to cover a longer stretch into New Albany. If I could make it to town, it would be another 32-mile day. Some of the best things about traveling this way are the little surprises that treat you without warning. Several miles down the road and off of the trail section, I passed a Texaco gas station, fully equipped with the usual assortment of runner-friendly goodies.

A friend's parents offered to take me in for the night. I wanted to see how far I could get before calling them to pick me up. I ran all afternoon and into the evening, finally arriving at the outskirts of New Albany at 8 p.m. I was exhausted. A sign even appeared and told me to stop. I walked up to a phone booth and called my contact from the parking lot of the "Save A Step" gas station. I also set up the next night's lodging by calling my father who lived in nearby Bloomington, Indiana. The next night we had fun catching up on all of the stories and eating at a buffet, where I ate five plates of food, three sundaes and ten cookies. Dad was impressed, as usual.

As I left town, two friends from college wanted to join me for the day. While enjoying their company, we witnessed a bizarre animal sight. As we passed a field of cattle, we watched a herd of cows grazing on the grass. Just as we passed one herd however, we spied one of the cows stick its head behind another cow's rear just as the front cow started to urinate. When this happened, the rear cow began drinking the urine! The whole event resembled something from The Far Side comics, if Bovine High Schoolers drank from golden fountains. As if the fanny pack didn't make running difficult enough, doubled over laughing in astonishment while keeping stride did the job. The day had been a fun change of pace from dealing with getting lost, running out of food, and explaining my trip to strangers. All of that would return the next morning and to a level I hadn't yet experienced.

After having spent so much time collecting all of the maps prior to my run, once the trip began I rarely stopped to plan out what was to come in each new section. I would merely start running each day and if I got lost or came to a junction, only then would I consult the maps. On a few occasions, this led to trouble and this day was one such instance.

The ADT joins the Adventure Hiking Trail (AHT) in central southern Indiana. Though similar in initials, the AHT is a much shorter version of trail. Only 27 miles long, the AHT loops through the woods with fine backpacker at regular intervals. I knew that I would be getting on a local trail but I was not aware that it didn't have any access to food or water. Armed with only dried apricots, cashews, and a few remaining crumbled cookies, I made my way to the trailhead. Merely finding the trail became a challenge. Just prior to getting on a county road, I phoned Mike, one of the founders of the AHT. Mike gave me some directions to get to the trail and described a bit of what to expect.

It always amazed me that the little-known remote roads, paths, and trails along the ADT were so hard to find. No one in the area had ever heard of the routes I followed, or at least the names I was told to go by. And yet, if I was very lucky, at some point prior to arriving at the necessary junction, I was given a name and a phone number of a person who had worked on that section-- typically some ten years ago. It took tremendous organization keeping all of those phone numbers handy and remembering whose name went with what. Cell phones were available at the time but coverage was spotty at best and I didn't want to carry the extra weight of a battery charger. What's more, almost half of the time if I had the correct person's name and phone number, and could find a pay phone, the person was either not connected with the trail any longer or had moved long ago.

Luck was with me that day, however, as Mike was home, knew much about the AHT, and ten minutes after I got off the phone, came driving up to me in his car. Despite having been given what sounded like very good directions from the man who created the trail, I still was unable to find it. After two hours of searching along county roads, I came to a farmhouse with two men working on a car in a shed. They asked me if I wanted a beer. To most, being lost in the woods, looking for a trail, and having 3,800 miles left to run, the offer of a cold beer would likely be a

Godsend. However, I don't drink and besides, if I was having this much trouble finding a trail while sober, I wouldn't want to try and find it under the influence of alcohol! They straightened me out and within minutes on the trail, a driving hailstorm began to fall from a seemingly blue sky.

I ducked into a nearby backpacker's shelter until the hail abated and then continued on. At my next break, I suddenly realized for the first time that, since this was a loop trail, I would likely end up back where I had started. Instances such as this require devotion to the trail as a whole. Sure, I could cut off the AHT and saved a day of running, but I would miss the experience of having traveled this section. By the same token, in the months ahead I could save 400 miles if I ran straight across Colorado rather than following the ADT's circuitous route.

This day the hail turned to rain and the trail turned to mud. Crossing a ravine, I came upon a middle-age couple not prepared for the threatening conditions. These pour souls had started what they thought was a three-mile nature trail but had actually gotten onto the nearly 30-mile AHT. When I told them that they were on a loop trail that was 27 miles long, they did not believe me. The woman said, "You don't understand. We have been walking for hours and hours and hours!"

"I believe it!" I said. They chose to continue the direction they were going. I never found out if they eventually made it back to their car or if they ended up drinking beers with some do-it-yourself mechanics in a shed.

That night I slept in a well-built but heavily vandalized old homestead. Dinner was a handful of cashews, apricots, and 18 ounces of water. The next morning I would push hard into Leavenworth for a good meal.

Finding a spring the next morning I filled both of my water bottles and used my small vial of bleach to purify the water for the first time on the trip. It was the first time I needed to use my bleach as there were enough houses, stores, and piped springs on the side of the road that it normally did not require it. The map showed I was nearing an old bridge across a river.

Little did I know that this was the same bridge I had canoed under dozens of times while leading summer camp trips down the Blue River to the mouth of the Ohio River. During those years it had become tradition, after checking the water depth for any obstructions under the surface, to jump off of the 35-foot bridge. On a few occasions I had climbed up the steel beams to the very top of the bridge and jumped from the 65-foot level. I considered jumping for old time's sake but, being alone, decided against it. Besides, I was hungry and didn't want to delay breakfast. I did take out my notebook and wrote a small note to the kids at my Camp. I hid this note underneath a steel beam and later wrote them a postcard telling them to stop and find my note the next time they canoed the Blue (Though they've looked many times since, they've still never found it).

Finally rounding a bend on a hill into Leavenworth, a white convertible stopped on the side of the road and the driver asked, "Are you the guy running all the way across the country?"

"Yes, sir," I replied.

"Well, there's an entire restaurant of people waiting for you just over the hill!" Holy smokes! What could this be about, I wondered? I got to the Overlook Restaurant and a woman was standing in the parking lot with a camera, waving her arms, cheering and yelling hello. Jean is the mother of Mike, whom I had seen the day before. He told his mother about me that night and, working at the restaurant, she wanted to meet me and give me a free meal.

She told me that the entire staff had been waiting all morning for me to arrive. They seated me at a table. I told Jean that I had been on the AHT and had eaten nothing more than nuts and fruit since yesterday morning. I told her I was also very thirsty. She noticed I was sweating from my morning run and adjusted the restaurant thermostat to make me more comfortable. They brought me a pitcher of water, five sodas, a great sandwich, and a piece of apple pie with ice cream. When I tried to pay, Jean said that the meal was on the house.

During the meal, each time Jean would seat a new party, she would point to me and tell them in a very audible voice, "See that young man over there? He's running all the way across the United States!" Each time she said that, everyone in the restaurant turned around to look at me, and smiled. With each new table, she would include more commentary, so that by the end of the meal, every table in the restaurant knew how many pairs of socks I had gone through, what the funniest dog in each state looked like, and how many times I'd been asked if I was Forrest Gump. She had made arrangements for me to stay in an Inn across the street free of charge but when we couldn't get a key to open it, she refused to be defeated. Without missing a beat, she drove me to a hotel, paid for my room, and asked what time I'd like to be picked up for breakfast! Her generosity was overwhelming.

The next morning, I thanked my new friend over and over. On my way out of town, Jean told me that Joe Tower, one of my high school teachers, had grown up in Leavenworth and pointed out where his parents still lived. I couldn't resist knocking. Mrs. Tower opened the door.

"Hello, you don't know me but I am a former student of your son, Joe."

"Well, come on in!" she said as if she'd already known me for years. I hadn't taken my pack off before she started showing me pictures past and present of her son and said, "Well, you just have to stay for lunch," as if there was no way around it. It was now 9:20 a.m. I thanked her for her kind offer but declined and continued west. At the time, I recall thinking nothing much of visiting the boyhood home and parents of my former high school teacher. In hindsight however, the act seems somewhat odd and gives me some insight perhaps into the level of extreme loneliness I was experiencing, despite the recent visits from friends and family.

Chapter 14
Trail Summit

Arriving in the quaint town of Derby, Indiana in the afternoon, I found a nice couple with cabins for rent. Just five miles earlier I had spoken to people about what I might find in Derby. They said that they could not think of anything but then confessed that they had never even been in the town! Dianne answered the door and told me that they did have cabins available. I told them that I was a friend of the Foots who had stayed there the a year ago on their bike ride and then asked her how much a cabin cost for a guy running 5,000 miles across the country. She told me that she could give me a discount to make it $50.

"Does that come with a breakfast," I asked.

"I don't know, we can ask my husband, Gary. He's pretty easy," she said with a smile. "Honey," walking around to the garage, "this young man wants to know if you will cook him breakfast?" It wasn't exactly the way I would have phrased it but everything turned out well as they invited me to be their guest and sleep in their "bonus room," a recently finished basement room with a full bathroom and Jacuzzi just outside. The trip just kept getting better and better.

That evening some friends of theirs came over and they had a party. Recently, Gary had bought a new fishing boat and couldn't wait to put the boat in the water to christen it so we had a christening party on the boat on the boat trailer on the driveway.

A boat blessing docked at an Indiana bed and breakfast.

Afterwards, Gary and Dianne invited me to have dinner with them at the local restaurant. While there, I saw a couple I had met earlier in the day. They said that they felt bad for not offering me water or a snack when I met them and so gave me money instead. I told them it was not necessary but they insisted.

After dinner, Bob Ramsbottom, a trail volunteer, came over to discuss the trails with me for the upcoming section. Bob is a retired schoolteacher and track coach and is volunteering to mark the ADT across southwestern Indiana. He had just finished marking a number of trails in time for me to come through. Hearing all of the hard work he was going through just for my arrival felt like a red carpet was being laid down just for me, except the carpet was an unbroken series of trail markers tacked to trees and posts. He says that he rides the trails on his mountain bike and nails up the markers. He had an enormous map of Indiana and gave me precise directions on the upcoming section. He also gave me the name of a farmer's home I would be passing. He told me to stop in and say hello if I needed anything.

Finally, while my hosts were getting ready for bed, I skinny-dipped in the hot tub outside, as my hosts had suggested. Loud cicadas and brilliant stars almost put me to sleep with the hypnotizing bubbles massaging my body. This was living.

The trail during the next day was the most tick-infested of any on the trip. In less than one mile of trail, I had over 100 ticks on my arms, legs, ankles, and shoes. Luckily, ticks don't just grab hold and start sucking blood without warning. They like to climb around. With my leg hair, when they crawl around on me I could feel them moving through my hair and I was able to stop to flick them off before they attached themselves. They were all different types and sizes and they were everywhere. At one point, the grass was so thick that I knew that if I stopped to flick off the crawling ticks I would only get more through the next section and so waited until a clearing to clean myself off.

After finishing the infested section of the Hoosier National Forest, I arrived at the house of Bob's friend, the farmer. He had just pulled into his driveway when I walked up. "Hello! Bob Ramsbottom told me to stop and say hi." We went inside and he poured me a cold soda as we sat in his kitchen. He served me a piece of Amish Friendship Bread and said that the dough had been reused continuously for twelve years. While I was enjoying his bread and soda, the conversation turned to the bad tick season as well as chiggers and he began telling me of his recent experience with the little vampires.

"I was lying down in a field because my back was hurting me and suddenly I felt an itch in my groin, so I scratched myself (which he demonstrated). But that didn't satisfy me so I scratched myself again (another demonstration in case I missed the first one), and that didn't satisfy me so I pulled my shorts down (no demonstration). He said his entire groin was covered in the "little fellers." At which point he said to his wife, "Honey, get the bleach." If you put a half-cup of bleach in your bath water it will take them right off, he said.

That afternoon the temperature soared into the 80's with high humidity, and I was frying on the pavement. Stopping at a convenience store I drank a half-gallon of juice in record time and followed it with chips and cookies. It was only eight more miles to St. Meinrad, a beautiful monastery and college with gothic architecture.

The next day was graduation at the college and I luckily got the last room in the campus motel. The furnishings were simple: bed, lamp, writing desk, telephone, and bathroom. I ate dinner in a campus tavern called "The Unstable" and had an enjoyable dinner talking with students while consuming my 16-inch pizza, breadsticks, and three sodas. One man, a 50-year-old former plumber told me the story of how he came to St. Meinrad.

"One day, I was working under a sink and God spoke to me and told me that this was not what I was meant to do. So, I'm 50 years old and finally happy," he concluded. It was hard to imagine how anyone could spend 30 years in a trade and suddenly think of that entire time as wasted or non-essential to his or her current life. I certainly hoped that someday I didn't look back on this trip as a distraction from my true calling.

With the high mileage days I had been accomplishing, I was looking forward to an upcoming brief vacation. The ADT Board of Directors had invited me to attend their summer trail meeting in Columbia, Missouri. Originally, I had thought I might be able to arrive at the meeting on foot, as the trail goes right through town. Alas, when the time came for the meeting, I was a few hundred miles away and needed a ride.

Still wanting to attend the meeting and give my input on the trail, Lu Schrader, the West Virginia coordinator, agreed to pick me up on his way to the meeting, but first, there would be Christmas.

The entire town of Santa Claus, Indiana is built, named after, and designed to have the feeling of a winter wonderland. To tourists, this theme is a large attraction to visit the town. To locals who live there, however, being exposed to a community infatuated with images of St. Nick seems as though it would be a breeding ground for Grinches. There are giant statues of Santa Claus at every corner, themed hotels, and of course, Holiday World Amusement Park. Two friends from college lived in town and I ran through their subdivision with street names like Bathalzar, Mistletoe Drive, Jingle Bell Road, and even Chestnuts Roasting on An Open Fire Lane! (Imagine writing that return address on your Christmas card 100 times!) That night we watched the final episode of Seinfeld.

The next morning, Lu picked me up and we made our way across Illinois and into St. Louis. At the hotel in Boonville, I finally got to meet the state coordinators. The coordinators include the widest variety of people I have ever met. There was a real estate agent, two mayors, a character portrayer, a cartographer, several retired persons, an Ornithologist, and a lawyer, to name but a few, all volunteers working tirelessly to create the nation's first coast-to-coast trail. I also got to meet Bill and Laurie Foot in person. Bill was a huge man, very fit looking and athletic. Laurie was also trim and kind. They were both eager to hear how my trip was going.

During the board meeting the next day, I learned about the status of the trail. The trail has had a long road to getting designated as a National Discovery Trail. First of all, there is not a trail category that the ADT can fall under. The National Scenic Trails act protects the Appalachian, Pacific Crest, and Continental Divide Trails because they stay in mostly wilderness areas, avoiding communities. The ADT travels through many wooded areas but also through the heart of some of the nation's biggest cities such as Washington, St. Louis, Denver, and San Francisco. Because of these urban sections, it cannot fall under the National Scenic Trails Act. Nor can it fall under the National Historic Trails Act because even though it does follow historic trails such as the Santa Fe Trail for 500 miles, it does not follow the entire Santa Fe Trail. Also, Historic trails must be one continuous trail and no more, meaning that you can not have a historic trail that is on the Chesapeake & Ohio Canal Trail and then joins the Santa Fe Trail later. Third, the ADT cannot fall under the National Recreation Trail heading because this heading is intended to be local short distance trails only. Therefore, with the uniqueness of the ADT it was necessary to formulate a new category of National Trails and the National Discovery Trails Act serves that purpose. All in all, I learned much about the trail and the workings of a non-profit organization.

Sunday morning we rode bicycles along a portion of a rail trail and stopped at a lunch depot for bikers and hikers. It was fun to think that in a few weeks I would be sitting at the very same ice cream stand, having arrived on foot from the east coast.

Chapter 15
California is a Magical Word

After returning from the meeting, I was a worried how my body would react after three days of rest. The next few days were a hot reintroduction to the lifestyle and rigors of crossing a continent on foot. Passing near the Lincoln Boyhood home, I watched a 24-minute video on the life of young Abraham narrated by a man with the kind of slow paced bass-range voice you might expect from a 1960 film on zebra behavior.

"Here, I grew up," was the title of the video. They had to give it a title that conveyed historical importance because Lincoln moved around so much in his life and they could not simply say, "Home of Lincoln." So they were going for the boyhood connection as he spent much of his childhood in this area. A roomful of antsy, fidgety third-graders sat through the video in pain, forcibly cooped up in a dark air-conditioned auditorium on a beautiful spring day. Little did they know that the smelly sweat-covered stranger in the back of the room was just enjoying a break in temperature and immensely enjoying watching yet another generation of kids be exposed to such a traditional school field trip.

Arriving in Boonville that night I entered the Una Pizza Restaurant to ask directions to the nearest motel. The owner said, "Well, if you are running that far, I'll be glad to help you out." Then he took my order for any pizza I wanted, free of charge. These merchants who offered me food didn't do so after I talked them into a donation or after "buttering them up" with a few stories of life on the road. Almost every time it happened, I walked in; they asked me where I was headed. I said, "California," and a plate of food would be placed in front of me. It almost made me wonder if the word itself had magic powers, "California." POOF! A cheeseburger would appear. "California." Zap! 14-inch pizza. "California." Blam – Dinner, laundry, bed, breakfast, *and* $20 cash.

The next morning, I got a ride from my motel room back to the trail and my driver, a gruff 20-something kid cocked his head to the side, looked far off on the horizon and replied to my trip with a contemplative, "... I can respect that," as if he has not thought much of his little town lately and I was something different.

Passing through a myriad of small towns, I arrived in yet another hamlet and decided to check my email in the local library. Keeping in touch with friends and relatives worked out extremely well when I could find access to the Internet. Typically, I would enter the local library, log onto my Hotmail account and check up to 30 messages that might have accumulated. In this particular library, as had occasionally been the case, only those with current library cards were allowed to use the computer. After signing to agree to the rules and regulations for use of the computer and policies of the library, I was issued my very own laminated library card and can now return to the Newburgh, Indiana Public Library should I ever want to check out a book or log on to their computer. Early on in the trip, I tried reasoning with the librarians, "You know," I would begin my debate of the rules governing computer use, "it's nothing personal, but I'm only going to be here an hour and then I'm probably never going to be back." But librarians like to follow rules; I now have membership and laminated cards to over a dozen libraries across the country.

A quick visit to Evansville took me along the Riverfront Trail. On the edge of town and with some time to spare, I stopped in the Caze Elementary School. After meeting the principal, the students were told over the loudspeaker to assemble immediately into the gymnasium for a special presentation. I told them about my trip and to be thinking about me during the summer and fall, as I would be finishing the desert and nearing the Pacific Ocean by trick-or-treating season of the next school year.

It was incredibly hot in the city in late May with radiant heat coming off the pavement, like I was sandwiched between the sun and a bed of coals. I stopped in front of a passing liquor store to buy a can of soda. After buying my drinks, I told him what I was up to and he immediately produced a party favor from behind the counter and handed it to me saying, "Here you go, to remember your visit to Evansville." Held out in his hand was a white plastic beer cozy with "Top Hat Liquors" printed on the side and a risqué graphic of a man's head in a top hat neatly framed between two leaning wine bottles suggestively looking like a pair of women's legs. I did not know what I was going to do with a plastic beer cozy, I did not have any beer, and my soda cans were now empty, but I thanked him and packed the drink holder away in my pack, adding two ounces to my nine-pound luggage. It would only be a matter of time before I arrived at the next post office and shipped another box of goodies to Lydia in Arizona. Oh, the treasures that awaited her!

While in Evansville, I also bought a pair of sunglasses and a new camera as my previous one had been dropped in a puddle and ruined. Both on the Appalachian Trail and the ADT up to this point, I had used an Olympus Stylus 35mm camera with great success but had managed to ruin two of them in water accidents. My third purchase was the newer version of the same camera but slightly smaller and with a built-in water seal to prevent such mishaps.

West of Evansville, the route travels through a confusing stretch of country roads and a railroad yard. Completely lost, I stopped a man carrying trash to the curb in the middle of a subdivision. He couldn't help get back on track but said he had someone inside his house who could. He escorted me into his home and I met his wife and a friend of hers sitting in a bedroom in the cool air conditioning. The friend in the room had conducted the census some years ago and knew the area very well. She gave me a detailed route to get back onto my trail. Curiosity overcame me and I asked them what they were working on. Built in the bedroom was a huge loom, which the women were working on in tandem and they told me that they have been making quilts together for some years. It seemed like such a happy existence, relaxing in a cool dark room with your husband and best friend all the while making beautiful quilts. I was equally satisfied with my existence, but at this particular time, sitting in a 70-degree room with a fully stocked kitchen nearby seemed a lot better then going out into that 90-degree searing sun and hoping to find a vague corridor that would take me to California.

The woman's directions got me to Burdette Park, a nice place for a picnic and a swim, but from there I was still confused as to where to go. In such times of confusion, I spent so long standing around, looking at my maps and taking in the surrounding landmarks that I inevitably got impatient with route finding. Eventually, I'd decide that if I'd just start running, at least I would be getting somewhere although this impatience rarely led to taking me where I actually intended to go. On this particular day I gave up looking for the route and impatiently glanced around for any kind of road that would take me west. I found one. It was a tractor lane in the middle of two fields of corn and even knowing I was headed for trouble, I set off down the muddy track.

Several hundred yards later, the lane petered out. I knew it would, of course. I came to a small ditch in the field and followed it to a larger ditch and eventually to a wooded stream. After crossing the surprisingly large stream, I spied a road a little further ahead. This turned out to be a private driveway and I followed it to a home.

Knocking on the door, an older man finally came to the doorway clad only in his underwear. "Tighty Whities," would be their scientific name. He was nice, however, and told me how to get onto a nearby road towards Mt. Vernon where a family had offered to take me in for the night.

Arriving in town I called the Vaal family and they offered to pick me up. Several reporters had been expecting my arrival, including a television crew from Evansville. I gave two interviews at the home and had a pleasant dinner with the family. Cathy, the wife, was preparing for a backpacking trip in the Smoky Mountains. With my experience from the Appalachian Trail, I went through her pack and helped her weed out several pounds of unnecessary gear. That night, a tremendous rainstorm came through the area and there was significant groundwater as a result.

In the morning, Cathy offered to drive me back to the trail and on the way there, the road disappeared into a giant pond in a corn field.

"Do you think we should try and cross it?" Cathy asked.

"I don't know. It's your minivan. Do you think you can make it through?" I replied.

"Let's try it," she said with a daring grin. We proceeded to drive through the puddle and nearing the halfway point, the van stalled. I looked out the widow. The puddle, much deeper than either of us had anticipated, was well over the wheels and halfway up the door panels. Cathy had spent the previous evening washing my clothes a series of times trying to get six states' worth of dirt and grime out of the fabric. She had done a great job. My socks, which had taken on a grayish hue since West Virginia, were now particularly white. I rolled down my window, crawled out and stepped into the new lake. The water came up to the bottom of my shorts. I walked around to the back of the van and pushed her out of the puddle. Just when we were getting to the other side of the water, a sheriff's car pulled up ready call a tow truck. I ran the last few miles of Indiana in sodden footwear, but brown socks are better than gray ones and I reminisced about the fine hospitality and looked ahead to Illinois.

Illinois' River to River trail really is over the water and through the trees.

Chapter 16
Over the River

Crossing the Wabash River on the shoulder of a narrow bridge, I entered Illinois and decided to celebrate entering my seventh state with a snack overlooking the river. Just as I was spreading out my variety of snacks on the guardrail, black clouds rolled in from the horizon and the wind picked up. It looked like a twister was coming for sure. I packed up my gear and started hightailing it to the first town. The storm came and went without severe elements and I eventually made it to Shawneetown, where I had arranged to meet John O'Dell, trail coordinator for southern Illinois. We met and he took me to the world's largest Kentucky Fried Chicken Restaurant. John's wife met us for dinner, and after retiring to his home, we watched a movie on television and John convinced me to take the next day off and rest up. He's very good at that. John is one of the kindest men I have ever met. He owned a camping store next to the ADT which uses the local River To River Trail. In fact, John was the man who spearheaded opening the equestrian trail to hikers, and his business catered to tourists, hikers, and locals selling camping gear, Indian trinkets, and the best hamburgers for miles around. John is also a volunteer Baptist Minister for four area churches and rotates among them throughout the month. On top of that he holds a doctorate in education and boards up to twenty horses on his property. He is a very busy man who somehow manages to assist with the ADT and help fellow travelers when they pass through.

After my relaxing day of hanging out in John's shop, eating hamburgers, and touring town, I ran through Garden of the Gods, a beautiful hiking and rock climbing area in the southern part of Illinois.

Over the course of the next few days, we set up a routine where John and his wife would drive me out to the trail in the morning. I would run 25 to 30 miles along the River-to-River Trail. One of them would then pick me up at the end of the day where we would proceed to Dairy Queen for ice cream and the comfort of home, a shower, the plush couches, and endless series of satellite movies on their big screen television. If life could have gotten any better, I didn't want to know about it.

Finally, I had run so far away from John's home that it was becoming impractical for him to shuttle me around and I was again on my own.

By midday I arrived in the small town of Cobden. The population of Cobden is a few hundred. I know because I saw all of them standing together in the center of town as I entered. Cobden had recently finished spending several years and 1.4 million dollars enlarging the only bridge over the only railroad track in the middle of town. The last bridge had lasted some 60 years and people were sentimental to see it replaced. There were fancy chairs lined up on one side of the bridge, blue Astroturf, a podium, flowers, public address system, several dignitaries, the local media, and about three hundred people watching it all. I had arrived within ten minutes of the grand opening of the bridge. The local high school band was lining up in uniform to play and march across. The mayor read a proclamation explaining how everyone was going to miss the old bridge but this was a time of change and today marked the start of new memories. I was standing behind two elderly women watching the ceremony and arguing whether the cement apple on the side of the bridge should be painted red or not. After the proclamation, the mayor cut a large ribbon, the band started playing and everyone marched across the bridge, totally unaware that one person in the crowd was using that small bridge to get to the Golden Gate six states away.

After leaving Cobden, I saw a sign on the side of the road, "fresh strawberries!" I stopped in the roadside market for my first fresh fruit of the trip and selected a pint of plump berries. Before finishing the third treat however, the entire family came out to talk to me while I ate them along with drinking several glasses of ice water. When I tried to pay, the father said, "You've got to be kidding. You're running across America. I think you deserve these." (California – Poof – Strawberries.)

In the late afternoon, I arrived in the even smaller town of Alto Pass. Several reporters had arranged to meet me in town and I arrived right on time. One, a television crew from a local network affiliate, wanted to do an interview with me, "*Live* on the scene." They had just acquired a new satellite truck and were eager to put it to use. That part of the state is quite hilly and they had to maneuver the telescoping antennae several times to get a good enough signal for broadcast. While waiting "on the scene" till five, a freelance reporter and fellow runner interviewed me. Finally, nearing five o'clock, we were getting ready for the big interview. The anchorperson was new to the industry and was surprisingly nervous about the upcoming segment. She was also quite young and kept repeating her opening line over and over in rehearsal, perfecting that all-too artificial emphasis newscasters seem to put on inflection.

"I'm here with *BRIAN STARK* in *ALTO PASS*. BRIAN is MARKING *DAY NUMBER 78* on his trip across America." The interview went fine, so well in fact that the station asked that I stick around and do another one for the six o'clock news. I agreed and wrote in my journal while we waited for the next, "*Live* on the scene." For having such an expensive truck filled with portable satellite technology, I thought it was funny that I had to stand around and wait for the next time slot rather than having the crew chase the news.

Later that night, the reporter reworked all of the interviews and clips of me running down the road and put it into a really nice 10 o'clock news segment that earned me some good exposure. That night I stayed with a woman who worked for the forest service and had a zoo of animals in her backyard. Foxes, dogs, horses, peacocks, greyhounds, rabbits, parrots, goats, cats, all running around in their pens, cages, the house, and even just around the yard. We ate 50 fresh fish for dinner that her boyfriend had recently caught.

The next morning, the route past town was quite overgrown and finding the trail was a miracle. Arriving at some kind of dude ranch, I asked a man for any information on water or food in the upcoming section.

"There ain't crap 'tween here and Grand Tower," he said.

"Ok, thank-you." Undeterred, I pressed on. Surely, there would be a few houses, a gas station, a diner somewhere, I thought. I thought wrong. Soon after, I exited the woods and got onto a series of levees along the Missippippi River.

Whenever you leave the woods, you can expect the temperature to rise at least 15 degrees, even more if you get onto pavement. The River-to-River Trail's westernmost segment is on dirt roads on top of levees for miles on end with no shade nor drinkable water in sight. I had been low on water even in the woods. Being hit with the full sunshine and a cloud of dust that rose from the dirt road with each step only further dehydrated me. I was out of water and very tired. The next known water source was at least ten miles further down the hot corridor. I had thought that the top of a levee would receive a cool breeze from the nearby river for the rest of the day. This was not so and for some reason the air seemed even more stagnant and still than it had been in the woods. Ahead and to my left, lay the Mississippi River, dirty, muddy, polluted, but liquid nonetheless. To my right was a murky swamp-like body of water. I needed water – and soon – but my options were few.

I passed a man mowing the levee in an enclosed county highway tractor and just held up my empty water bottle. He simply shook his head and kept mowing. Just as I was trying to decide whether to drink out of the river or the swamp, I spotted a person sitting in a vehicle parked on the side of the road a half-mile ahead at a railroad crossing. There was no logical reason for this person to be in the middle of nowhere on such a hot day. I surmised he worked for the railroad and was working on the tracks. That, or he had tracked me down from the recent television broadcasts and was waiting to either up my dose of lead or give me another free pint of strawberries. He must have been wondering about me also as I appeared as a tiny bobbing object from over two miles away, slowly getting bigger as I closed in on him.

"Oh," I thought, "if only he stays there until I can catch up to him, surely he will have a water bottle, a breath mint, or some stale coffee that I can drink." Visions of this mystery driver turning around when I was within fifty yards of him and driving away made me panic and I picked up the pace. It was all on the line now. If this guy couldn't offer any help, my situation would become dangerous. Without him, it would mean a swamp diet for sure.

Luckily for me, as I got closer, this man must have realized that I was thirsty out in this strip of desert dividing a brownish green ocean because when I was within fifty yards, he didn't turn around and drive away, but instead got out of his vehicle. Walking around to his trunk just as I was arriving at his van, he emerged from the back holding out an ice cold Pepsi-Cola with bead sweats dripping down the sides simply saying, "Take it!" I thanked him, holding back tears only because I couldn't produce them. I drank the soda in a matter of seconds.

"Wow", he replied as I shook the last drop from the can without stopping since opening it moments earlier. "Would you like another one?"

"Yes, please." I eventually had four cans of the drink before my thirst registered the aid and I started feeling bad about draining his supply of refreshments. When I finally started cooling down, I was able to ask him what on earth he was doing out here on this Sahara like median.

He explained that he was a train spotter and had driven several hundred miles across the state to take pictures of trains crossing the trestle over this swamp. By listening to a train radio in his van, he could determine when the next train was coming and he had simply been sitting on the shoulder waiting for the next train to pass. It was only a few minutes away at this point and he took out his camera and tripod and prepared for the coming train. The locomotive rounded a corner and crossed the trestle. As the train drove by, the conductor waved out the window at us and we returned the greeting. I thanked my new friend again and pressed on with revitalized spirit to the next town of Grand Tower.

Train spotting in the backwaters of the Mississippi River.

My fame had preceded me as word had been left in the local store to be on the lookout for me. I was introduced to the mayor and received a message from John O'Dell that a man in a nearby campground wanted to offer me a place to stay the night.

Grand Tower has seen better days but it has a nice laid back existence, as do many of these towns that once catered to a bustling mining or railroad economy. Grand Tower is noted however as the western terminus of the River-to-River Trail and is the starting line of a statewide trail run each year.

After a lunch in the local restaurant a cute young waitress came over to me and asked, "Do you mind if I sit down next to you?" She was sweet and asked me some questions like, "Don't you get tired? I know I would."

She had with her a paper plate and a permanent marker and glancing over at a booth of older men spying us, said that they had told her she should get my autograph. I drew a picture on the plate with each of the states I was crossing and wrote how Grand Tower had the best B.L.T. sandwiches in America and gave it to her.

Just then a large man walked into the restaurant saying, "There he is!" Fred Houston was one of the managers of the local Devil's Backbone RV Park on the river on the edge of town. He had been on the lookout for me and had finally tracked me down. He bought my lunch and talked as if he already had everything figured out for the night. Fred and his wife Delores had a home in Grand Tower but it was being renovated so they had retreated to their camper trailer in the park for the summer. Fred let me use the shower house in the park and after cleaning up, I found Fred and a park employee arranging a stack of patio cushions on picnic tables under a picnic shelter. This, I found out, would be my bed for the night.

For dinner, Fred and Delores drove me to a nearby town and he said, "Order anything you want on the menu, it's on me!" I looked over the selection and after a time Fred asked, "What'll you have, steak?"

"Actually, I think I'll have a salad and some chicken strips," I replied.

My selection apparently didn't chime with what Fred's expectations of my appetite should have been and he mildly lashed out with a series of comments on my choice, "Chicken Strips! Are you crazy? If I was running across the entire United States and someone came up to me and told me to order anything I wanted on the menu, I sure as hell wouldn't order... (and this he emphasized) 'Chicken Strips!'" He later apologized saying that of course I was welcome to order whatever I wanted. But I know, in the back of Fred's mind, somewhere in Grand Tower, Illinois, there is a steak with my name on it.

That night we sat around his camper with a group of other park residents until the bugs got bad and I decided to retire. Living on the edge of the Mississippi River, people have had a few hundred years to deal with the biting mosquitoes. When common bug spray failed to work some time in the late 16th century, people apparently began wearing, spraying and using any and all chemicals, cleaners, and perfumes they had laying around the house to try and keep the bugs at bay. The most effective cleaner depended on at what point in history you were looking at.

For instance, when I was hiking the Appalachian Trail in 1995, the current practice was to spray Avon's Skin So Soft on your skin and the rumors were that nary a blood-seeker would travel your way with such a defense. I tracked down a local Avon salesperson and explained that I wanted to buy a small bottle of their Skin So Soft as I heard it smelled so bad that it was the preferred chemical over DDT. Armed with this new weapon, not only did I end up with smooth soft skin on the trail, but proceeded to attract more hordes of black flies than had attacked me before using the product! I even have a photograph of my bottle sitting on a bridge in Maine, with the lid covered with thirty Black Flies who seemed not to be able to get enough of the anti-potion.

In the summer of 1998 A.D. in the hamlet known as Grand Tower, the current repellent of choice was Downy Dryer Sheets. By rubbing the sheets on your skin, as the locals claimed, the mosquitoes wouldn't bother you a bit. Possible guesses for up and coming repellents I figured were, roofing tar, Ding-Dong Cream Filling, and gasoline. Watch for it in camping stores this season.

With my complimentary supply of dryer sheets wiped up and down my arms and legs, and over my ears and face, I retired to my picnic bedroom smelling like a cuddly stuffed teddy bear. No sooner had I laid down on my sleeping bag did I proceed to get eaten alive by mosquitoes, honed in on the local repellent of the week.

For two hours I tried to swat those pesky biters away. Who has been teaching them that the human ear is the ideal landing zone? It was clear that I was not going to get any sleep, and having a 37-mile day to look forward to prevented an all-night swatting vigil. At 11 p.m. I simply could not take it any longer and decided to improve my situation. Where do you go for help in the middle of the night in a campground? I looked for any moving object and found one. There was a man walking across a field. I figured this to be one of the men whom I had been sitting with in the lawn chairs earlier. I was to soon find out that he was not.

I approached the dark silhouette moving across the grass without a flashlight and greeted him. "Excuse me, I'm trying to sleep under that shelter over there and I just keep getting eaten alive. Do you know of a building where I could get away from these insects?" His first question was what was I doing here and did anyone know I was sleeping on the tables. I then figured out he did not know who I was and quickly explained my trip and how I had become an invited guest of the campground.

He finally said a bit hesitantly, "Well, um yeah, I got a camper over there with an extra bunk in it. You're welcome to sleep in there."

"Oh, that's great," I replied, relieved at the thought of anything that offered protection without the use of fabric softener.

We walked together across the field and when we got to the camper he reached for the aluminum door handle and paused asking almost as an afterthought, "You don't have any... guns or knives do you?"

"Um, no," I said.

"Ok," he replied, and in I went, not thinking to ask the same question of him.

The camper was tiny, one of those near bubble shaped jobs on two wheels with two single beds on either side of a narrow hallway. I immediately lay down and went to sleep but woke up off and on to see that my host was watching television and drinking beer until 3 a.m.

At 7 a.m. I woke up, thanked him, and quickly took off. Fred and Delores had gotten up early to cook me breakfast and not finding me on the picnic tables the next morning had assumed I had left early. They were relieved to see that I was still around but sorry to hear of my long night. Delores made me a great pancake breakfast and I got on the road, hoping to make some miles before the heat came on in the afternoon. Another television crew had interviewed me in the campground that evening and the exposure paid off as several cars pulled over during the next day to wish me luck and see if I needed anything.

My goal was to get to Chester, Illinois, home of the creator of the cartoon character Popeye. There, I would pick up my fourth pair of shoes and another highly anticipated large stack of mail. Ten miles into the day a man informed me, "There ain't crap between here and Chester, 22 miles!" I don't know what the fascination is with feces in southern Illinois but it seems to be a common judge of services.

On a similar note, the Happy Feet were getting directions one day on the ADT from a man when he said the following in response to a distance question,

"Yeah, you just go up about 3 farsees, and you'll see it on the left."

"Excuse me?" they had asked. "Just what is a 'farsee'?"

"Oh, well, you go up the road for as far as you can see, and then you go again, and that's two farsees." When I heard this I assumed the man did not travel much at night.

Along the way, I stopped at a passing house for some water and met Dave, a man working in his garage. He had seen me on television the night before and gave me several bottles of cold spring water from his refrigerator. He also said that he and his wife would be heading up to Chester later that day and would be on the lookout for me. Several miles later, my lack of sleep and dehydration were catching up to me and I decided to take a short rest on the side of the road. I was so hot I didn't care if I even made it off the road. I pulled out my Tyvek ground cloth and laying it on a section of the shoulder, partially under the shade of a nearby tree. I woke up some twenty minutes later, and focused on two small boys standing over me, likely wondering if they had just come across a corpse.

I opened my eyes, startled them with a, "Howdy, boys," then stuffed away my gear and continued down the road as they stared at me awestruck. Not long after, a Suburban pulled up alongside me and stopped on the shoulder of the road. True to his word, Dave had found me on his way to Chester and had brought along a few more bottles of water. He and his wife invited me into their truck where I got in, closed the door, and sat in the air conditioning for five minutes while I drank the water and visited with them, enjoying the comforts of an automobile, even if it wasn't moving.

At 4:30 p.m. I made it into Chester, and after eating two snow cones in record time, made my way to the local post office. I love going into the post office. It never takes longer then a few seconds for the postmaster to realize who I am and that they finally get to unload the stack of mail they have been holding for a month and a half. In Chester, I got the biggest batch of mail yet: a new pair of shoes, three boxes of food, and thirteen letters! To conceive carrying that much would have doubled the contents of my pack! I called a local motel manager and he said he would be willing to come pick me up and take me to the motel.

I was sitting on the steps of the post office, trying to imagine what wonders were contained in all the correspondence on my lap when an elderly woman walked up to me on her way inside.

"Are you walking far?" she asked with a sweet hush.

"Well, yes actually, all the way to California." I said.

"Oh, I think that's great! Is this your pack?"

"Yes," I answered.

"Can I heft it?"

"Go right ahead." She smiled as she lifted it, gave a small giggle, then went inside. When she came back out she held out her hand and said that she wanted to give me something and when I took it from her I counted up $1.72. I thanked her and she wished me well. After getting cleaned up and reading through all of my mail at the motel, I took a walking tour of town. The characters and setting of the cartoon strip Popeye came from shops and the people in the town at the time. "Whimpy," the overweight unmotivated hamburger eater was based on the manager of the local theater in town. I had a nice visit in a sporting goods store where the owner gave me a long sleeve Nike shirt as a keepsake of her town.

The next day, hydrated, rested, and revitalized, I set off north now towards St. Louis, bound for the crossroads town of Prairie Du Rocher. The trail for the day was along a beautiful country road next to the river. As soon as I left town I ran past the Menard Maximum Security Prison. It had been awhile since I had seen so much barbed wire in one place. The road I was on was so small and unassuming; I feared I was off course as it ran right through the prison employee parking lot. I worried a tower guardsman was going to mistake me for an escaped prisoner. It turned out that I was not lost, but as I ran past the prison I wondered what could have been going on in the inmates heads had they seen me running past. Even more, what would they think if they heard of my trip? I was just a man on the road, having exceptional luck with the generosity and kindness of strangers. The day before I had been given a nice shirt for free and been handed money. The day before that a man had found me on the road and let me sit in his car while I drank his cold water and sat in his air conditioning. The day before that a couple had bought my lunch, dinner, and breakfast, another man invited me to stay the night in his camper. To contrast this seemingly utopian lifestyle with the harshness and severity of hundreds of thousands of coils of barbed wire and lookout towers with armed guards, I could not think of a pair of more diverse lifestyles than the inmates and I. I wanted to stop and share my story with someone on the inside, but didn't have the courage and kept running.

Taking a short tour of the site of Fort Kaskaskia, I learned how the immense fort had once been standing high on the hillside and how battles and floods had caused its demise. A tour of Pierre Menard's home (for which the prison was named) was educational and the cool interior was another nice break from the heat outside. In the town of Modoc, I stopped in a bar, the only local enterprise still in business. Downing two cokes, I hit the road again and stopped soon after at the Modoc Rock Shelter, the longest known habitat used for human shelter in all of North America, so it claimed. It didn't offer quite the protection I had expected. The Rock Shelter is merely a bubble of rock protruding out from a sheer wall and a historical marker noted that the site had been used since 8000 b.c.

By finding shady and sometimes cool spots to rest throughout the day, I finally arrived in Prairie Du Rocher and found the only lodging in town, a bed and breakfast. Weary now of prices in such places I asked how much they charged for a night. Jan, the proprietor was very nice and asked how much I typically paid for a bed and breakfast. I explained that I had paid everything from free up to $90 for such a lodging. Then she asked what I thought was fair. I was in shock. No one had ever so openly negotiated with me before. I said that $25 would be a great deal and she agreed to it. I got cleaned up and ate the best chef salad of the trip in her restaurant. The salad was so good in fact that I had a second one. Fresh greens mounded the plate, honey mustard dressing, fresh strawberries, Feta Cheese, and *chicken strips*. It was truly amazing. I also had two side dishes and three root beers. These were no small salads mind you. Having finished the second salad, I ordered dessert, which finally elicited a gasp from the other couple in the restaurant. When finished, I was secretly still hungry and, not wanting to put on a show any longer, went down the street where I ate two snow cones with ice cream. Still not satisfied, I bought a bag of Reese's Cups and three soft drinks in the local grocery store for late night snacks.

Finally, the big day had arrived where I would enter St. Louis and run under the giant Arch. I had thought about the excitement of seeing it from afar. The metal sculpture would serve as a welcome sign to my eighth state from ten miles away.

The ADT enters the city on a series of levees along the Mississippi River. I had taken an alternate route for the last few days to stay near services while it was so hot. Now that I was closer to the city I needed to get back onto the levees. I had a message that Marvin, a local runner who had been volunteering to mark the trail. I called him hoping he could give me directions to stay on the ADT. He told me he was going to meet me and personally escort me into the city by running along side. We started the ten-mile stretch of levee up to the Arch.

"What do you do for a living?" I began.

"I work for the railroad," he said.

"Oh, really? There sure are a lot of active tracks in this part of the state," I replied. "Just the other day, I was in the middle of nowhere and was drinking sodas with a man who was taking pictures of trains crossing a trestle."

Just then he got quiet and said, "Were you standing in front of a minivan in your running clothes?"

"You're kidding!" I said, "That was me!" Sure enough, Marvin was the train conductor I had waved to 100 miles earlier as I stood behind my train spotter friend drinking his cooler of sodas.

During the course of the run he told about life on the rails and how the shifts are long, and the different people he's encountered hopping rides in his empty cars. He also explained to me that since train employees work such long shifts, and sometimes have to wait hours for an approaching train to pass on another branch of tracks, that they often carry plenty of water and food in their locomotive. He then said that there is an international symbol for asking for food and water from passing trains. He demonstrated these sign languages by rubbing your stomach for food, tipping an imaginary glass up to your mouth for water, or my favorite sign, though I'm not quite clear how it works, forming a roof over your head with your hands to ask where to sleep. Marvin explained that most railroad companies have barracks built every several hundred miles along the tracks and many of them are equipped with vending machines and are rarely locked. He said that if you need a place to stay and form the appropriate sign, a passing conductor would shout or point out the window the direction and the distance to the nearest bunkhouse. This bit of information excited me very much as I was envisioning staying in a slew of these shelters all across Kansas. Alas, try as I might, I only found a few buildings that looked as though they even resembled such shelters and all of them were either locked or empty.

The route up to St. Louis is very dramatic. For miles the traveler is on a long series of hot, straight levees with no end in sight. Then, suddenly, the St. Louis Arch appears. It slowly grows bigger until suddenly, the levee road becomes a giant casino parking lot. From the edge of the parking lot, you buy a ticket from an ATM-like machine on a staircase; take an elevator up one story to a metro, and cross the Mississippi River on the historic Eads Bridge. In the space of a few short minutes, you go from the impossibly long experience of the levees, to being whisked across the river in a city train and dumped out in a beautiful city park. Though slated to reopen to pedestrians in the near future, the Eads Bridge served as the third point where the ADT traveler must use public transit on the trail.

Chapter 17
Coffins, Coons, & Kittens

Only two landmarks along the trail conjured up immense powerful emotion, the St. Louis Arch and the Golden Gate Bridge. Both of them were easily identifiable and marked, without question, a specific geographic location. The mountains of Colorado were fun to see, the major rivers held my interest for a time, but the power of a single massive man-made structure that I could see approaching, that I could run right up to and touch and say, "Now I am here," and point to a map knowing exactly where I was filled me with a sense of exactness that I rarely was able to experience. A river continues. Mountain ranges are too big to touch with one hand. Cities begin at a fuzzy line after miles of sprawl. Only the monuments offered exactness. And when I arrived at each, I felt as though I was home. I didn't want to leave. Every step near them felt good and safe and sure.

Arriving at the Arch, Marvin followed me into the Museum of Westward Expansion in the basement of the Arch and bid me farewell. I rode up the leg of the Arch in the egg-shaped elevator and enjoyed the view of the city from the top. Returning to the bottom I toured the underground museum. Being left-handed and right-brained, however, I toured the circular museum counterclockwise instead of the other way around and so, it appeared, the country was doing fine until Lewis and Clark came along and unsettled everything.

The next morning a television crew met me. They wired me for sound and filmed me running on a fitness path. It was a Saturday and there were gobs of people out and about on the recreation trail. It was athletic overdose. I hadn't seen this many people exercising since the Washington Mall and I felt the near irrepressible urge to go up to each one and ask, "Hi,

I'm Brian. I'm running to California! How far are you going? (Imagining that every one of them was also on some gargantuan trek). The few people I was able to make eye contact with responded to my initial greeting with a disappointing head nod or a half smile.

The next morning, arriving at the Missouri River and the adjoining town of St. Charles I was very excited, as I would finally begin the highly reputed KATY Rail Trail for 200 miles from St. Charles to Mid-Missouri. Years ago, when the line was still active, the M-K-T (Missouri-Kansas-Texas) had been the central transport between Kansas and Texas. Now, with interstates and more widely used semi-trucks, the K-T or KATY has been transformed from its overgrown rails and ties and now offers nearly 200 miles of uninterrupted crushed, rolled gravel for the biker, hiker, and runner.

The KATY was amazingly easy to get on, just head towards the giant floating casino, hit the gravel path and turn right.

My dad and brother Eric planned to meet me at the end of the day in Defiance, Missouri. Eric had just finished the certification for his pilot's license. They rented a single engine plane, put two bicycles in the back seat, and flew from Indiana to a small airport just outside Defiance. We met that evening.

The three of us stayed at a bed and breakfast owned by Al and Carol Keys. They were excited to have me staying with them and had a fax from a producer of the CBS Saturday Morning Show. American Hiking Society suggested to CBS that the network interview me from the road live over the telephone during National Trails Day, which was the next day. I called CBS and we set up the interview. They faxed ahead the questions, told me how to call the direct line and how their operators would patch me into their studio system.

The next morning at 7:15 am, I called the network and a technician patched me into a series of lines all the while asking, "Brian, are you still there?" Included in the fax were the four questions the reporters were going to ask me. They instructed me to try and be relaxed, "as if talking to an old college chum," the fax read.

The questions were, "You don't always get to food or lodging at night… how's that going?" "How many pairs of shoes will you go through on this trip?" "When will you get to California?" and "Why in the world are you doing this?"

I had expected the questions to be asked in order, and I spent a few minutes writing out my responses to each. While I was on hold, I could hear the show being taped over the telephone. First, I listened to a segment on a contaminated breakfast cereal, then a clip on a S.U.V. crash test, and finally an interview with a former astronaut schoolteacher. Finally it was my turn.

First came the greeting, "Brian is running across the United States on the American Discovery Trail and he joins us now in Defiance, Missouri, just west of St. Louis. Brian, good morning."

With a sky blue plastic telephone in hand, sitting at a wrought iron table on an enclosed porch, I was ready. I had my questions right in front of me. I had my prepared answers right next to the questions. I was ready for anything. "Brian, first of all, why are you doing this?"

"What?! That's the fourth question! TIME OUT! I have the questions right in front of me and that's not the first question!" But I didn't say any such thing. I quickly turned to my second page of questions, all the while asking myself in a panic, "Why AM I doing this? I don't know."

Just then I saw the second page and remembered my response. "I wanted to see the country from the perspective of the settlers," I said as coolly as possible.

I was still alive. They only asked two more questions and then the interview was over. The whole thing lasted less than 30 seconds. We sat around the television and watched the quick interview shortly after. Everyone seemed impressed with the outcome.

Since it was National Trails Day, various trail clubs were hosting public celebrations to raise awareness about the importance of trails. One such celebration was being held in St. Charles, right on the KATY Trail where I had been the day before. The organizers there had invited me to make an appearance. So directly after watching the CBS program, we drove back to St. Charles.

We found a small crowd of dignitaries, reporters, and trail enthusiasts inside a bandstand in Frontier Park. I greeted them, gave a brief overview of my trip and conducted several more interviews. After weeks of relative isolation, the media buzz that day was a welcome experience.

After all the morning's hoopla, my family shuttled me back to my place on the KATY and resumed my run- I on foot and my dad and brother on bicycles.

Later in the day, we came upon Walt Root, an interesting man and fellow traveler. By this point in the trip, I was able to identify the afternoon joggers from those doing a more strenuous trek. There's a look about you when you haven't done regular laundry, when your muscles and skin shine from miles of uninterrupted effort. These bodies are generally easy to pick out from a field of rollerblading, spandex-wearing, afternoon health nuts. I spotted Walt from a quarter mile away. I could tell he was pulling a huge load. He had perfect form, for pulling a cart. By the way he moved, it was obvious this man could cover 20 miles without breaking a sweat. As he got closer, I could see he was also watching me, analyzing my gait and trying to figure out my story. "This should be interesting," I said to myself. When we finally stood in front of each other, it was as if we already knew everything about one another except for the small details of starting and finishing locations. I could imagine the cold rain and wet nights he had endured. I knew about the questioning stares from patrons as he ate deli sandwiches in supermarket parking lots. We stood face to face without talking, smiling in acknowledgement for a moment.

I soon learned that Walt wanted to do something about all of the nuclear weapons being built and stored around the world. He decided that the best way to stop the promotion of world destruction was to pull a coffin-shaped box on an ox cart across the country.

He began in Washington, D.C. two years earlier and made his way to Oregon. On the way, while crossing Alabama, a Lincoln Towncar struck him. His hiking partner was thrown 50 yards and broke both legs. Fortunately Walt escaped serious injury, but his coffin was demolished and it took him two weeks to tape it back together. Eventually Walt got back on the road, finally arriving in Oregon where he turned around and went back to Washington. When I met him on the KATY Trail we were simply crossing paths. On the sides of his cardboard coffin were all sorts of anti-war messages about stopping the production of nuclear weapons. One such slogan was, "War Victim." Reading this, I asked, "Oh, were you in the Vietnam War?" To this he replied, "No man, we are ALL victims of the war!"

I bid him farewell and the Happy Feet eventually met him three months later on the C & O Canal Towpath the weekend he finished in Washington. He told them he remembered meeting me on the KATY.

The next morning my dad and brother said a quick goodbye. It had been a great weekend, and I enjoyed seeing them but wished they could have stayed with me longer.

That day, I once again adjusted to the solitude of being on my own, of no one knowing who I was, where I was going, or even more painful, from where I had come. I passed through a few small towns with no businesses. Into the even smaller town of Treloar, I was thirsty and wanted someone to talk to. I ran through one of the small neighborhood streets and found a soda machine and a pay phone. I bought three soft drinks and called my friends at Camp Palawopec, which had been on my mind a lot lately.

Jill Braun answered the phone. She was one of the counselors whom I had led numerous trips with while spending summers as a camp counselor.

"Hello?"

"Hi, Jill, this is Stark."

"Stark! Where the hell are you?"

"I'm in Treloar, Missouri." I had happened to call the first day of Camp and all of the staff was arriving as I was talking to her. That made it especially difficult to not want to hang up and fly home for the summer. The first week of each summer is spent mowing grass, repairing cabins, and clearing trails. It was also a time to catch up on news from the school year, and is always regarded as a special week in the program.

That day, I tried to convince myself that this was really the place I wanted to be, the place that I needed to be. I had spent 13 years at my summer camp and it was time for a new experience. Even so, it was hard running that day, knowing that with each step I was getting farther and farther away from the patch of woods that taught me a love for camping and adventure.

At the end of the day I got to a road leading to the town of Hermann, several miles away. A young man gave me a ride into town where I walked up to the first motel I came to. The manager was cleaning the rooms.

"How much for a guy who just ran here from the East Coast?" I asked her.

"Thirty dollars," she said without turning off her vacuum.

"Does that come with a continental breakfast?"

"No."

"Do you have non-smoking rooms?" By this point in the trip, my senses were peaked from the hundreds of miles of fresh air, and I found that smoking rooms really bothered me at night. She said she had just scrubbed down the walls and counters in each room and so even "smoking" rooms were, in her mind, "smoke-free." She also said that, if the last tenant in the room did not smoke, the room would also qualify as "smoke-free," simply because it did not have fresh smoke in it. "Hmmm," I said. "Perhaps I'll take a look around town."

The next lodging was a bed & breakfast. "$79 a night, but since it's a weekday, we could probably go $65." "Ok, thanks, perhaps I'll be back," I said again. Finally, at the far edge of town, I came to the Hermann Inn, the only AAA approved motel in town. Clean rooms for $37, donuts for breakfast, and HBO in the room. It was the perfect solution.

In the morning, it was pouring rain. I couldn't get a ride back to the trail and ran the several extra miles before I started the day's run. By mid-afternoon, having run all day in the rain on the deserted trail, I came to the small and near non-existent town of Bluffton, Missouri. There were only two places to stay in Bluffton and both of them were Bed & Breakfasts.

The first one looked nice enough and even had a separate cabin for rent, but standing in the rain for 20 minutes proved futile as no one was home, nor was there any indication that they were open for business. I pressed on to the second lodging, and this is when things got interesting.

Knocking on the home of the only other lodging, my host came to the door wearing a T-Shirt - just a T-Shirt! He invited me in and, still a bit surprised by the attire of my host, I fumbled as we negotiated a price for the night. He then asked if I would like a dinner as well. There were no restaurants for miles and with only soggy crackers and a single Twizzler to my name, I accepted.

After the negotiations were over he apologized for his lack of attire saying, "You'll have to excuse me. I'm the president of the Co-Ed Naked Bikers' Club." This also took me by surprise so I asked for clarification as to just what he meant by that.

Apparently, this man and his friends do a lot of bicycling on the KATY. One day a few years ago in the blistering heat, he decided that he was going to cool off as he rode. This he did in the buff, and over the years it has become something of a tradition between him and his friends.

I was cold, hungry, and soaking wet. Nothing was going to keep me from a dry, warm bed that night, not even a naked biker.

After a dinner prepared with fresh vegetables from his garden, he said that he had a hot tub in his backyard and that I was welcome to get in and loosen up after my big day of running. I agreed that the water might feel good and gladly accepted. When I did so, he said that he thought he would join me.

"Oh? Okay," I said. I wore my running shorts and he put on a bathing suit and we walked across his backyard to a small cinder block building containing his spa. As soon as we got in, Doug reached over, turned out the lights, and started lighting candles around the hot tub. He told me several stories of how difficult it is to keep women from taking their clothes off while inside. Personally, I was perfectly content leaving my shorts on!

The next day I was determined to make it to Jeff City for a 35-mile day. I employed my now popular method of long distance days by using the 15/5 method. By running for 15 minutes and walking for five, you can cover great distances without wearing out your body. One set of 15/5 generally came out to about two miles of distance. By using this method across Illinois and Missouri, I was able to build up my stamina without undue fatigue. Later on in the trip, I could run much longer distances without stopping or tiring.

In the late morning of that day, the temperature was on the rise and I stopped in Steedman for a Coke. The bar was just opening when I arrived, and the bartender and I watched an episode of *The Price is Right* on his television. During commercial breaks while I was now sipping my second Coke, I explained my trip and how I was starting to think that if I could get all the way across America, I might have a good chance of becoming a contestant on the game show. The bartender seemed impressed and wanted to give me a trinket to remember him by. I was expecting another beer cozy, but this time I was given an oversized neon-green plastic flyswatter with the slogan, "S.O.B., Steedman's Only Bar".

It was so funny I couldn't refuse it. In return I gave him one of my "Transcontinental Runner" business cards. He then gave me a plastic card that said, "Don't touch my drink, I've gone to pee. S.O.B." I didn't know what I was going to do with either of these gifts, but I did know that I would love to see Lydia's expression when she received them in the mail.

Twenty miles later I arrived in Jeff City and treated myself to a decent motel and a wonderful meal in the Hotel DeVille while a local reporter asked me questions. Conducting an interview in the fancy dining room made me feel somewhat justified for wearing my running attire while surrounded by sport coats and evening dresses.

I was nearing Columbia where I had attended the trail board meeting several weeks earlier. Darwin Hindman is the Mayor of Columbia as well as the Missouri ADT state coordinator. He had told me that he and his wife were looking forward to having me over when I came through town.

We had a nice dinner on their back porch, although the telephone was ringing off the hook as it does in many politicians' homes. The Mayor arranged for a reporter to come over and interview me for the newspaper. The next morning, just before we left to get back on the trail, I gave a short radio interview from their home. It was the first such interview I had done on the trip. I enjoyed the way it let me tell my stories in detail and with enthusiasm, rather than trusting a reporter to write down the information correctly and to portray me in an accurate light.

Darwin drove me by his office before heading back to the trail. In his files he had a copy of the diary that the scouting team had written while hiking, biking, and driving the route ten years earlier. It was a thorough source of information and, even though severely outdated in places, was quite helpful.

Over the past few days I had been receiving an array of e-mails from a writer for *Walking Magazine*. At first, I was under the impression that the magazine wanted to write an article on the ADT, the KATY, and me. But I eventually learned that the article was to focus on the KATY. I also had originally thought that the writer wanted to run or walk with me for a few days, which also turned out to be inaccurate. During the night at the mayor's home, I finally reached the writer by telephone. She was staying in a series of bed & breakfasts along the KATY and, as she explained, would enjoy meeting me on the trail. We figured out that even though we were traveling in the same direction, since she was walking ahead of me and I was running, I would overtake her at some point the next day.

From the point when Darwin dropped me off on the trail the next morning, it took all of 18 minutes to catch up to her. The KATY is an abandoned rail line and, as one might expect, the terrain is very gentle, straight, and unobstructed. Like spotting the man in Illinois sitting in his van on the levee from two miles away, I slowly began to make out the image of a large green object up ahead on the trail. For a few minutes I would have sworn that it was a deer, bear, or large pack animal, as it constantly swerved from one side of the trail to the other. There were clearly no obstructions on the trail to cause some one or some thing to zigzag in such a crazy pattern. It reminded me of those old-fashioned cars at amusement parks that drive themselves along a narrow track. Even if you try to drive off the lane in one of those cars, the low metal track pulls the car back to the other side. That is what this person was doing but on autopilot and without any controlling median.

Sure enough, as I got closer, I could make out that the large green object was a huge backpack. When I was within one hundred yards, she noticed me and turned around and waited for me. I got up to her and introduced myself, and she asked if I minded walking with her for a little while. I was happy to and as soon as we took off I sensed that she wanted to swerve but by this point I had become such a miser with my mileage that I wasn't about to add even a foot by swerving with her. So we walked together and I kept her on track, heading straight for the remainder of the morning.

An hour later we stopped for a snack, eating trail mix and candy while sitting on a fallen log. She explained how she was a freelance writer and *Walking* was just one of the many magazines for which she wrote articles. She also went on to tell me about the many countries she has been to on writing assignments. I had to admit, it sounded great, getting paid to go somewhere exotic, all just to write an article about it.

Oddly enough, she wasn't asking me any questions about my trip. I had thought the whole reason we were getting together was to shed some light on the variety of people that travel the KATY. Later on the trail, we were met by another freelancer, this time a photographer, whom this writer had hired for a few days. Now I figured that the writer wanted to get a picture of me running on the trail, but this wasn't the case either.

She had hired the photographer to take pictures of her on the trail and told me that I could go ahead and they would catch up with me at the next restaurant for lunch.

Arriving in Rocheport well before the media pair, I immediately went to the ice cream shop where I had sat with the members of the ADT board after our Sunday bike ride over six weeks ago. I sat in the very chair where I had sat the first time, watching Harv smoke his pipe. I even had an ice cream cone. Leaving my memories of my time with the ADT board, I walked next door to the writer's scheduled lunch stop. The writer was out for a four-day walk along the KATY, looking forward to free meals and lodging, and thinking about what angle this story would take. By all accounts, it sounded like a trouble-free trip that anyone in his or her right mind would be elated to be asked to go on.

During lunch, I chatted with the two media people. After a few stories about my nearly 2000-mile trip thus far, the photographer turned to the writer and asked in a consoling tone, as if she was deep in the trenches of war, "So, how are you holding up? Do you think you will make it?"

The writer responded, "Yeah, it's tough, but I'm hanging in there." Neither of these remarks had even a hint of sarcasm. A professional writer for the premier walking magazine had just walked for two days in a row and had a day and a half to go when she was trying to keep the faith that this "torture" wouldn't last much longer. I hated to admit it, but I had become snooty. Just imaging that someone had paid this person to fly to the trail to hike for four days, and had paid for her food, her lodging, a photographer, and a salary, while I was doing all of these things for 5000 miles on my own didn't make sense. After the meal, I wished her well, thanked her for the lunch and conversation, and decided to press on.

Arriving in Boonville that afternoon, two teenage girls riding their bicycles caught up to me and decided to ride along side me for quite some time. They were friendly enough but they were also the kinds of girls that you know are headed for trouble as soon as boys start taking an interest in them. I was answering their questions as we made our way into town and while crossing a major road, they both flung their soda bottles as far as they could into a field. "I think you might have left something back there." I said as I passed them for the 400th time. They just laughed.

When we got into town, they devised a plan that to them seemed like a discovery that equaled sliced bread.

"Hey Mister, you know what? My mom drives the taxi in town and we could call her and she could pick us all up, and she could put our bikes in the trunk and drive you to a motel!"

"Uh, thanks, but I'm alright." It turned out that their idea wasn't bad as the only motel was two miles away on the other side of town. I ran the extra mileage and got a room for two nights. I was beat up, dehydrated, and needed to update my web site.

During my day off, I walked through some of the older neighborhoods taking in the fine homes. Sitting at the library, I wrote an update article for my hometown newspaper, *The Republic*, in Columbus, Indiana. After writing the story on the library computer, I e-mailed it to the paper. This library, like most others, has a one-hour limit of computer use per person per day. Just as I was sending the email, the librarian walked over to me and said, "I'm sorry, but your hour is up. You'll have to leave now."

This might be a good time to mention that I was the only person in the library! I had not even begun to update my web site, which is a main reason I decided to take the day off anyway.

The American Hiking Society had been covering my trip in their newsletter, and they lined up the national interview with CBS but, for the most part, promoting the ADT and raising funds for AHS's National Trails Endowment was up to me. Therefore, often times I had to work extra hard to convince newspapers that just because I didn't have a "front person" arranging interviews for me, my trip was still a newsworthy story. Making time during the run to gain media exposure was hard enough, but convincing obstinate librarians to flex the rules of computer use was futile.

The next day, I went to the lobby for my continental breakfast and there were only two donuts left.

"Excuse me. Do you have any more donuts?" I asked the receptionist.

"No," she said. "We ran out."

It was still early in the morning and I knew there must be more guests that would be coming into the lobby for food. I figured that as long as there was one donut on the tray, they weren't going to consider themselves "out" of donuts and that if I took both of the donuts, then they would have to go get more. Just as I planned, as soon as I took my two donuts, a family of five came in through the door and realizing there were no donuts left, took matters up with the receptionist, who, after giving me a quick glance, sent someone out to the store to get more.

Boonville was an important town on the ADT for at one time the KATY trail ended there. It has since expanded at least 30 more miles westward but when I came through, it meant getting off the smooth, trouble-free gravel bed and readjusting to maps, road signs, and getting lost at least three times a day. It also meant the beginning of the Santa Fe Trail, a historic autoroute that I would follow all the way to Denver, Colorado.

Only portions of the original bed of the Santa Fe Trail exist. Wagon wheel ruts can still be seen carved by the thousands of settlers looking for a better life and merchants transporting their goods to the various outposts. Today, the Santa Fe Trail is a scenic driving route paralleling the official one as much as possible with cast iron historical markers dotted along its course.

Exactly at noon, I came to a roadside junction of the interstate and stopped in the Dogwood Restaurant for two B.L.T. sandwiches. B.L.T.s had become something of a tradition for me on the road. There was just enough food to make me feel fed, but not enough to weigh me down. The best B.L.T. I had on the trip was in a small town in western Indiana. The cook had inserted a third layer of toast between the bacon and the lettuce and tomato, forming a kind of club sandwich without the meat. Ever since that wonderful meal, no other sandwich could compare, but I always tried, hoping for a version that rivaled it.

It's amazing how many different ways a B.L.T. sandwich can be presented. Some were burnt. Some had only shavings of meat in the bacon; the rest being whole strips of fat. The lettuce might be wilted or only one leaf. Other times the whole thing might have been dominated by a half of a head of lettuce. Some were cut into quarters, others halved. In eight months of having B.L.T.s whenever possible, I never had the same sandwich twice.

By mid-afternoon I arrived nine miles farther along in Arrow Rock, Missouri. Never before in a town so small have I been so surprised. With only a population of 70, the residents of Arrow Rock have somehow managed to develop nine bed & breakfasts, a nice theatre, lots of interesting shops, plus over half of the town is listed on the National Historic Register. Arrow Rock is very similar to my home in Nashville, Indiana -- an artists' community with small-town charm where everyone knows each other. They are both kind of an Andy Griffith's Mayberry, if Barney Fife had done pottery.

As luck had been a continuing aspect to my trip, it again was the case when I entered Arrow Rock. The citizens were celebrating "Juneteenth," an annual city-wide celebration complete with gospel singing under a circus tent in the town square, an ice cream social, and a professional traveling musical troupe performing, "Children of Eden" in the playhouse that night. Every room was booked in town and the cast of the musical had even filled two bed & breakfasts.

I got the last bed in town. In the upstairs common area of one bed & breakfast there was a cot in a cubby secluded by a thin drape. This bed I was told was being offered at a discount, and I took it. There was a nice campground nearby but predictions of rain and, more importantly, the thought of social interactions with actors pulled me in.

After eating a generous bowl of ice cream and listening to some gospel music under the circus tent, I went to have a look around town. I poked my head into a few craft and antique stores and went over to the theatre to see about getting a ticket for the show. They were almost sold out but since I was by myself I was able to buy a single ticket in the middle of the fifth row, best seat in the house. When I showed up for the performance, however, I felt more like sitting in the back. I was clearly the only person wearing shorts, and especially nylon running ones.

I swallowed my pride and made my way to the middle of the row where I sat for three hours between women wearing heavy perfume, which wafted over me, monopolizing my suffering nostrils.

The show was excellent. God was played by a very large, well-built black man. The rest of the cast was white and so it made his presence seem all the more striking under the stage lights and the colorful outfits. During different songs the actors came out wearing elaborate animal heads to transform themselves into animals on Noah's Ark.

The next morning's breakfast conversation was interesting. I talked about life on the road. They talked about life on the stage. One of them, a young man who had played Able the night before, was going to magically become Huckelberry Finn in just three days. We had a good time, but I needed to get back on the trail and bid them farewell so we each could continue our unusual careers.

Only a few miles out of Arrow Rock, my happiness and good feelings were swept away as I came upon a raccoon who had been recently hit by a vehicle. It wasn't the first time that I had seen a dead animal on the side of the road. The fact that this animal was lying on the side of the road was not what struck me. I had begun the tradition of apologizing to each dead animal on the side of the road, almost feeling responsible for the destruction of each one's life. After all, if it wasn't for our endless network of roads and barreling machines, this creature would likely still be alive.

"Sorry little fella," was a typical sentiment I would whisper down to the lifeless body on the road. Just as I was apologizing to this raccoon, I saw, out of the corner of my eye, that he was in fact still alive. He must have recently been hit because even though he was in very bad shape, he was laboriously breathing. I stopped and turned to examine him. He had been hit hard. Immediately I could tell that at least three of his four legs had been broken by their position. Feces had been squished out of his abdomen, his eyes were glued open, staring darkly ahead at pavement level, and his tongue was white and swollen, hanging out and laying on the pavement. He made a wheezing sound with each inhale of air.

"What can I do?" I thought. I'm just a guy on the side of the road running to the ocean. But then I realized that this raccoon and I were on the same level. We were both living and working on the side of the road. I had carried no weapons and it very easily could have been me that was taken down by that metal beast. Had it been I that was lying, dying, and frying on the pavement in the scorching sun, I certainly would have wanted someone or something to help me. So I tried to think back to past memories of what dying things want. First and foremost, instinct told me to put this animal out of his misery, to stomp on his head and end his pain. But worries of not stomping hard enough, or missing his head and hitting his back prevented any such action. Then I remembered all of the old western movies I had seen. Anytime a cowboy had been shot, just before they died they always whispered in a hoarse cry, "I'm so thirsty." I somehow decided that this was just what this raccoon was thinking and with my ten ounces of water, poured some into the cap, and dribbled this on his tongue. Immediately, with each inhale of breathe, I could hear a faint, "slurp, slurp" of him trying to drink the water as best he could. Who knew how long he had been lying on the hot road? The sun was getting hotter by the minute and the only other thing I could think to do was to stand over him, using my body as a sunscreen and letting my shadow fall across his body. I stood over him for twenty minutes. I began to wonder if there was anything else I could do.

On the side of the road I found some tall reeds and I made a makeshift stretcher out of them. With this I carefully rolled the raccoon onto the stretcher and dragged him off the road into the weeds. That was it. At least he was off the road. I figured that now he either had a fighting chance or a proper burial. I bid him farewell, said sorry once more, and ran on.

I was out of the next town by eight miles when I heard a far off, "Meoooooowww." It was coming from the fields beside me but was somewhere between the endless horizon and a vast farm to my left. Stopping on the side of the road, I fixed my eyes until they picked up on the movement; a kitten was running towards me from the field. I picked it up; it easily fit in one hand. It wasn't wearing a collar, and it seemed very glad to have found someone.

Taking out my "animal hospital" bag of supplies, I set up shop on the road once again. Taking out my water bottle, I poured water into the cap and let the kitten drink out of the cap. He was still meowing so I decided he was hungry. I had two packs of cookies in my pack and crushed these and set the crumbs on the pavement. The kitten started to eat them when a car drove up and stopped next to me.

"Do you need a ride?" the people in the car asked.

"No, thanks, but this kitten does. I just found him in this field. Do you want him?"

"No. What are you doing out here?"

"I'm running to California. Look, will you be willing to take this kitten? I really can't do anything for him out here by myself."

"No. How long have you been running?"

I was getting pretty disgusted that they were more interested in finding out about my trip than in helping this kitten.

Their last question was, "Are you going to be famous?" I had wanted to say, "Yeah, I'm going to be the guy that starts the non-profit organization, 'CPFJWDPOFK,' Capitol Punishment For Jerks Who Don't Pull Over For Kittens." But I held myself back as they drove off.

When I set the kitten down, he looked up at me, meowed endlessly, and clung to my legs. I finally just picked him up and started walking. I carried him for three miles. It wasn't so bad, I thought. I could get used to the weight of a cat, couldn't I? It could learn to balance on top of my pack, bounce along with me to the Pacific Ocean. However, I came to a farmhouse and decided to make one more attempt at adoption when a woman answered the door.

"Hi, my name is Brian and I'm running to California and I found this cat. Do you want him?" The woman willingly adopted him and I continued down the road, happy to have helped someone else out for a change.

Later in the day I finally arrived in Lexington, a very historical town due to the battles it has seen. A woman at the Historical Society told me about the famous Battle of the Hemp Bales. Lexington was built on a hill and at one time the town had been held by a group of people defending it from the hilltop. The opposing army, trying to charge the hill and not having protection from gunfire, gathered great round bales of hemp from the nearby valley. With these, they rolled them up the hill hiding behind the bales. The bullets easily shot through the bales, and they rolled back down the hill. At the bottom of the hill, still determined, the army soaked the bales in a river where they became sodden with water and very heavy. They then rolled the now saturated bales up the hill again. This time it worked to deflect the bullets, and they overtook the town.

After my museum tour, I searched out the local fire station. I spoke to the fire chief and he invited me to stay the night in their bunkroom. That night I got a taste of the life of an on-call fire fighter.

After dinner, we sat around watching television before we finally went to bed. All was working out very well until around 1:30 a.m. when I woke up standing in the middle of the bunkroom trying to turn off the massive alarm clock that was coming from all directions. When I finally got my senses I realized that a call had come in and everyone had hopped out of bed to go to the rescue. Even with the new understanding that this could happen I found myself making the same alarm clock mistake only and hour and a half later.

I pushed on the next day through the small town of Wellington where, one week later I read in a newspaper, the town was nearly wiped out by a microburst. The planned stop for the day had been Sibley, Missouri, just about fifty miles from Kansas City and my next state line. I chose to stay there because the scouting team's diary had said there was a hot dog stand in town. This, I planned, would be dinner and breakfast.

Arriving in Sibley, the postmaster in town sadly informed me that there was no food in town and so long as she could remember, at least nine years, there never had been. How dare a hot dog stand close ten years after a couple biked up to it, ate a wiener, and wrote about it in their journal? Don't they know that other brave souls are wandering around the country relying on what existed a decade before?

Only a few hours earlier I had passed a road leading to the small town of Buckner. There was no lodging in that town either, but there were several places to buy food. If the character of a ride into town is any indication of the upcoming experience to be had, I might as well have pressed on to Kansas City. The man that picked me up and took me to Buckner was driving a homemade wrecking truck, pulling a pickup truck.

We drove the long way into town on back roads because, as my driver told me, "I don't have a license and me and... the cops don't get along too well." He spoke as if he had dealt with them on several occasions. I didn't ask any more questions.

Chapter 18
Mr. Bruiser

The tow-truck vigilante dropped me off in town where I proceeded to eat at both restaurants in succession. A full Mexican dinner at a walk-up taco stand followed by several milkshakes and fries at a nearby A & W Root Beer stand quieted my appetite. I confirmed that there was no lodging in this town and, although people told me there were plenty of motels "just 20 miles away," none were here where I needed them.

I went into Plan B, which entailed introducing myself to the personnel at the local fire station. This had worked well the previous night. The only problem was that the fire fighters were at "Haz-Mat training," according to one fire fighter's wife. I waited outside in the drizzling rain for them to return. Eventually, the wife invited me into her home next to the fire station. Our discussion quickly turned to my trip and my many adventures. She suddenly said, "I've got two dreams of my own."

"Oh?" I asked.

"Before I die I want to see a mountain and an ocean." I was stunned.

"Why don't you just go this weekend?" I asked, knowing that some kind of mountain couldn't be more than a day's drive away.

"Oh no, I've got the kids to take care of and my husband's working. We could never do that." She brushed aside my idea as if even the possibility was a lifetime away.

It was then that I realized how fortunate I was to be having this adventure. Here I was having the time of my life. I'd already seen one ocean on this trip and was headed for another. I was going to be enveloped in the Rocky Mountains for a month, then the Sierra Nevada later, and this woman just wanted to see one before she died!

126

I offered to watch her kids for a weekend while she went and saw her mountain but she didn't think it would work. I suppose each of us has to find our own mountain in our own time.

Not long after our discussion the fire fighters returned. After going through the proper channels, they told me the station is volunteer only and isn't staffed full-time. Because of that I had to find other lodging. It was now a solid rain at 8 p.m., and I still had no place to go.

I searched out the local church. People at several churches along my run had let me sleep in their fellowship halls or Sunday school classrooms. The only person inside the local sanctuary at that hour was the custodian who wouldn't even open the glass door to hear what I wanted.

Now I was venturing into unexplored territory. This hopeful – and slightly – desperate seeker of human kindness tried the local police station in hopes of a jail cell: closed.

Finally, I searched for lodging for the first and last time of the trip at the local tavern. With my dingy grayish-white shirt, fading nylon shorts, and a smell that can only come from 90 days of running in the same outfit, I entered the bar and sat on a stool hoping to go home with a stranger. Acting faster than my brain could keep up, I turned towards the man next to me at the bar and struck up a conversation.

How do you start a conversation that results in going home with someone? If I could have been an attractive female it would have been no problem. But if my outfit and smell didn't give me away, my beard most certainly would have. I was at a loss, so I asked, "How's it going?" For the first few minutes the man next to me didn't even look my direction, much less respond to my overtures. After several minutes of persistence however, he slowly began warming up to me. Once he realized that I was running from coast-to-coast and simply needed a dry place to stay in town he gained interest.

Every few minutes, almost in mid-sentence, he would stop himself and ask, "And you're not gay or anything, right?"

I just laughed in wonderment at the possible categories covered by "or anything" and said, "No. Not gay *or anything.*"

Once he was convinced that I didn't pose a threat, he called his buddies over from a local dartboard tournament. Soon I had a collection of men standing around me wearing ballcaps with sharply creased bills and Carhartt jackets, all smoking, drinking, and trying to think of some place I could spend the night. Many of them had suggestions of other people's homes that I could try. Oddly enough, none of them suggested their *own* homes.

Finally, one of them asked, "Why don't we just put him in the truck and drive him up the street to Mr. Bruiser's's house?"

A murmur of "Oh?"s and "Ya'think?"s went through the group. "Sure, Mr. Bruiser will take anyone in," the first said.

Moments after getting into a truck, we pulled up to a dark single-story home two blocks from the bar. I was envisioning what Mr. Bruiser would look like. Would there be a bouncer at his door? Would ZZ Top be blaring out of his windows? None of the images I conjured up made me feel particularly confident or comfortable.

The driver said, "Wait here."

He disappeared into the dark house without even a knock. A moment later he came out and said that it would be okay, and I was to go inside and sleep on the couch in the living room.

Not a creature was stirring in this small neighborhood home. With a name like "Mr. Bruiser" I was expecting a livelier atmosphere than the tavern. My barstool friend drove off, leaving me to fend for myself in this dark, strange dwelling.

My vivid imagination conjured up a series of scenarios. What if the guy hadn't even talked to Mr. Bruiser? What if Mr. Bruiser didn't even exist and this stranger just told me to go into a home he knew nothing about? What then? I inched my way into the black living room of the man whom I still had not met.

With just enough streetlight I could tell that there was already a bedroll on the couch. Apparently, a different local had already suggested a different guest take Mr. Bruiser's couch for the night. I took the floor, laying out my sleeping bag and climbing in. The night of June 17th was incredibly hot in this open-air billet without a whisper of a breeze. Within seconds I was too hot and had to leave my down sleeping bag. Still too hot, I took off my shirt. I was eventually lying spread-eagled, damp with sweat, and bare-chested on this man's carpet, sleeping bag kicked to the side, and my pack beside my head. All of a sudden a large woman walked in wearing a voluminous nightgown. Enter *Mrs.* Bruiser.

She noticed a hapless bare-chested stranger on the carpet and, flipping on the light, exclaimed, "What in the hell are you doing in here?"

Apparently, when my bar friend sought permission for me to spend the night, Mrs. Bruiser was left out of the approval process.

I tried explaining the situation to the large figure with the smoldering red ember sticking out of her mouth.

In my haste I spouted out a running apology in one breath. "I'm sorry-I am running across the country and I got into town with no place to stay and I went to the bar and met a guy who brought me here and said that he had talked to Mr. Bruiser and that it was okay and I'm just here for the night and I'll be gone in the morning..."

At the same time, the real Mr. Bruiser was mumbling from a nearby bedroom that I was a schoolteacher and it was okay. Fortunately for me she concluded, "all right" and went to bed.

I slept until 5 a.m. when I awoke to the strange feeling that I was being watched. When I opened my eyes, still bare-chested and spread-eagled, I saw two people chain-smoking and staring at me from the couch, 2 feet away. Mrs. Bruiser and the couch guest had decided they couldn't sleep and, to occupy their attention during a smoke, chose to watch The Brian Channel.

If there ever was an inspiration to get in an early morning run, this was it. I still had not actually met Mr. Bruiser, but decided that was one experience I could forego. I thanked Mrs. Bruiser for her hospitality and hit the pavement a little earlier than usual, bound for the comfort of Kansas City and its thousands of air conditioned smoke-free hotel rooms, "just 20 miles down the road."

With my early start, I reached the outskirts of Kansas City by 9 a.m. With time to spare, I stopped in the Truman Library and Museum, taking in the 47-minute film and having a look at the exact replica of the Oval office in Harry Truman's day. I was particularly impressed with the amount of gifts to the past President, which were on display: cabinets from around the world, oriental rugs, gold figurines, sculptures, and other priceless items. It was quite a collection.

Getting a room at a Shoney's Inn, I waited for the big day. Lydia was flying in the next morning for a weekend visit!

On our first full day we decided, of all things, to go to the movies. I was starved for movies and there were many out that both Lydia and I had agreed to wait and see when we were together. We spent the better part of the day in the theatre, hopping from one movie to the next. We saw *The Truman Show, Six Days and Seven Nights,* and *The X Files.*

After dinner we had a look around town. The day had flown by. Lydia's flight was to leave the next afternoon and neither of us wanted to do anything Sunday that would make us sad that it was our last day together. So we went to the one place where you can keep your mind off such things as traveling and work: Kansas City's Worlds of Fun Amusement Park.

The operator on the phone warned us of a crowd of 12,000 with an average ride wait of 40 minutes. We went anyway and, with threatening dark skies, the most we waited for any ride was three minutes. We rode every ride back to back all day long, only stopping once for a snack of curly fries and a giant Coca-Cola.

This was a mistake. Back on roller coasters such as the *Mamba*, *Orient Express*, *Timber Wolf*, *Detonator*, and *Cyclone* our tummies were beginning to feel the effects of grease, ketchup, and carbonation.

At 2 p.m. it was time to leave and get Lydia on her plane. We got to the airport and sadly walked back to the gate we had been at only 48 hours earlier. Just prior to her visit, we both felt that the weekend was not going to be enough time to see each other. Lydia called the airline to see about extending her visit and they told her that it would cost $170 extra to change the ticket, not to mention the extra night for a hotel room. Trying to say goodbye, I told her I would see her very soon in Utah. We kissed goodbye and she walked down the ramp and got on the plane.

During a previous visit to see me in Indiana, I had waited for her to get on the plane and fly home and watched for it to take off. After sitting at the gate for a very long time, the passengers finally deplaned, as they had to replace a part on the airplane. The airline gave each passenger a meal coupon for food in the airport while we waited three hours for the plane to be fixed. Ever since then, I've always waited for the plane to take off to make sure there are no problems.

This plane was also sitting at the gate for a long time. Finally, and as if the subject of a mirage, Lydia came running out of the gate eagerly looking to see if I was still around. The plane had been overbooked and she had *graciously* volunteered her seat, for the tradeoff of a $300 flight coupon and a first class return flight home!

The next flight wasn't until the following morning so the airline also gave her a free night in a Mariott Hotel plus a meal stipend. Moments after we were sad that the weekend had ended so quickly, we were suddenly being given a free hotel room, meal, and a free plane ticket to boot! We now had the rest of the day and night to spend with each other. With amusement tickets still in our pockets, we drove back to Worlds of Fun and rode all of the rides again until closing time when we watched the laser light show and went back to the hotel. Sometimes things just have a way of working out.

The next day I was happy and light as I ran through Overland Park, a giant subdivision in Kansas City. I spent the night with relatives of the Happy Feet. Their relatives have four boys, and I got into a spirited conversation with them. I asserted that Lucky Charms Cereal is far healthier than more popular "health cereals." I'm not sure I convinced them, but who can argue with the diet of a guy who's running across the country?

Once I left town, now officially in Kansas, I got on the familiar combination of dirt and gravel roads that the ADT calls home wherever local trails do not exist. Several miles out of Overland Park, and now back into the countryside, I came upon a feed store that had seen better days. The faded, peeling clapboard siding hung as if the entire building might collapse in a good wind. The large picture windows stared blankly across the western-style plank porch. Inside, the storeowner looked as though he had been waiting for some time for anything to happen. It all contributed to the look of a set from an old western movie.

"Howdy!" I said as I entered the store.

"How are *you*?" came the slow reply. The man was in his 70s and looked as if he hoped a severe fertilizer shortage would take place any moment. The worn wooden floors had obviously held more excitement in their day. The now near-empty shelves had been stocked to the hilt in days past. But now, I was the only customer in sight, and perhaps even the only one for the month by the looks of things.

"Do you have any water?" I asked, holding up my empty water bottle.

"You know, we never got that in here," he said as if it was some kind of mystery to him as to why his store never had a sink.

Looking behind me, I asked, "Is this an ice cream freezer?"

"Yes, but I haven't plugged that in for years."

"Oh," I said sadly.

I was about to press on when he piped up with, "We have Cokes, though." I bought two and he proceeded to tell me about life in "the old days."

His father started the feed store back when local farming was in its heyday. All of the local farmers used to come from miles around to stock up on chicken feed, hog feed, horse feed, and thousands of other farming staples. Since then, however, the smaller farmers had sold out to large farming companies and these large companies buy their feed from giant suppliers. So the local farmers' market went by the wayside and this man stands at his register every day, hoping it's not so.

His only sales these days he tells me are an occasional bag of dog and cat food. I tried to imagine the slow transition of five farmers standing around in their overalls talking about the buck they just shot, or the calf that was born sideways, to the modern-day housewife coming in wearing a rainbow-colored jogging suit to buy some Fancy Feast cat food for Fluffy. It felt mildly depressing.

Later that day I made it into Spring Hill, Kansas. During the trip, an important aspect to my rest and recovery each day was a good night's sleep in a clean, dry bed. Television, a telephone, and a good meal went a long way to reviving my spirits, too. The positive effects of motels were appreciated and necessary, but having stayed at a few lodgings in a row, I would begin to feel as though I were cheating myself from experiencing this adventure to its fullest. Wouldn't I see more of this country if I forced myself to camp out in town? Isn't the whole point of the trip to see America and meet the people in it? If so, how can I say I am getting to the point if I lock myself up in a motel room each night, complete with all of life's luxuries?

Typically after a 35-mile day, my sentiments would be that I had seen enough of the country for one day and wished to retreat to a motel. However, on lower mileage days, around 20 to 25 miles, these questions would haunt me and I would be forced to bypass the lodging in search of something that offered more adventure.

Such prodding encouraged me to seek alternative accommodations in Spring Hill, Kansas. I stopped in at the local fire station. The fire chief gave his special permission and invited me to stay the night. Later that night, the firefighters bought me a half-gallon of cookie dough ice cream. I could get used to this. After watching them play 007 on their Sega video game, I did my usual show-and-tell, displaying what I carried in my pack and sharing a few stories from days on the trail.

Checking my email one last time in the fire station, I had a message from Nick, a friend of mine from Indiana. Nick had tried to find me when I was running across southern Indiana. Over the telephone, I learned that he had driven for ten hours, going up and down every county road in my area. I felt bad that he had tried so hard to find me without success.

Maps for the ADT were very rare when I was running the trail. Even for me to know where the trail was became a daily challenge. It's no wonder then, that Nick and others had a hard time finding me. Keep in mind that since the ADT route finders chose the most remote, scenic, and lightly traveled byways, such paths can be nearly impossible to find.

Nick's email in the fire station told me he was driving across the country, moving from Indiana to Washington State. On the way there, he thought he would take another chance at finding me and would drive across Kansas in search of me. My mother had told him that I should be just west of Kansas City on a series of back roads and she rattled off a list of small towns I was to go through.

Nick's email said, "Stark, Nick here. Drove through Spring Hill, Kansas yesterday looking for you. I went into the grocery store and asked the clerk if there were any trails in the area and they said that Spring Hill is pretty much a, 'what you see is what you get' kind of town. 'In that case can I have these deli sandwiches?' Good Luck, Nick."

The grocery store Nick had written about was directly across the street from the fire station I was in. I had missed him by one day.

Getting an early start the next morning I saw two deer walk out of the woods and move onto the road several hundred yards ahead of me. They saw me but weren't startled. Instead of bolting off into the woods, they simply trotted ahead of me down the road. A moment later, a truck came over the hill from behind me. At the same time another truck came over a hill ahead of me. At the base of both hills, where all of us were about to converge, was a long cement bridge over a stream. I knew something interesting was going to happen. The deer saw the truck coming towards them and stopped on the bridge. They turned around but then saw the other truck coming from behind. I stopped in the road to watch what would happen.

Why the trucks didn't stop I'll never know but the deer panicked and both at the same time jumped off of the bridge, falling some 40 feet to the streambed below. I was in total shock. The trucks continued on without stopping.

I wanted to shout, "Did you see that?" Running onto the bridge, I looked over the cement wall that now had fresh deer hair on it from their bellies scraping it as they plunged over the side. Looking down into the valley below, the underbrush was too thick to see their demise, but I hoped for the best.

That afternoon I arrived in the colorfully named town of Osawatomie and headed straight for the visitors' center, temporarily located in a tiny air-conditioned one-room shed. Inside, I was greeted by a couple manning the shed center. They were very excited about my arrival. I drank several bottles of water as they pelted me with questions about my run.

They felt my stories were newsworthy and called the local paper. Soon a reporter arrived and interviewed me. Afterwards the couple told me that they were going to try and get me a complimentary motel room for the night. There are only four people on the visitor's bureau committee who can give funding approval for such a purpose. Luckily for me, two of the four were with me in the shed.

They called the other two on the committee, and all four agreed to pay for my motel room. One of the board members also owned the motel where I would be staying, and he generously went along with the motion. They were nice people who certainly knew how to treat a visitor royally!

Running back through Osawatomie the next morning, I passed a park that is host to a cabin once used by John Brown as a stand against local slavery activists. Having passed the arsenal attacked by Brown in West

Virginia, I enjoyed my continuing history lesson. Making historical ties like this were some of the most rewarding events of the trip.

Leaving town I got on the Flint Hills Nature Trail. The Flint Hills is a rail trail project that is planned to be open in the near future. In 1997 a crew came in and took up many of the rails and ties but the large rocks of ballast were still present and made for tricky footing. I considered myself lucky that the ties had been lifted and removed just a year earlier because I believed doing so uprooted what may have been a lot of weeds which would have made for rough going.

There was a large debate going on between the rail trail supporters, who are many, and a select few farmers whose property through which the railroad right of way passes. Some believe that the right of way should be eliminated and the land returned to the surrounding property owners. A few of the more adamant opponents have even physically bulldozed the elevated right of way across their fields and planted crops on the land.

I knew nothing of the differing opinions about this issue and set off down the rail trail to have a look at its progress. Even though the weeds had been recently pulled up from the center of the levee, the brush was still full grown on the sides and was so thick that it blocked what little breeze there was that day. Adding to the stagnant air, the black color of the ballast on the rail bed only intensified the heat by radiating it back towards me. Growing quite thirsty, I stopped at a passing house to refill my bottle. Not only did the mother and daughter give me ice-cold water from the refrigerator, but they also handed me a cold glass of iced tea. We sat on the porch and chatted for a few minutes before I thanked them for the refreshment and started off again on the rail line. From the reaction they gave me when I told them I was running the rail line, I gathered they didn't get too many visitors this way on foot.

"You had better be careful on that thing. You can go for miles and not pass a single house or road. And it's hot out there."

"Thank you," was all I said and pressed on. Several miles further, I chatted with a construction crew who shared some of their ice water with me. Entering a small town later in the afternoon, the only business was a row of three soft drink machines. I stopped and drank a soda from each. Some men working on a water main nearby cautioned me against following the rail trail any further.

"You can't go down that way," one of them said without even looking up from his ditch.

"Why not?" I asked.

"Last year someone went in there and burned down one of the bridges. No way around the water." Taking their recommended detour would have meant adding several miles. I decided to see if there really was "no way around it."

Sure enough, two miles down the trail, the levee came to an abrupt end where someone had torched what appeared to have been a fine wooden trestle across a stream. The streambed below had quite a bit of murky water in it and did not look at all inviting. I searched my surroundings, trying to think of a way to cross the expanse. The stream was a small one, perhaps forty feet across and the bridge had burned right down to the blackened telephone pole stumps sticking just inches out of the water. On the right side of the bridge the stream made a sharp turn where it paralleled the rail line. Across the stream at this point was a decent sized tree, fallen across the stream.

If you have a mental image of a tranquil woodland setting with a giant tree trunk stretching across a pleasantly flowing stream and a couple wearing starched white outfits and sun hats sauntering across their natural bridge, forget about it.

Just getting to the tree took 20 minutes, even though it was only ten feet away. I had to maneuver through a matrix of fallen branches, twisted vines, and immense thickets. When I finally got to the tree trunk, I realized that the crossing was going to be a bit trickier than I had thought. Rather than one nice straight tree across the water, what I had seen was actually three different trees. I would have to hop across and hope that none of them would break or sink into the water. The stream itself was barely moving. It seemed to carry more pond scum than liquid. Slightly surfacing above the murky depths were dozens of sharp pointy broken branches of various sizes. Falling into this quagmire would not only mean soaking my pack, shoes and socks, but a good possibility of injury from the sharply pointed branches as well. After 45 minutes I was across the water but now had to negotiate a wide ditch of brambles back up to the continuation of the rail trail. All in all, my forty-yard detour had taken just over an hour to negotiate while unsnagging briars and branches from my pack, feet, and shirt. My legs had become a matrix of red lines, with blood dripping from larger wounds. I had crossed the "uncrossable," but the descriptions from the workman in the ditch had not been far off.

One trail opponent, a match, and a lost trestle.

I arrived in the small town of Ottawa by evening and approached two teenagers asking them for a ride to the nearest motel. They agreed to give me a ride one and a half miles away to a Days Inn.

As I climbed into the car they turned to me and said, "Yo, dude! Check this out, no key needed!" Whereby they turned the keyless ignition and started the car.

The next day I decided to stick to the highways, not wanting to negotiate around other burned bridges. The Data Book I was using indicated that the next town, Osage City, had a motel. I was glad to read this for it meant that at the end of a long hot, 35-mile day, I would be treated to a clean bed, television, and a meal.

The temperature climbed into the 90s, again with high humidity and stayed there for most of the day. Arriving in town, I found the motel I had been looking forward to. It was, quite likely, the worst lodging of the trip. Never before had I stayed in a motel made entirely of sheet metal. For

$30, I got a television with cable but no remote. Sure, I can run 35 miles day after day, but make me get up from the bed to change the channel and there's going to be trouble! To change the channel on this television, I had to push a button on a cable box bolted to a desk. The television was mounted on a pole on the wall and, while standing at the cable box and changing the channel, I could not see the television screen unless I leaned way back as if in a back dive position. Pulling back the thin cotton bedspread, I found five dead bugs laid to rest on their oversized casket. The none-too-clean bathroom offered a shower stall but no soap. Also interestingly, the bathroom had a heavy steel door, but the only locking mechanism on it was a flimsy latch hook.

To top it all off, the entire motel was being overgrown by some massive bushy monster. It was even overtaking the doorways into the rooms. To open the door even part way required a battle with nature as I struggled with several major leafy arteries of the beast blocking my entry.

My heart sank as I took off the next morning to find that the day before, I had stopped 200 yards shy of a brand spanking new fire station, offering tame shrubbery, bug-free sheets, and, very likely, bar soap.

The night before I had called a contact near Topeka who was a friend of my college roommate Robert Webster. His friend, Mike, or "TeKa-MeKa-Gan" as his trail name goes, had hiked a chunk of the Appalachian Trail with us in New England. I told him I would call him from Admire, the next town, where he agreed to pick me up for the night.

Arriving in Admire, I was at a loss for services. The only restaurant in town was only open on Sunday afternoons to catch the church crowd.

35 miles between towns and a nickel short for the drink machine.

I needed a pay phone to call Mike in Topeka and found an open Methodist Church. A woman cleaning the fellowship room there told me that the only public phone in town was at the high school mounted near the front door. I found the school across town. The phone was in a small metal box. It did not have any change slot and looked more like a security phone than a pay phone, but my calling card worked nonetheless.

Mike agreed to pick me up, and I retired to the back yard of the school where I rested under a picnic shelter, drank water, and wrote in my journal. An hour later he arrived with his wife, Cathy. Mike had placed a cooler in his backseat, fully stocked with soda on ice, my kind of guy.

When we got to his house, Mike asked, "Now, you're not one of those vegetarians are you?"

"No, sir."

"In that case, would steaks be alright for dinner?" he asked with a smile. Dinner was excellent and I checked my email and reminisced about life on the Appalachian Trail with my host.

The next morning we got an early start back to Admire as I wanted to make the 25-mile run to Council Grove and my next batch of mail before it got deathly hot. Starting the day's run at 8 a.m. I arrived at my destination at 3 p.m. and took a quick tour of town. Besides the excitement of picking up my new pair of shoes and any number of letters and goodies from friends and family, I was glad to be at another site of interest in my trail book.

Reese Lukei Jr., the national coordinator for the ADT, had written a guide to the trail with a selected list of interesting sites along the way. While on such a long journey, just the knowledge that I had gone 30 more miles across a state was not enough to keep me feeling like I was getting anywhere. The two real gems I used to judge distance were Reese's guidebook and the Weather Channel.

In the entire 4,800 miles of the southern route of the ADT, there are 24 identifiable historic structures pictured in Reese's book. I looked forward to seeing them all. So far, I had either missed seeing some of them or a large number of them had been removed. An old, one-room jail calaboose in Council Grove was one such structure I had been looking forward to seeing for hundreds of miles. Even more than touring the site, I mostly just wanted to be able to hold up my guidebook with the page open to the jail and look in front of me and see that I was actually at that point in the book. This was one way I used to measure that I was actually getting somewhere.

The second way was by the weather channel. When the weatherperson would give the national weather, I could look all across the country and point to exactly where I was, where I had been a week ago, and then trace my finger all the way back to where I had started in Delaware. That was my favorite part, thinking all the way back to the beginning of it all.

Chapter 19
Ad Astra Per Aspera

With guidebook in hand, I walked down Council Grove's main street and found the calaboose, now nothing more than a cement slab in a city park. When I asked what happened to the jail, I got differing stories from several people but all said that it had been removed no more than two weeks ago. Some people told me that it had been taken down to have the wood restored while others simply said it had been hauled off to the dump. The preservation tactics of the town further baffled me as I went down the street a bit more.

I came to a tree stump beside the road, clearly dead and severely rotting away. But it was an historical stump and the town had seen fit to preserve it.

The Kansa Tree Stump, as I found out, was the very place Native Americans signed the Santa Fe Trail Treaty allowing the trail to travel through their territory. Now, some 150 years later, the stump needs all the help it can get.

Several years ago, the city erected a shelter over the stump to keep rain and snow off of it. Then, panic set in among the townsfolk. The stump developed a crack in the middle, and it slowly began to rot. "Have no fear," someone apparently thought, and came back from the hardware store with a bag of cement mix. After mixing a bit of water, they poured a great mound of cement into the crack in the middle of the stump. The entire stump affair delighted me.

If my night in Osage City was terrible, the motel in Council Grove clearly made up for it. As I walked up to the motel, I was fearful that I wouldn't be able to get a room. The "No Vacancy" light was illuminated, but I decided it wouldn't hurt to try. Luckily, they had simply forgotten to turn the light off from the night before and they did have rooms.

The Cottage House Inn and Motel is a first rate complex. Guests have their choice of posh bed & breakfast rooms in the main lodge or less expensive motel rooms in another building. I opted for a motel room and was blown away to find that for my $30, I received a non-smoking room with a king-sized bed, cable, HBO, remote control, shower, hot tub, writing table, and refrigerator. I was also able to get a very nice continental breakfast. I was in hog heaven! I reserved the room for two nights, as weather reports predicted the temperature to soar into the 100's the next day.

The following morning after breakfast, I set off for the post office to see what treats I was to receive. It felt like Christmas. I had been giddy for days. The postmaster recognized me right off and produced four boxes of snacks and 15 letters. It wasn't quite a record but plenty to pour through for the afternoon. A reporter wanted to interview me and took a picture of me standing in front of "The Madonna of the Trail "using a Polaroid Camera. A series of "Madonna" statues was made possible through the work of a committed group of women. In each state the Santa Fe Trail passes through, the Daughters of the American Revolution have erected a stone statue of a woman with children. The statues are dedicated to the pioneering women who lost their lives to famine, disease, and hardship traveling across the country.

Footwear before and after – three weeks and 500 miles.

After my day off I should have made an early start, but I couldn't pass up the highly reputed Hay's House Restaurant which didn't open until later that morning. The wait proved to be worth it. Along with my order of pancakes, I had the best ham I have ever had in my life. That meal featured the kind of cuisine where with each bite you sit back and say out loud, "Wow." Sitting by myself I didn't mind that others could hear me as we were all chanting in unison.

Towns on the roster for the day were Delavan and Herington. After an interview at the Herrington newspaper, the reporter offered to drive me around town giving me a tour of my "home" for the night. In order to share most of the metropolis with me, he managed to drive nearly every street in a confusing matrix of patterns so that finally when I was completely confused as to where everything was, we arrived back at the newspaper.

"Wow," I said. "Where was the post office again?"

"Right over there," he said. "We just came from over there."

After the tour, I found the city pool. Some years ago the parks and recreation department was considering closing the pool because they weren't getting enough business to pay for its operation. Then someone came up with the bright idea that as long as they weren't making any money, why not just let people swim for free. That is what they have been doing for several years, and the pool is crowded every day of the summer. Neighborhood kids can wallow in the sky blue water with their friends free of charge. I went for a free shower and dip in the pool, washing away the miles of grime and cooling off amidst the sea of splashing kids.

Over the course of my trip I had several goals. One of them was to be invited to swim in a family's swimming pool. I could just see how it would happen. After spotting the blue treat in someone's backyard I would walk up to the front door, introduce myself, and ask for some water. After drinking several glasses, I would slip a comment into the conversation about how incredibly hot it has been and that the heat is like a hot air dryer blowing on me for weeks at a time. At that point, with a bit of luck, the homeowner would offer me a swim in his pool. If that didn't work I could always sneak into one, I figured.

Alas, much to my chagrin, nothing like that happened on my run. I did have more than my share of generosity, but I always hoped I would be able to go up to someone after he or she had invited me into their pool and be able to say, "So you're the one. I've been waiting to meet you."

After my time in the city pool, I went about looking for a place to sleep. I remember somewhere in the driving tour that we passed a fire station in town. I set off looking for it and a hopeful bunk for the night. Frustratingly, I couldn't find the fire station! It was hard to imagine in a town of only a few hundred people how anyone could walk for over an hour being lost in neighborhoods looking for such a landmark. I was at my wit's end and ready to give up.

Just then I saw a woman, possibly an apparition, riding a horse down a neighborhood street towards me. I asked her if she knew where the fire station was. After assuring her that I did not have a fire to put out, she told me that she was on her way to the local horse arena and would show me the way. So I walked next to the equestrian as we crossed the town.

She got me to the fire station, which also turned out to be the police station. They informed me that the fire station was day shift only and did not have bunks. Another one of my goals had been to sleep in a jail cell. They did not have any private cells in this station, and I did not feel like taking the chance that someone else might be "invited" to share the cell with me. They did tell me that I was allowed to sleep in the city park next to the swimming pool. They said that they would make a note that I was there and would patrol the area a few times during the night for me.

Walking back across town I found the park. It was shaded, offered a few picnic tables, and a stage. It was only 4 p.m. when I picked out a table to sleep on. Still wanting to confirm that there was no other available lodging in town, I set off again in search of a motel. I found one on the edge of town. The sign in the window said, "Closed. Go ½ mile further to The Sleep Inn." That sounded inviting and I made the trek. On my way down the highway, I started asking myself what it would take to get me to stay there. "Ok, it's got to have HBO, decent cleanliness and under $30. If it has all that, then I'll stay. When I arrived, the man said he had a room for $20. For my $20 the room offered HBO, a full bathroom, and a kitchen - not a kitchenette, but a <u>full</u> kitchen.

I don't know what made me do it. Perhaps it was the recurring nightmares from the crappy apartment-deal in Little Orleans, Maryland, but I turned down the motel and retreated to my police-patrolled city park and free choice of picnic table beds.

In a grocery store I thought I had overheard someone saying that the pool was open until 8 p.m. I laid down at 8 only to feel like I was on center stage. The security lights for the pool and park flooded the entire area of town, and I felt as if every person walking by was wondering what I was doing lying on a table. It turned out that the pool didn't close until 10 p.m. and the kids were being understandably noisy until well past that time.

The next morning I awoke to find that it was July 1st! Another month had gone by! It was time to start thinking about how I was going to spend my 4th of July. With an early start at 6 a.m. I set off to arrive in the town of Tampa, Kansas for the night. The HappiFeet had recommended I contact a man in Tampa who had helped them out when they biked through town. Meeting the HappiFeet for the first time in a grocery store, their new friend offered to put them up in the Community Hall for the night and even provided a meal for them.

When I arrived in town, I learned that this Samaritan had been in the hospital for six weeks. "My blood's got no oxygen in it!" he said in a slurred speech over the phone to me. With that connection falling through, I decided to push on a bit farther, hoping to reach Hillsboro, but first I needed some food. Stopping in the only restaurant in town, I ordered the special: salad bar, dinner roll, drink, and lasagna with corn. It all sounded like a good deal for a fair price but the predominate color at the salad bar was brown, the corn and roll barely did anything for me, and worst of all, the lasagna was the most interesting concoction of "pasta" I have ever seen. I was handed a plate with a small puddle of brown gravy, two squares of ravioli, and three quarter-sized hunks of beef.

It is funny how the mind plays tricks on you. Earlier that morning, while I peeled myself off the stone-slab picnic table, I had wondered how I was ever going to run the 19 miles to Tampa. Now, with my lodging having fallen through, only a light snack to propel me, I was pushing on for an additional 16 miles. For inspiration, I recalled Kansas' motto, "Ad Astra Per Aspera - To the Stars Through Difficulties."

While I was eating my meal, three construction workers sitting at the bar overheard my phone call with the man in the hospital. It wasn't hard to overhear conversations in unappealing restaurants like that. Everyone seems to sit, dazed in front of their puddle of gravy with ravioli placed in front of them. When I hung up the phone, the three turned around and started asking me questions. They said that it sounded like I was headed past their work site, and that I was welcome to stop in and fill my water bottle from their cooler when I went by.

Several miles down the road I did so and waved to my new friends. Looking at the map, I realized that Hillsboro was going to be three miles off the trail. Having run 35 miles that day, I didn't want to add three more if I didn't have to. I decided that when I got to the highway leading into town I would hitchhike in. As I neared the highway, I started casually throwing my thumb out if a vehicle was coming from behind headed into town. I wasn't even stopping on the side of the road. Suddenly, and without warning, a giant, white pickup truck screeched to a halt beside me. "Get in!" the driver commanded. I was being kidnapped!

Chapter 20
Kidnapped

With three unofficial miles ahead of me, I wasn't going to pass up any ride into town. After quickly getting into the truck, he asked, "Where are you headed?"

"Well, I was hoping to get to Hillsboro for a motel. You see, I'm running across the United States and I need a place to sleep for the night."

Almost cutting me off, he slammed on his brakes again, started to make a "U Turn" while asking, "Why don't you just stay with us? I'm a dairy truck driver going to my night shift. I'm running a little behind schedule but my wife is home and she'll take good care of you."

"Ok," I said, still a bit shook up from what was happening. We sped back to their country home past endless farm fields. Stepping inside his nice farmhouse, the man said, "Honey,-this-is-Brian.-He's-running-across-the-country-and-needs-a-place-to-stay. Give-him-some-dinner,-and-he-can-sleep-on-the-couch-and-I'll-see-you-in-the-morning. Ok?"

The whole introduction had taken maybe 30 seconds, and he was back out the door, headed to work. The family has two young daughters. One of them had gone with her father on his delivery route. The other one was home with her mother and me. Things were a bit awkward at first, seeing as how this man had just dropped off a total stranger to spend the night with his wife and daughter in their new home. Fortunately, the wife seemed to take it all in stride and soon we had my laundry in the washer and had agreed on Sloppy Joes for dinner.

The family usually goes for a horse ride every afternoon and they had been getting ready to go when I arrived. The mother hinted that she could use a day off from the ride, so I accompanied her daughter on horseback as we rode across the cornfields together. I had never thought about it before but would not have imagined that Kansas horseriders simply ride across the grain fields when they ride. When we returned from our nice tour through the countryside, the mother had finished making dinner, and we ate a great meal while watching the video, "Pure Country."

Just before bed, we decided to watch another video, "Murder at 1600." I slept great that night on the overstuffed couch. As we went to bed, there was a knock at the door. It was 10:30 pm. The mother decided it must have been the water man coming out to check the pressure in the water system but I have never heard of a utility worker coming to a home that late on a non-emergency call.

Later, she expressed her gratitude that I had been there to protect them from strangers. How odd, I thought. She was glad that there was a stranger in the house to protect her from a stranger knocking on the door late at night.

At 8 a.m. my "kidnapper" came home from his shift. There had been a bad storm that had slowed him down. As soon as he came home, he started playing with the kids, and started another video, "Conspiracy Theory." He tried his best to get me to watch the video with them.

"It's a real bad storm, Brian. You'd better stay here on the couch, eat donuts, and watch this movie with us." It was very tempting, but I really wanted to get to McPherson by evening, 25 miles away. I watched the first ten minutes of the movie and was just about sucked in but forced myself away, thanking them for their genuine friendliness and hospitality.

The ADT through Kansas, as close as I could figure, is on a series of county roads, most of which are dirt. The Foot's Data Book listed the necessary towns that the trail goes through but rarely did it list the name of the road.

I figured so long as I got through the right towns and saw the historical sights, and was on a lightly traveled road, I may as well be on the correct route. I picked a road. All of the county roads in Kansas are built on square-mile grids. Just pick a road and stay on it was my theory.

Just as I was enveloped in miles of fields with no homes to speak of, the storm announced itself. Loud thunder, occasional lightening, and very heavy rain came all at once in a trio of sound, light, and water. Within minutes the dusty road turned to mud and then to peanut butter. With each step, my shoes sank into the road several inches. As I would try to push off for the next step, my other foot embedded in the road would squish and slide back two feet on the slick surface. I figured if I had gotten stuck and trapped in the mud I might have been found, eventually. Anyone could have followed my sink – slide tracks for miles until finding me.

The going was so slow! I had been forced to stop running almost immediately after the rain began. I was never going to make it to McPherson this way, I thought. At the next mile mark and cross road, I turned and made my way, sinking and sliding towards Highway 50. It offered a paved surface and a better chance for services throughout the day.

The heat and miles over the last few days had taken their toll, and I stopped in a Best Western hotel. As I walked into the lobby the manager took a look at me, pulled out a sheet of paper and asked me to check my name off the list. He was about to give me a room key. I didn't know what he was talking about but I was readily willing to become Leo Miller or Gern Schnekerly if it meant a free room.

When I studied the paper for a moment, he hesitated and asked, "You're with the bike ride, right?"

"Um," moment of truth, I thought, "no."

"Oh, sorry." He told me that a group of people bicycling across America had arrived that day and were staying in the motel. I walked around the hotel to the pool area where I spotted a group of gangly bicyclists, pouring over their vehicles with black toothbrushes, hotel washcloths, and rags. They had apparently also experienced the rainstorm I had just come through. I walked up to one man cleaning off his bike and struck up a conversation.

"Wow, where did you guys start?" I asked.

"California," he said without further contribution. I asked him a few more questions but each was met with a bored response as if he had gone through this interrogation from curious onlookers before. He told me about the Ryder truck that followed them, the lunch break each day, the bike mechanics who came to their aid, and the outlined maps they were handed each morning, as well as the fact that they were staying in Best Western hotels every night of the trip. Then I mentioned my trip.

"Your ride sounds like a lot of fun. It must be neat to share the trip with other people," I said. "I'm running across the country and it sure would be great to have someone else along with me." At that point the biker stopped giving his gears the Oral B and looked up at me for the first time. I loved every syllable of it.

"You mean, actually 'running'?"

"Yep." A few other bikers overheard our conversation and came over to meet me. I ended up having dinner with the group in the hotel's buffet restaurant. Not wanting to be outdone by anyone's appetite, as well as having a gargantuan hunger from the last few days, I put down an adequate eight plates of food, combining fried chicken, mashed potatoes, corn, tacos, salad, pudding, and three sundaes into the jostling pantry more commonly known as my stomach. The bike ride, I found out, is a commercial business that makes the trek every year. On each trip at the midway point, they hold a talent show. The tradition was taking place that night, and I was invited to watch the annual event.

During the talent show I witnessed a juggling act, a stand-up comedian, a singer, a piano recital, stories, poetry, and at the end, a pie eating contest. Many of them encouraged me to participate, but I felt that it was their group activity and I should remain a spectator. Also, having just shoveled down eight heaping plates of food, the urge to shove down an entire pie in record time wasn't on my list for a nightcap.

These bikers were going a long way, but they had many conveniences that I did not. They could coast down hills for miles and have food and hotels awaiting their arrival each day. Plus, they were given a detailed map each morning with the day's route, water stops and lunch. Even so, it was great to meet other people doing something similar to my trip. To their bafflement, I kept telling them that I regarded them as equals to me. They ignored this comment and kept peppering me with questions. One of which was the typical, "Why, Brian?" This I could not answer. I had answered it hundreds of times to convenience store clerks, motel managers, and police officers. Those people were understandably curious because they weren't doing anything similar to my run, and may have been looking for an inspiration or a reason to contemplate such a trip themselves. They would be satisfied with my honed sound byte, "Because I wanted to see America from the pace and perspective of the settlers." Or if I was tired, I might give the reason, "Because it's there." Occasionally, I gave the excuse that I was on my way to see my girlfriend in the west. All of these were part of the big answer, but when you are asked such a question, it is impossible to answer in a way that will make the trip seem sensible. Therefore, rather than try and satisfy their curiosity, which is impossible most of the time, I would use the opportunity to entertain myself. I could even give such an illogical answer as, "You see, I've got this third ear and it's turning purple and there's a doctor in Wichita who can acupuncture it," and they'd be just as satisfied as if I had really tried to give them an honest reason.

But this group of bikers, even though using a different form of human power, must have had the same sorts of reasons that I had for touring the countryside and so I justified the reason for my trip by saying, "I'm doing this trip for the same reasons you are."

After the talent show a few of them took pictures with me. One of them, Jane from California, offered to take me out for a snack. We walked across the parking lot to a convenience store and she said, "Ok, I've got my Visa Card, so GO WILD!" It brought back memories of my chicken strips in Illinois but I was still full from dinner and only picked out a candy bar and a root beer. "Is that all?" she asked. "Go on, get anything!" I also picked out a pint of ice cream, my sustaining element that enables the big miles. She also gave me her address in California and told me that she would take me in for a night when I came through.

The next morning, the bikers were eating at a private buffet in the restaurant so I got an early start on the road without a goodbye. Over the past several days, I had been getting very weary in the late afternoon. My key focus at those times was that if I could keep going, I would get to a clean, cheap motel with HBO and a nearby restaurant. If I could run the whole way there, I would finish all the faster. I also noticed, however, that when I finally did get to a town at the end of each day, I was switching gears so quickly that getting clean, having an interview, and eating a meal, that I wasn't taking the time to appreciate that I had accomplished another day on the road.

When I was wearing down on this particular day, I told myself that the first thing I was going to do when I got to a motel was to lay on the bed and take a few moments to appreciate that I had made it through another day. In fact, I might even treat myself to a cry. Weeks later, I would realize that much of my problem in the late afternoons was a combined effect of the heat and not enough electrolytes in my water. Once I began mixing sports drink powder in my water bottle, the going was much, much easier.

This proved to be a painful afternoon. Coming across a lonely man having a not so good day at his garage sale, I stopped in for a gander and to ask for water. He gladly brought me three glasses of ice water. My grandmother's birthday was coming up, and I had my eye out for an appropriate gift from the roads of America. This man had a tremendous collection of old fashioned glass telephone insulators. My grandmother used to have an extensive collection of them on her windowsill. There were green ones of all shapes but she also had an impressive collection of the more rare colors, red, blue, and purple.

This man gave me one of his green bell jars and I carried it for ten miles down the road to Lyons, Kansas. There is only one motel in Lyons, and I just happened to arrive on its re-opening day. In fact, I was the second person to check in and consequently filled the motel. Apparently, the managers are still in the process of finishing all of the rooms.

As soon as I got to the room I started to get ready for a nice long cold shower, but then remembered my oath to stop and appreciate that I had arrived. I took time to sit down, to reflect on the day, appreciate my progress and look forward to more. Just then, I realized that it was nearly 5 p.m. Without showering, I dashed across the town square to the newspaper

office where I caught Judy Jones, editor of the local paper, just before she
headed out the door.

"I'm sorry to catch you on a Friday as you are closing, but I've just
arrived in town and thought you might like to hear about my trip." She was
very nice and did a wonderful hour-long interview asking lots of questions
and taking time to get the information correct, one thing many reporters
struggled with. As the interview was wrapping up, I told her my most
recent story about getting the bell jar for my grandmother, and she offered
to mail it to her for me, which she did.

The next morning was the 4th of July! I wanted to be in a decent sized
city for Independence Day and tried to reach Great Bend, Kansas for a
fireworks display. It was another one hundred-plus-degree-day and I still
had not figured out the correct balance of drink powder in my water bottle.
I eventually trudged into Great Bend. I decided that the day called for
a nice room in a fancier hotel, and I found one at a Holiday Inn with a
Holidome.

The nice thing about the motel I chose on this particular day was that
it had an airport shuttle. Since I was a guest, the motel was willing to take
me to the fireworks display at the fairgrounds on the edge of town and
pick me up afterwards.

After being deposited near the fairgrounds, I sauntered around the
vendors selling elephant ears, snow cones, cotton candy, candied apples,
and all the other things that look so good until you take your fourth bite
with a mouth full of sugar. Past experience has shown me that midway
through a serving I swear that I'll never eat the mega-sweet thing again. I
learned this lesson again as I worked my way through a delicious looking,
giant cone of cotton candy. Even after the sun had gone down, it was
still so hot that the cotton candy was melting faster than I could eat it. I
was eventually left with a glossy clump of pink goo adhered to my mouth,
fingers, and paper cone. Earlier I had lamented being alone on the holiday,
but now, looking at the mess I'd made, I was glad no one was with me to
see the sticky goo covering my arms and chin.

As full darkness descended, wives pulled their husbands from the
antique car display and their children from the animal exhibits and took
to the field for the fireworks. I had brought my hip pack, so I spread out
my Tyvek ground cloth to lie on. As I lay on the ground staring up at the
brilliant explosions in the sky, listening to the music blaring from the public
address speakers -- "Coming to America" by Neil Diamond -- I thought
about where I was, where I had been, and all the people in my life who
were in many other places.

I thought of my family, probably sitting on my brother's pontoon boat on a reservoir in Indianapolis. I thought of my father and his wife sailing on Lake Monroe in Bloomington, Indiana. Lydia was likely camping on a mountain in her true "let's celebrate the holiday by camping" fashion. I also thought about where I had been three years ago.

Standing in a shoulder-to-shoulder crowd in Auburn, Maine with my trail friend Mosez, his family had taken us home for a weekend off of the Appalachian Trail and treated us to an endless supply of donuts, pie, sodas, and hot dogs. Mosez was a recent high school graduate and had missed his super-swamping four-wheel-drive Jeep while on the trail. He made up for lost time on the Fourth of July. With thousands of people tying up traffic trying to leave the downtown area in their cars, Mosez took to the medians. We were driving on, over, and along median strips, curbs, and yards as we made it home in record time to lie around and eat more donuts, pie, and hot dogs.

Now, three years later on another adventure, I was adding one more memory to this festive holiday. The night ended with a much milder drive home in the motel shuttle van. On the way, I was treated to an array of distant fireworks displays.

Since Kansas is extremely flat, you can see all the neighboring towns' fireworks for miles around. Small clusters of multi-colored explosions were going off in all directions. The day was also special as it was my four-month anniversary on the trail, as well as the halfway point in miles covered.

I was already over halfway across Kansas but was quickly tiring each day. As longtime distance runner Jim Henderson said after running 70 miles during a 24 hour run, "I was very tired *of* running. But to my surprise, I wasn't at all tired *from* running- even after 14 ½ hours of it." I could relate to Henderson's sentiment. The act of getting up each morning, ignoring what might be coming on HBO in 20 minutes, going outside and sweating on the side of the road for 12 hours was becoming redundant.

Another day of hurting throughout the afternoon brought me to Larned, Kansas, where I chose a Best Western. It was the first time in the trip that I had ever noticed being charged for a "bed tax."

"Excuse me?" I asked as I saw it on my bill.

"Bed tax. The state requires it," the manager said.

I wondered what the manager would have said if I had replied, "Well, then just skip the bed, and I'll sleep on the floor. I'm really just here for the television."

From my string of long afternoons of running and the incredible heat lately, I decided to take a day off in Larned. I was able to update my web site from the library for the first time on my own, which made me feel pretty good about my computing skills. I mailed a box of trinkets home and went for a tour of the town.

Whenever I had an extra hour or so in a town, I liked to tour local museums. The one I chose in Larned was the Central States Scout Museum. The building has seen better days. The sign said "Closed" but I knocked anyway and a man in a white t-shirt came to the door and let me in. This man has made collecting Scouting memorabilia his life. Or at least, it used to be his life. Now, his life seems to be looking at the burnt-out spotlights, noticing more leaks from the damaged roof, and keeping enough space on his coffee table for the next frozen dinner.

After I paid my $1 admission fee he told me that I could walk around on my own, or he could give me a tour himself. There is no beating a personal tour, so I gladly accepted his offer. The museum is based in two large rooms, with dozens of glass cases, shelves, tables, and wall collections. There was an extended family of mannequins dressed in Scout uniforms from around the world, with every artifact connected to the outfit claiming, "Be prepared." But despite the very impressive collection of Scout lunch boxes, knives, thermoses, hats, briefcases, patches, and tents, the museum is overpowered with a lack of upkeep. My guide gave me an array of reasons why this was leaking or that didn't work. He said that he has volunteers who are supposed to come in and work but many of them never fulfill their commitments. Also, as one might imagine in a Scout Museum, a large percentage of his visitors are Scout troops. This being the case, many items on display have shown the wear and tear of sugar-rushing, field-tripping patrol members. Hands and entire arms of mannequins are cracked, taped, and hanging limply. Glass-top display cases have been leaned on too hard and have 18 layers of clear tape holding the cracked pieces together with taped signs saying, "DO NOT LEAN ON GLASS!" Also, I was told how some of his collection has disappeared over the years. Despite all the downfalls of the museum upkeep, the collection itself was the most impressive I have ever seen.

On top of one wall, running from one corner of the museum to the other, is a collection of hundreds of Scout mugs on pegs. There are booths dedicated to scouting organizations from different countries. He pointed out the rare items in his collection, a limited edition Scout S.O.S. code panel, rare flashlights, compasses, Scout matches, and books with the temporary inclusion of girls into the organization. He has even built a "hostel" in his back room which is being slimed by a mysterious green ooze dripping from the ceiling. For $3 per person, a troop or small crowd can rent the bunkroom and throw plastic mattresses on the floor. There is a shower room, restroom, and an air conditioner that doesn't work.

After the tour, I went up the street to the edge of town for the best meal around. I was treated to a Kansas specialty for dinner: Chicken Fried Steak and *Deep Fried Corn on the Cob*.

My day off had been a good one but it was time to cover some ground. Looking at the map, I realized there wasn't any lodging until Jetmore, just north of Dodge City, 46 miles away. There were a few outpost towns that would likely have a gas station and maybe a bar but no word of a motel. With an early start, I decided I would see if I could make it.

Leaving town at 7 a.m. I reached Fort Larned, a historic trading post, just as it opened at 9 a.m. After a quick tour of the post, I was back on the road and racking up the miles.

Stopping in the "Just One More" bar in Rozel, after 16 miles, I put down two Cokes and filled my water bottle.

Twenty-three miles down, and I was ready for more refueling. Entering Burdett, I ate at a café and had a late lunch of the typical double B.L.T., soda, and sundae.

At mile 33 for the day I arrived in Hanston, my planned stop should I be in bad shape. I caught a late dinner just as the store was about to close. Two corn dogs, two Cokes, cottage cheese, and three ice cream sandwiches, and I was revitalized and ready to tackle just 13 more miles to Jetmore. Two men in the restaurant recognized me from the nice news article in Lyons and peppered me with questions and well wishes. That gave me a boost, and I was looking forward to running through my first Kansas sunset as I made my way to Jetmore on this evening run.

Using my tripod and timer, I took some self-portrait sunset pictures with me running past grain fields with the setting sun in the background.

At 9:20 p.m. I turned into the Jetmore Motel and got my longed-for reward -- a $20 room where I could rest my exhausted body. "Job well done," I thought.

Across the street at the gas station, I got the only food available at that time of night: a personal pan pizza, a quart of chocolate milk, a bag of chips, and three candy bars. When I started thinking about it, I had consumed an impressive amount of food in one day! I also finally realized that the food had greatly helped me keep going. It just so happened on that day the small towns were spaced out in perfect segments for re-supplying the weary runner.

Next stop, Dodge City. I had been looking forward to this city for 2,000 miles, only because of what I had seen in National Lampoon's "Vacation" when the Griswald family enters Dodge and Clark gets blown away with a shotgun blank in a bar. I was soon to find out that Dodge was nothing like the movie.

Breakfast the next morning was in one of the most colorful restaurants I had been in. William Least Heat Moon wrote in *Blue Highways*, "There is one almost infallible way to find honest food at just prices in blue-highway America: count the wall calendars in a café."

As I neared Dodge the next morning, I stopped in one such multi-calendar restaurant. Beyond the monthly photo timetables, my attention was caught by the numerous signs and notices taped to the wall.

Taped above my booth was my favorite sign, "Men, please remove tools from back pockets before sitting down. They are ruining the upholstery." The food was, as Mr. Moon would have predicted, incredible.

Later, as I was approaching the next town, I passed by a green information roadside sign that said, "Scenic Overlook."

"Hmm, what could that be about in Kansas," I wondered. Running to the pullover to join a few other people getting out of their cars, I was shocked to look at the vast field below. The "scenic overlook" it turned out, was a view of a commercial feedlot. Thousands of cattle were crammed into gated yards, waiting for their demise. The smell of these lots was overpowering. I had noticed that as I got closer to Dodge City, more cattle trucks were passing me on the road.

It is said, "All roads lead to Dodge." This is because many of the major trade routes went through Dodge City. With the suffocating stench of cattle on my hot days of running along the side of the road, I was soon muttering the phrase, "Get the hell out of Dodge!"

After asking a fellow tourist to take my picture next to a metal cow made of welded horseshoes, I set off for the main entrance to Dodge City.

The closer I got to the heart of the city; the more it seemed feed trucks were passing me every minute. The combination of the blazing sun, truck engine exhaust, and a bothersome pelting of fecal matter with each cattle truck flying by at 60 miles per hour, made for an experience in the Dodge City area that I'll never forget. I figured it was time to be MOOving on!

From the movie, "Vacation," I was most looking forward to running up dirt "Front Street," walking along a plank sidewalk, and seeing all the old buildings. As it turned out, "Front Street" had been taken down some time ago and moved across town. It now was replicated at two-thirds size in a commercially operated theme park. That disgusted me, and I opted instead to take a trolley tour of the town. Buying my ticket for the hour-long ride, I sat in the Visitors Center as I had been instructed and waited for the upcoming tour. Twenty minutes later I found that the trolley car had left without me, and I missed the tour.

My visit to Dodge City was proving to be less than I had expected. Not wanting to have wasted the entire afternoon, I found the newspaper office and got an interview, then a room at an Econo Lodge. I can't speak for the entire Econo Lodge chain but this location in particular was keeping in tune with the experience I was having in Dodge. The air in my room was overpowering with a reeking body odor I was sure wasn't mine. The floor was creaky and sloping and the entire franchise seemed ready to fall into the nearest feedlot where it would become another scenic overlook.

The next morning while I was checking out and contesting a "pet charge," another guest was complaining about a $67 phone charge for a call he said he didn't make. The manager kept insisting that no one else could have made the call but the guest was adamant that the charge was an error.

The customer did say, "A few times we found the phone on the floor 'cause it's, you know, wobbly and everything." The manager finally called the operator, but the called number was unpublished so she had to call it herself and ask who lived there and if they had talked to anyone in Dodge City at an Econo Lodge the previous night. I would have loved to hang around and see what happened, but I had stalled too long already and left just as she was making the call.

Passing a gas station on my way out of town, I found the local paper and there was a feature story on me on the top of the front page!

As I was leaving town, people were yelling out their windows to me, "Good luck, buddy!"

"Hey, are you that guy going all the way to California?"

"Yeah."

"Go get 'em, man!" along with a host of honks, waves, and other greetings. Perhaps the Dodge experience hadn't been so bad after all. One car was a black Miata sports car that pulled over onto the shoulder of the road.

"Excuse me," the driver said as he got out of his car, "Are you the guy running to California?"

"Yes, I am!" I said with a smile.

"I read about you in the Dodge City paper this morning and wondered if you needed anything." I thought for a second. I was a few miles out of town and figured water might be hard to come by, so I asked, "Well, if you have any water, I could fill up my water bottle." He said that he is a minister in town and that he didn't have any water in his car, but he would be happy to go get me some. I told him it wasn't an emergency and he said okay and wished me luck on the rest of my trip.

A half hour later, he returned and produced a quart of cold spring water. He had driven ten miles to a gas station to get me the water. I appreciated his 20-mile detour and thanked him profusely.

Revived now, I endured another hot 20-mile day on the road to Cimarron, where I picked up a batch of mail. My father sent me another 100 "Transcontinental Runner" business cards. Lydia sent me some snacks, and my mother sent me my upcoming Colorado maps.

Next stop at the library, I was accessing my email where I met Dan Ferguson, pastor of the local Methodist Church. Dan was reading the Dodge City paper when I came into the library, and he recognized me from the story. He was also a runner and, after asking me several questions, invited me to stay in his church for the night. He set me up in the fellowship room in the basement, fully equipped with carpet, air conditioning, and an adjoining full-service kitchen with lots of leftover food, which he said I was welcome to have, except for the grape juice. I think there is a universal rule against drinking grape juice out of a Church kitchen anyway.

The next morning on my way to Garden City, I was making my weary way on the left hand shoulder of the road when a car slowed down from behind me. I never knew what was going to happen when a car stopped near me. Would they have a gun or a cooler full of iced Cokes? Would they be cute and flirty or hairy and interrogating?

This time it was the KLV News Blazer, an affiliate of NBC based out of Wichita. The anchorman was on his way to Garden City and recognized me from a recent newspaper article, even though there'd been no accompanying photo of me. He pulled over and we did a short interview. Near the end of the interview, he got a call to go cover a story and said he would try to find me later in the day.

Soon after, a recreation vehicle making a very expensive sounding screech passed me. On the back right side of the trailer, the rear tire had come completely off the rim and the family was driving the trailer on the rim. Sparks were flying off the metal frame, and there was a noticeable amount of rim worn away on the pavement. The man pulled over in the next town of Pierceville to try and fix the wheel. As I past him he told me about a nearby feed store. I ducked in for a few sodas and ice cream bars. While I quickly ate in the store, the cashier told me that I had to see the "World's Largest Hairball in the Kansas Room of the Garden City Library while I was in town." It sounded like a definite plan to me. I thanked her for the tip and headed back out, hoping not to miss the TV anchorman.

Just two miles out from Garden City, the white Blazer pulled over again and this time he wanted to videotape me running on the road. He had a ride-along passenger with him; a schoolteacher was on summer break and joined him for a few weeks. He asked the teacher to drive the Blazer while he sat on the tailgate and videotaped me running behind them into Garden City. For some reason, the teacher had great difficulty driving the Blazer at the same speed that I was running. My pace had been honed over the past 2,400 miles so I knew it was the truck and not me that was moving inconsistently. She would tap the gas, and they would zoom way ahead of me. The anchorman would call up to her, "Um, ok, slow down a bit." She would then stomp on the brake sending him flying to the front seat, and I would quickly catch up to them and actually start to pass them. "Ok, um speed up just a tad," and they would fly away again.

I finally arrived in Garden City where I found a nice hotel for the night. The newsman said that the clip would be on the evening news and when I checked into the hotel, the staff offered to videotape the broadcast for me.

With lodging in order, I couldn't wait any longer to see the hairball. Others had told me it came from the stomach of a cow and was about the size of a beach ball. Walking down the street to the public library, I asked the librarian, "Where's your hairball?" She gave me a frown and said that so many people had been coming into the library just to see the hairball and not to read, that they moved the hairball to a museum at the zoo. Sad and hairball-less, I retired to my room hoping for better prospects of a hairball day tomorrow.

My segment on the news was a good one. That should give me a few more honks over the next few days, I thought.

In the morning, I mailed the videotape with the news to Lydia and ran over to the zoo museum, but it wouldn't be open for quite awhile. Thus, I left Garden City without seeing the World's Largest Hairball, much to my disappointment. (I'm not sure why seeing the hairball became such a goal for me, but two years later, while on a marketing campaign for the trail, I fulfilled my dream and met the hairball.)

My improved conditioning was measured by the stretches I could run without stopping. I was starting each morning with a full hour's run, followed by a short walk, then a 40 minute run, walk, then the 15 / 5 format until I finished. If I took a long lunch, I was able to finish with another 40-minute segment.

When I arrived at the road leading off the trail into Lakin, two teenagers picked me up. They had just received a 1970s van for free from their dad's friend. It was the supreme high school cruising vehicle. The day before they had put shag carpet under the benches. They had also painted the pea green outside a matrix of black and white racing stripes. The van itself had a "three on the tree" transmission and the brakes were a bit intermittent. They dropped me off at the Dairy Queen where they worked, and I got an early dinner and a nearby motel room at the Santa Fe Trail Inn.

The room was cheap and decent. There were a few bugs and no telephone in the room but that was to be expected in that price range. In the tiny bathroom, when you sat on the toilet you had to store your legs under the sink. Good design for a multi-tasker.

All day I had been in the mood for a nice dinner, but for some strange reason all of the restaurants in Lakin are closed on Saturday nights. That left the Phillips 66 or Dairy Queen for dinner. I chose DQ, but my chicken sandwich at Dairy Queen didn't even look like a relative of the pictured fowl on the menu.

Next stop on the map the following day was the town of Syracuse. There didn't appear to be any more services in Syracuse than Lakin, but anything beat camping in the weeds with no food. When I arrived in town, I was pleased to find a merry couple who had devoted themselves to renovating the motel, adding twice as many non-smoking rooms and offering an affordable price.

There was a movie theater in town and this week's movie was "The Truman Show." I had seen it with Lydia in Kansas City, but since we had missed the first 15 minutes, I went to see it again.

Leaving town the next morning, hoping to reach Colorado by noon, I got an early start at 6 a.m. and got on River Road, for my arrival into Colorado. The heat of Kansas had been a challenge, and I was ready for the cooler climate of the Rocky Mountains now only days away.

Colorado offers a whopping 869 miles along its southern route.

Chapter 21
Colorado!…I think

The only indication that I was crossing into my tenth state was a break in the fence line on either side of the road. Colorado does not greet you immediately with majestic views of the Rocky Mountains. In fact, for the entire eastern half of the state, Colorado looks identical to Kansas. I had been told this but still, when I crossed the state line, I hoped for some noticeable difference.

Accepting the fact that I would have to cover some miles before seeing the famous mountain range, I surveyed my surroundings. On the side of the road was a windmill and underneath the mill was a working spigot, which I sampled three quarts from before sloshing on.

By mid-afternoon, I arrived in Holly, my first town in Colorado. I ate lunch in The Tasty Plate that had signs on the walls such as, "No Smoking – Enjoy Your Food More." I love managers willing to post signs like that.

Just as I started eating, two women, traveling from Montana, walked in and asked to sit in the smoking section. After being told that there was none, they complained all through lunch about the heat that they had to walk through to get from their smoke-filled car to the air-conditioned restaurant.

Holly doesn't offer much in the way of services. A main street with a few bars, a city hall, and a Mexican diner called "Porky's" pretty much sums up the town. I went to the library, which had closed 20 minutes earlier. In the same building as the one-room library was a public meeting room. Tacked to the door of the unlocked room was a note, "Please check with County Clerk for use."

I walked to the city hall, and after speaking with a city employee, was granted permission to sleep in the meeting room. It was somewhat dusty but fully stocked with back issues of magazines and several meeting tables, on one of which I made a bed that night.

Thanks to an early bedtime, I awoke fully rested at 5:30 a.m. Setting off in the darkness, I aimed my sights for Lamar, just 25 miles away. In the mid-afternoon, a Lincoln Towncar slowed down several hundred yards ahead of me and stopped. "What's going to happen this time?" I wondered. Then the back up lights came on and the car sped and swerved in reverse towards me at twice the speed it had been traveling forward. I stepped off the roadway out of the car's path.

The car stopped next to me and one of the two elderly women inside rolled down her window asking, "We passed you four hours ago, where are you headed?"

"California," I said.

"Oh, can we give you a lift?"

"No thanks. You see I'm running there."

"Oh, we have to hear about you!" And they proceeded to swerve forward, driving off the road to talk with me for a few minutes. After a brief chat filled with a healthy dose of, "Isn't that something!" and "My goodness," they wished me well and swerved away.

Ever since Dodge City, I had been seeing signs for the Cow Palace Best Western Hotel. "Just 3 hours ahead in Lamar" the sign had said back in Dodge. Each day or so I would pass another billboard claiming, "Just two more hours to the Cow Palace!" then "One hour to Cow Palace." I had been keeping track of the time it took me and when I finally reached the famed landmark, it totaled 156 hours. How could I stay in a hotel that had such inaccurate times on their signs? Even more, the hotel rooms were $72. Choosing to forego the famous hotel, I jogged across the street for a $45 Days Inn with continental breakfast.

A reporter with a digital camera came to interview me at 6:15 the next morning and took some pictures as I left town. He gave me excellent directions to follow my route, and I headed to Las Animas.

Running across the dam of the John Martin Reservoir, I met a family parked on the dam and they gave me a Coke when they heard about my trip. So many people handed me food, drinks, and support that it seemed apparent that there was a network of agents on the lookout for me, helping me along. While I was drinking my cola on the dam with a nice breeze coming off of the reservoir, the family couldn't believe that I had recently run through Garden City. They told me of 78 rival gangs in the town. To get into a gang, prospective members have to walk up to a stranger and stab him. They said that just a week ago a man was mowing his yard and was stabbed with a knife. I was glad I hadn't heard about these gang problems until after I had left the town. I told them the only problem I had in Garden City was that I didn't get to see the world's largest hairball.

Passing a bait shop on the shore of the reservoir, I stopped in for lunch. After picking out and paying for a selection of Gatorade, candy, and crackers, the man asked what I was up to. Upon hearing about my trip he said, "Well why didn't you say so," as if I was some long lost friend of his who he'd never take money from. He then pushed the cash register button and gave me all of my money back.

After a night in Las Animas, Colorado, I arrived at Bent's Old Fort National Historic Site. Rangers at the park give guided tours, and I was the only one on mine. Having a keen interest in this historical trading post on the Santa Fe Trail, I asked many questions during the tour. The poor high school intern had to keep answering all of my questions during the tour, then try and remember where he was in his memorized speech.

It was strange to be the only person representing a tour group and hear my guide say things like, "Now if you'll look over here folks, I mean, sir, you'll see bottles of Florida Water in the store. The settlers used to get very dirty and smelly when crossing this country. When and if they finally arrived at Bent's Fort, they would douse themselves with this 'cologne' and have a big night at the bar with the women."

Eric, my older brother, was having a birthday soon and I was on the lookout for a unique gift. In the Fort gift shop were plates of pressed tea. Very heavy and ornamental on one side, the tea powder was once pressed together for shipment. I was told that these plates were actually what were dumped into the Boston Harbor, rather than round bags of tea powder often depicted in historical cartoons. When shopkeepers received the plates, they would take a small saw and cut corners off the plate for individual sale. They looked somewhat like a large chocolate bar. I bought one and carried the ten-pound beast in my pack to the next town of La Junta.

An overpriced motel forced me down the road to a much cheaper and friendlier MidTown Motel for $28. It was really the potted plants and the clean white lampshades in the windows that drew me in. A medium pizza with all the toppings and a quart of ice cream for dinner topped off my day, and I was soon fast asleep.

. I again got up at 5:30 a.m. ready for an early start, but my chores for the morning prevented me from leaving town until midday. At the post office, I received a package from my former high school coach, Rick Weinheimer. As I sent him post cards along my trip, he shared them with his students and posted my progress on a bulletin board. He did this through the spring semester and then resumed it the next fall. During a few classes, Mr. Weinheimer had his students write me letters cheering me on as I ran. I received one such package in La Junta. There were 25 letters waiting for me, and during breakfast, I responded to each student by writing them short replies. I was also finally able to mail off the heavy plate of tea to my brother as well as the usual assortment of expired maps to Lydia.

Arriving in the small town of Rocky Ford that evening, I got a motel room and spent the evening checking in with family and friends. Later that night I received a phone call from the Foots.

They never cease to amaze me with their demonstrations of keen memory. They had heard from me a few days earlier and guessed that I would be in Rocky Ford. Bill Foot remembered back to a year earlier when they had biked the ADT and gone through Rocky Ford. With all the hundreds of towns and the thousands of motels they had passed along the way, Bill was somehow able to remember that the only motel in Rocky Ford was called "Melon Valley Inn." He then called information and got the number and was patched through to me by the front desk. I was in shock. It was great to talk with him and tell him of my recent adventures.

Saturday, July 18 turned out to be quite a day on the trail. I ran an easy day to Fowler. As I left town, I found myself running under a crop duster working on a series of nearby fields. There hadn't been much to photograph lately so I took out my camera and, standing on the road, began to take a picture of the plane. The pilot must have seen me shooting him because as I stood in the middle of the road, he began doing stunts for me. He flew under several power lines, did dives towards the ground and swooped along the rows of crops several times. It was really neat and when the show was over I gave him a big wave and continued on towards Fowler.

Several miles further, as I was passing a feedlot, a herd of cattle came running towards me. Hundreds of cattle crowded up to the fence as they got as close to me as possible. When they hit the fence line, they stood silent, staring at me. On occasion, when other cattle have done the same thing, I had felt as if a speech was appropriate, so I usually gave them one.

"Oh, um, hello. I didn't know I was the speaker for today," I would start. "Um, my name is Brian. I'm from Indiana and I am running from Delaware to California. I hope the grass is good today. Are there any questions?" As with the previous such speeches, my audience stood silent, chewing their cud while watching the roadside entertainment. They were a tough crowd!

Crossing the Huerfano River later in the afternoon I came to a junction in the road. I wasn't sure which way to turn and sat down on the roadside guardrail to check my map. Guardrails are really wonderful places for pedestrians to take a break. The top of every guardrail I came across had a bend to it that made sitting possible if not fairly comfortable. The height was just about right for an improvised chair. I was sitting on the guardrail when a Colorado State Trooper pulled up in his mighty cruiser.

At first he just sat in his car looking at me. I acted as though I didn't notice him, but really, I was looking forward to our interaction. I was doing nothing wrong. Sitting on the side of a highway, I might have appeared a bit suspicious but I knew that I could not be in trouble for sitting there.

The Colorado State Trooper radioed in to headquarters that he was about to interact with a hitchhiking vagrant. Stepping out of his car, the outlines and puffiness of his bulletproof vest were apparent through his uniform.

Sauntering up to me in true suspicious police style, he asked, "Are you hitchhiking?"

"No."

"No?" he asked with an air of disbelief. "Well, do you mind telling me just what you are doing out here?"

"Sure," I said. "I'm running across the United States and just thought I should check my map at this junction to make sure I take the right road that will get me to California."

"Uh huh. Do you have any identification?"

"Sure," I replied. I had been looking forward to this for the entire trip. I reached into my pack and pulled out one of the business cards that my dad had made for me. They read, "Brian Stark, Transcontinental Runner, Delaware to California on the American Discovery Trail." Dad had even fit a small picture of me running onto the card.

I produced this business card for the state trooper, and he looked at it for a second. I also offered him my license but he seemed satisfied with the card I had given him. Eventually he figured I was harmless enough, wished me well with a chuckle, and drove away, convinced I was not about to rob the First National Bank or kidnap a dog. I could just imagine the scene if I was being pursued after having committed such a crime, "He's traveling five miles per hour," the cops would say. "We'll never catch him!"

That afternoon, as I was into the mileage groove and could feel the upcoming town pulling me in, a car driving towards me slowed down and came to a stop on the left side of the road. It was a black Miata. I gave a large wave to the driver, instantly recognizing him as the preacher who had pulled over a week ago outside of Dodge City. He stepped out of his car with a huge smile on his face.

"What in the world are you doing out here again?" I asked. He said that he was on his way back from a convention in Las Vegas and, thinking that he might run into me again, had brought water with him this time!

After giving me another quart of spring water, he asked, "Brian, would you mind if I said a prayer for you?"

"Not at all," I replied. He put his hand on my shoulder and, standing on the south shoulder of Highway 50, often called the Loneliest Road in America, with occasional feed trucks whizzing by, a prayer was said for my safety and success.

When I arrived in town, I approached the only motel right beside the highway. The parking lot was full of cars and the "NO" red neon vacancy sign was illuminated. I decided to plead my case and inquire about an empty janitor's closet. My hopes sank as the woman at the desk nearly laughed me out of the building when I asked if there was anything left.

"You've arrived on Missouri Days. You won't find anything, anywhere, of any kind for miles around." That didn't sound good.

Leaving the motel, I stopped at a gas station to buy a large drink before I set off once again to seek lodging in a lodgeless town. While I was drinking my quart of Iced Tea in front of the convenience store, two carloads of kids met in the parking lot. They were planning a lake party later in the day.

"Yeah, Reggie's bringing his boogie board, my parents have all the food, but they'll be gone. We'll see you there." It sounded like a lot of fun, and listening to all of it was enough to make me consider asking them if I could tag along. Chances were good that there would be an empty couch or even a bed that night at the party. Good food, a little water skiing, and the camaraderie of older high school students would surround me. Although I was tempted by the diversion, I didn't approach them. The day was far from over, however.

I set off for downtown and, while running down the main street, passed a sign in a medical clinic that said, "Free Medical Screening." This should be fun, I thought, as I walked in for a free exam for the fun of it. Several people were standing around in the lobby sipping free frozen drinks from a Slushie machine and a man greeted me.

"How are you?" he began.

"Well, you tell me. Can I get a free screening?"

"Sure, come on back into the office." We walked into a small room. I had not told him of my current marathon-a-day exercise schedule and waited to see how his equipment would rate me. I hoped he was going to put me on a treadmill with wires and sensors, diodes, and plugs. I imagined his quizzical expression, as my fitness level would be registering off the charts. He did nothing of the sort. I sat in a chair beside his desk as he produced a James Bond type box with a somewhat scary looking series of wires and electrodes. He told me to relax and lightly touched an electrode to the knuckle of my index finger. Then he turned and looked at his computer monitor. He told me that this method of testing worked on the Chinese theory that all of the body's organs and key operating systems could be monitored through the knuckles of the fingers. By placing his electrodes on my digits, his computer was analyzing how the rest of my body was doing.

I impatiently awaited his reaction when he would see the results on his monitor jump off the screen.

At first, he turned to the monitor and stared for a second before saying, "Hmm, that's interesting."

"What is it?" I asked, expecting him to tell me that my results were superhuman.

"Well, I'm sorry, but I can't test you."

"What? Why not?" I asked.

He told me that I had an unusual hypersensitive condition in my body in that my nerves were very close to my skin and that this condition was throwing off the system. Apparently, there has to be a minimum distance between the nerves and the electrodes to take accurate readings and my nerves were simply too close. He also accurately guessed from this condition that by personality, I was a "rush-rush, run around" type of person that was always "go,go,go."

From the initial results, he did pick up that I was in very good shape and asked out of the blue, "You wouldn't happen to be running across the United States would you?" I was flabbergasted. When he told me that my nerves were too close to my skin, I figured it was at first a ploy to explain having temperamental equipment but now I was genuinely impressed with what information he had been able to gather.

"Wow, yes, I am! How did you figure that out?"

"My sister owns the motel in La Junta and she told me last night you stayed in her place."

So much for scientific theory, I thought.

He was very friendly, however, and when I asked if he knew of any other place in town besides the motel to sleep, he said, "You could just stay here in the office."

He had opened his business less than a week ago. To allow a total stranger to sleep in his brand new office filled with expensive medical equipment, workout stations, and a Slushie Machine was a very trusting thing to do. I gratefully accepted.

It was still early in the afternoon and he suggested that I go over to the city park to see the festivities. This led me to ask just what the celebration was all about.

I'm not entirely sure that the man's explanation of the festival is historically accurate but this is what he told me.

In the 1800s, as the settlers made their way across the nation, a few of them died along the way. A few others made it all the way across the country to California. And the rest stopped somewhere in-between. The Missouri Days Festival is an annual celebration to remember that a group of settlers stopped their wagons in the middle of an endless prairie and said to each other, "How about here?" and founded the town. At the town park I found an impressive crowd of families competing in horseshoe tournaments, children's sack races, three-legged races, bingo, and a visiting carnival. It was a great afternoon. I watched some of the races, consumed an elephant ear and a large coke, and then decided to try one more ball of cotton candy.

Next I played two games of Bingo. In my second game I won my first Bingo game ever in my life. Net winnings: $8.50.

In the evening I went back to the medical clinic and met the owner again. He told me I was welcome to stay anywhere in the office. He logged onto the internet at his desk and told me I was welcome to access my email as well as update my web page for as long as I wanted while there. He also invited me to have as many Slushies as I wanted. I thanked him but didn't respond with enough zeal to convince him that I was going to rip into the syrup and melted ice treats, so he pressed harder.

"I want to see every flavor of that thing gone when I come back in the morning!"

"I'll do my best, sir." I said. That night, I replied to lots of email that had built up, and I made many revisions to my web site, which was something I had needed to do for some time. My memorable day ended with three bedtime Slushies before my teeth begged me to stop so they could thaw back to room temperature.

Leaving at 5 a.m. the next morning I was eager to put miles away early before the heat got to its full intensity around 3 p.m. I was so eager to get on the road that I decided not to go back two blocks to re-supply on snacks for the day from the only gas station open at that time of morning. I was headed for Pueblo, and from the looks at the map I figured it was going to be a decent-sized town with nice lodging. With the motivation of food, I was able to put in 15 miles on an empty stomach early in the morning.

Throughout the morning, as with every recent morning, my eyes would scan the horizon while my legs did the work. I was looking for the first sign of the Rocky Mountains. Since the Appalachian Mountains, I had envisioned spotting the Rockies off in the distance, slowly growing in stature as I crept westward in four-foot strides. Is that it? I saw something just slightly darker than the surrounding blue sky at the edge of the earth. It appeared to be floating on the horizon as an enormous blue lump. I had seen lots of mountains in the distance and I knew to look for their telltale-jagged contour, the pointed peaks, and the abrupt change in horizon. No, that's just a pack of clouds, I figured. Shouldn't a mountain range start small in the distance and grow larger as you approach? What did it mean when this one was already enormous from a distance? Miles and hours later, still not having eaten that day, I began struggling to make miles. Maybe it was a mirage, but the blue object was getting darker and more defined. It simply looked too huge to be a mountain. Everything is supposed to look small when surrounded by endless nothingness, and yet, this object appeared to be the end of the nothing. Ok, so it is the Rockies, I concluded. How on earth am I going to get over that? The thought of it was exciting and terrifying at the same time. Sure, I could run a marathon a day on the flat, with convenient lunch stops and bargain motels to keep me company, but how would I fare with snow, confusing trails, and running at 11,000 feet? Not to mention being days between HBO and the daily allotment of king size candy bars. Maybe this trip wasn't such a good idea after all. I decided to see what the day had in store for me and began looking for inspiration to get back into the mileage groove. Most likely, by not starting with any snacks, my body was simply craving energy.

At 11 a.m. with only 10 miles to go to Pueblo, a man in a van pulled over into a driveway next to me. He got out and walked up to me asking, "Hey, man, where you headed?"

"California."

"Well hell, man, come on up to the property. I'll give you a cold drink!"

I was soon to find out there was a second man living on this parcel of land. For anyone who plans on inviting a stranger into their home or even simply onto their property as this man was, don't start introductions like he did, "Hey, John, I got another one." Much to my relief I soon discovered my new friend made a habit of offering hospitality to each passersby.

There was a garden shed on the property where the older man, who actually owned the property, lived. He was getting ready for church. My friend was living in the yard on a bed that was simply sitting on the dirt next to a nightstand with a radio, lawn chairs and a few books sitting on

spools. Picture a living room with no walls and furniture salvaged from
an abandoned loading dock. We drank Coke's from a dorm refrigerator
and sat on lawn furniture. He told me about all the people he has invited
to stop "in" and have a drink. He told me of the woman who was driving a
covered wagon pulled by oxen. This woman was only a few weeks ahead of
me, I found out, and I had hoped to catch her. He also told me of numerous
bikers and hikers, and even the time when he believes First Lady Hillary
Clinton drove by in a limousine, although he couldn't get her to stop.

Sugarized, I thanked him and pressed on, trying to beat the predicted
110-degree high that would be due a few hours later. I finally arrived in
Pueblo and checked into an overpriced hotel just as the heat was searing
at 3 p.m.

I had planned to run 25 miles to Canon City or Florence on the next
day, but when I awoke I was dehydrated, tired, and stiff. I reevaluated the
map and looked for shorter options for the day. The residential community
of Pueblo West was about half the distance away and although the Foots'
Data Book made no mention of services in town, I decided I would try my
luck at finding a motel once I got there.

Just as I was leaving the town of Pueblo, I noticed the Pueblo Chieftain
Newspaper office on the edge of town. I had called them earlier but, as
with many large papers, it can be difficult to break into the newsroom
and be assigned a reporter when other "shoot 'em up" or "he took my dog"
stories are breaking across the nation.

I walked in the office just as they were opening. With a stroke of timing
luck, I was assigned a reporter simply because the planned assignments
hadn't yet been delivered. During the hour-long interview, I enjoyed
gauging his reaction as he slowly began to figure out my trip and piece it
together into a story. That article ran on the front page of the sports section
and eventually came back to haunt me three weeks later.

When I arrived in Pueblo West that day, a father and his son on their
way home from an unsuccessful day of fishing gave me a ride across town.
They dropped me off at a Best Western where I collapsed in the room
content to recover through a room service dinner and erasing the pain of
the day in front of a television. After dinner, once it was much cooler and
I had rested some, I ventured out of the hotel room for a snack. A quarter
of a mile away, I consumed an 8-pack of tacos at Taco Bell, a large Blizzard
at Dairy Queen, and finally a gas station for an assortment of candy bars
and crackers for the next day.

In the morning the front desk clerk gave me a copy of the Pueblo
Chieftain. My picture came out great. The staff photographer had wanted
to get a good picture of me but did not have the time to drive me to a scenic

section of the trail, so we took the picture in the newspaper staff parking lot. Question: How does one get an action shot in a nature scene while in the middle of a paved parking lot? Answer: Have the subject stand in a grassy parking median, kneel as if tying his shoe, and stand over him shooting down. The picture was great.

As soon as I left Pueblo West that morning, I was in the most expansive region I had been in yet. Miles upon miles of flat, mostly vegetation-free terrain and no structures to be seen sent fear though me as I quickly began to wonder if somehow the desert had started before I got over the mountains. If so, I was grossly under-prepared for such conditions. Five miles down a small highway and still having passed no building, water source, or tree, I spied what looked to be a house. It was getting hot at this time and with only 3 ounces of water left, I decided to stop in and ask for some cold water.

When I arrived at the building I realized that it was not a home. It was the lodge of a private campground. Numerous signs warned "Non-Campers - Stay Away!" and "Do Not Use these Facilities." There were signs such as, "This is NOT a public rest area!" and "NO broken down vehicles permitted!" and "This facility is for registered campground users only!"

Needless to say, it didn't convey a very inviting impression as I walked up hoping to score a drink.

The lodge was closed so I cautiously walked towards the back of the property in search of some water. While I was standing in an empty campsite, clearly trespassing, a woman walked over to me as I was filling my bottle from a spigot.

"Excuse me, what are you doing?"

I explained my trip and apologized that I had gotten water without permission and that I would be gone right away. She didn't call the police but my time spent there was none too long. As I ran down the highway, I couldn't help marveling at the range of attitudes I was encountering on this trip. With a belly full of water and my bottle topped off, I relaxed back into the meditative mode and continued staring at the massive blue outline before me.

After running through the sweltering heat and much more of the same arid, piercing stretch of endless road, I arrived in Florence, Colorado. It felt like an oasis. My short stint in the desert-like conditions that morning made me wonder if I would be able to conquer the real deserts of Utah and Nevada in a few more weeks. Better get over the Rocky Mountains first, I figured.

As I was running through Florence, a Four-Wheel-Drive Blazer pulled over ahead of me and two attractive young women got out. They waited for me to run up to them, and when I did, they introduced themselves. The two were co-owners of The Pour House, a nice coffee shop in town and they had read about me in the newspaper that morning.

"I just had this *feeling* that I was going to see you today!" one of them said to me with a warm smile.

They invited me to stop in their shop and have anything I wanted. Food, coffee, tea, cookies, it would all be on the house. That was a very nice invitation but mixed in with the offers of food, they both made several comments that I was *more than welcome* to use their restroom. "Oh, you'll love it; it's a great bathroom!" they said. Little did they know how resourceful I could be given a public restroom. I stopped in their shop and enjoyed a fresh-brewed iced raspberry tea. The afternoon wasn't over however, and I had to pass up the chance to sleep in another restroom.

I wished I had made it into Florence the previous day; I would have loved to stay there. Besides accommodating coffee houses, there are plenty of lodgings and the town's main street has a very inviting charm. Reluctantly I pressed on and that afternoon I finally arrived in Canon City.

The ADT follows a recreation trail along a beautiful rushing river as it nears town. As I entered town, I just happened to pass the local newspaper office. I wondered if they wouldn't want to print a story on me since a much larger paper had already run one that day. As I entered the office, it turned out that the sports editor was scratching his head trying to decide what to put on the front page of his paper. I was his answer.

We did a fun interview and he latched onto my trip very quickly and seemed to be getting some good stories down. Afterwards, he wanted to photograph me running along the trail I had just come in on. After the photo shoot, he gave me a driving tour of the city, orienting me to its fine services.

After he dropped me off at the library, I spent an hour reading and responding to wonderful e-mails that had piled up in just a few days. Next, I went to a Goodwill Store. My only clothes consisted of a summer outfit and my windbreaker. I knew that I would need warmer clothes as I ascended the Rocky Mountains, so I bought a cheap fleece vest and shirt for camping in any sudden temperature changes.

While in the mountains, I knew that reliable water sources might be far apart, so I bought a small CamelBak water pack that was lightweight and did not collide with my hip pack when worn together. I also got a haircut and beard trim in Canon City. When I was done with all of my errands, the post office had already closed and my mail would have to wait until morning.

With a cheap room at a motel, I opened my windows and received a personal serenade as an acoustic guitar concert was underway in a city park below my room. The next day was to be my greatest ascent of the trip.

I awoke at 6 a.m. and ate a double order of French Toast as I stuffed envelopes of the Pueblo article and sent them to relatives. I got to the Post Office as it was opening. Waiting for me in the mail was a letter from Dick Bratton, Mayor of Green Mountain Falls, Colorado. He had caught wind of my trip and volunteered to assist me as I ran through his part of the state. "Assist" is really not a strong enough word. "Carry me like an angel," is more like it.

His letter to me said, "Brian, congratulations on making it to Canon City! As soon as you receive this letter, call Mike at the local Church. He has agreed to put you up for the night in the Church and get you a meal." I was really upset that I had missed a free night and another chance to share my trip with people, but I called Mike anyway and thanked him for his offer, then called Dick and told him I would be arriving in Cripple Creek later that day.

The ADT ascends from Canon City to Cripple Creek using a lightly traveled narrow dirt road called, "Shelf Ridge Road." The distance between the two cities is 24 miles and in that near-marathon distance, the traveler ascends 5,000 feet in elevation, climbing to 10,300 feet. Dick said he would meet me for a meal in Cripple Creek at 3 p.m. I told him I would try my best to make the appointment.

I had been warned that there was absolutely no water for the entire ascent to Cripple Creek. This turned out to be partially inaccurate but not knowing, my pack was sloshing with liquids when I left town. I had two full 20-ounce water bottles in my pack, plus my new water bladder, 80 ounces in all or five pounds of water. As it turned out, there are many homes along the road for the first ten miles of the ascent. Stopping at one home that sold eggs, the woman nicely told me to drink as much as I wanted.

Running up the mountain, I looked over the sheer drop-off to my right that led to a lush valley below. I saw one canyon filled with meadows and trees with an abandoned ranch, forlornly situated in the center. I wondered who would let a home in such a beautiful setting rot away to nothing. I decided that after my run I would return, move onto that ranch and fix it up, just as soon as I renovated the Counterfeit House in Ohio, that is.

Climbing uphill all morning and into the afternoon, I came to an abandoned mine shaft two miles after I had run out of water. Cripple

Creek was founded in the mining days and hundreds of abandoned mine shafts attest to its heritage. A steel grate had been placed over the very large opening but someone had cut a hole out of the bottom of it. I crawled in and sat just inside the entrance on a rotting board letting the naturally air-conditioned breeze blow against me.

The temperature must have been at least 30 degrees cooler sitting in there and I actually became quite cold within a few minutes. I filled my water bottle from a stream flowing out of the mine and crawled back outside, sitting in a spot where I was half in the baking sun and half in the tunnel of cold air blowing onto my back. I treated my mine water with a drop of bleach but never actually risked drinking it. Lydia had warned me over the phone not to drink any water out of mines as she'd heard that one of the main ingredients used in mining long ago was arsenic with cyanide.

A mile further uphill a green Blazer met me with a man inside who said, "You must be Brian! Hi, I'm Dick Bratton!" He had been waiting for me in Cripple Creek and since it was after 3, he decided to drive down the road and see if I needed any help. He handed me an ice-cold quart of good water, which I drank in one helping. Then he offered to take my pack into town so I wouldn't have as much weight to run with, which I gratefully accepted.

When I ran into town at 5 p.m. and entered the main street of Cripple Creek, I was greeted by a small crowd of people from the local Parks and Recreation Department clapping and cheering me on from the sidewalk. Dick had called them earlier that week and arranged for them to greet me as I entered town. They handed me a new Cripple Creek Parks and Recreation T-shirt and a water bottle. We sat in their building eating donuts and drinking orange juice while we got acquainted. They had also agreed to put me up in the Hotel Saint Nicholas for the night, a beautiful establishment overlooking the town.

Dick and I met a local reporter at a casino restaurant that night for an interview and dinner. Cripple Creek is one of three towns in Colorado that legally offers gambling. The town was founded in the days of mining but now is starting to come back to life based on its draw from high altitude, small stakes gambling.

After dinner, I sat at a table and played a few hands of blackjack wearing my tights and new Cripple Creek shirt. Lady Luck didn't do me any favors that night, but I already felt like a winner with the support I was receiving from Mayor Bratton and his City employees.

The next morning during a continental breakfast in the hotel lobby, a couple from Texas recognized me from my CBS interview on National

Trails Day in June. The man handed me some folded bills saying, "We'd like to help you out."

After mailing a lot of heavy trinkets home to Lydia, I left town. I had been under the assumption that Cripple Creek was on top of a mountain. But when I left town I discovered I was still going uphill and it looked like it would be that way for quite a long time. I was not prepared for this and struggled uphill for much of that morning. I did have one motivation, however. Since the town is one of three in the state to offer gambling, it is a hot tourist destination, and dozens of giant tour buses were making their zigzag way down the mountain towards town and the ever-hungry one-arm bandits. As these tour buses would near me, I would see half a bus of passengers crane their necks out the window in disbelief that someone was running up this steep mountain at high altitude. I could just imagine the comments being said inside those buses, "I hope he's not going too far with that pack." "Better him than me." "How'd you like to be out there with him, Esther?"

As I neared the top of the pass, I was approaching the Molly Cathleen Mine and its guided tours. I looked at my watch and the remaining hill ahead and said, "Oh, why not." I knew the mine would be a bit touristy but having just come from Cripple Creek, I was in the mood for something a bit touristy.

A young woman at the ticket booth gave me my ticket and told me the next elevator would be going down in 20 minutes. A sign near the elevator warns people not to take anything extra with them on the tour: no strollers, no large cameras, no backpacks, and no bags. Apparently, to simulate a true mining experience and to maximize the number of tourists per tour, they cram as many people in their "authentic" elevators as possible. Without excess baggage, there is much more room for an extra arm, shoe, and knee.

I stored my pack behind the counter of the very expensive jewelry shop selling gold from the mine and stood in line for the next tour. As our guide prepared to take us down the shaft, we were handed raincoats to wear to keep the dripping rock from getting us wet. An old reproduced metal sign outside of the elevator entrance read, "Warning, According to City Ordinance Code 637.4, It Is Unlawful to Fart in Elevator."

Several of the tourists got a kick out of that sign and were having their photographs taken next to it surely planning on telling their families back home about that sign made just for them. When I saw how tight we were going to be packed into the elevator, I hoped they would control themselves for our 1000-foot plunge into the earth.

Our tour guide was a retired gold miner who led us into the steel cubicle that would take us into the bowels of the mine. There were about 20 of us in line and after the first five got in, we started wondering how many were going to fit. Our tour guide just kept calmly saying, "Keep going, move to the back." We already were in the back. It became a challenge to suddenly try and get as thin as possible as the elevator was already full and our guide was still shoving people in. He later told us that in the "old mining days," they used to cram twice as many miners in these cars.

Finally, with ten of us in the four by four foot cage, the steel door was latched and locked closed and we descended five feet and stopped so that the second half of the group could board the second elevator directly above us. Once everyone was in, and with 20 shoes just inches above my head, body parts with various odors pressing in on all sides of me, we began our slow decent, passing by numerous abandoned tunnels that had a single electric light placed in them to give us a view of how far back they went, seemingly forever. In the four and one half square miles in the mining district of Cripple Creek, there are over 2,100 miles of mines underground. It was, therefore, inevitable that mine shafts were going to run into each other. When this happened, as it often did, the workers were pleased. Not only did it mean that with the connected tunnels there was going to be better air circulation, but that there would be at least twice the help should an accident occur.

During the loop tour through a shaft we also learned that mules were actually born and raised in the mines and worked their entire lives pulling carts full of ore uphill on tracks towards an elevator. Once the animal right's activists heard about this atrocity, they forced the miners to get the mules out and use manpower instead.

The tour was good and, at the end, we each got a nugget of ore with a few specks of gold. I placed mine on an informational sign at a rest area along the highway. Sure, I could carry plates of pressed tea and beer cozies, but solid gold was merely a trinket to cast away.

With a late start that morning after the mine tour, I reached Woodland Park, Colorado in a strong thunderstorm. Dick found me on the highway in the rain and followed me into town where he picked me up and drove me to his home in the picturesque town of Green Mountain Falls, just west of Colorado Springs. The next morning I was to pick Lydia up at the Denver airport for a four-day vacation that would include, oddly enough, hiking!

Chapter 22
The Rockies

After driving up the interstate in my rented economy Geo Metro getting dream-like mileage, I met Lydia at the airport. Even a Geo Metro feels like a NASCAR racing machine when you're used to a six-mile per hour pace. We decided to spend our vacation weekend doing an arcing tour of the Denver area. We started in Boulder. It is a great college town but, unfortunately, the prices are better suited for the well-to-do summer tourists, and we reluctantly checked into an over-priced motel that offered one of the last available rooms in town.

The next morning we strolled the pedestrian mall with its constant supply of street performers. Their acts were as varied as their outfits.

The first guy was standing on top of a one-sided ladder, balancing in the air by walking the ladder back and forth. He was juggling different objects at the same time. For a finale, he juggled flaming batons.

Another man was a contortionist and folded himself into and through a variety of tiny cubes and cylinders. One was a very small plastic cube, which he was able to somehow scrunch himself into. Another was a very narrow 14-inch pipe. He first folded himself in half and then proceeded to fit the pipe around and through his body. Seeing his shoulders go through looked very painful. He also stood on a platform and slowly bent down with knees locked, touching his elbows to his feet. Watching his back elongate and stretch looked like a snake's jaws unhinging while trying to swallow an animal twice its size.

After I left town, I read about another performer who uses only a long red, white, and blue chain. He takes the chain and lays it in an outline of the United States and has spectators stand on the space where they are from. Then he proceeds to tell them their zip codes and creates stories about all the people standing on his "map" while restating their zip codes. He reportedly has memorized over 48,000 zip codes.

We wanted to spend the next day touring Rocky Mountain National Park so left Boulder and headed north. On the way towards the park, we stopped in the gambling town of Black Hawk and won some money playing Blackjack at the tables. We actually left with heavier wallets!

Being a summer weekend, there were almost no vacancies in the park-bordering town of Winter Park. We finally gave in and coughed up the fee for a four-star condominium at Silver Springs Resort, fully equipped with a dining room, full kitchen, and full-sized indoor hot tub. Unfortunately, all of the traveling left us too tired to enjoy the hot tub, and we went straight to bed after dinner. The next morning, we slept so late that housekeeping had to kick us out at checkout time.

We headed inside the park that nice Sunday afternoon and found that a few other people had decided to join us. We stopped in a food pavilion on a mountain and had a $10 baked potato.

It never ceases to amaze me that people will fly from all over the world to go to the most spectacular national parks in our nation and the first thing they do when they get there is go to the cafeteria and buy an overpriced hot dog. Of course, the park service figured this out long ago and thus adjusted their prices accordingly. Imagine a day when the national parks did not even offer food! Heavens! And people actually had to bring a picnic basket! And where would they have parked without lot attendants directing traffic in parking lots like inbound planes at Chicago's O'Hare Airport telling you, "You can't park there. That space is reserved for our recreational vehicle guests."

After our midday snack, we meandered past herds of people trampling the fragile alpine tundra next to signs saying, "Please stay on the trails."

Trying to escape the masses, we chose to hike a three-mile trail up Deer Mountain. Happily the trail had very few people so we were able to enjoy the view in peace and solitude.

The next morning was our last day together for awhile and I had a busy schedule. I had an appointment in Golden, Colorado with a woman from the Colorado Trail Society. Dick had arranged the meeting and told me the Society was prepared to do anything and everything to help me out for the next several days since I would be on their trail. The people I met were very friendly and provided me with all of the maps I would need to travel across that part of the state and even cautioned me about tricky places to watch out for.

The Colorado Trail is a 400-mile long hiking trail that mostly runs north and south from Durango to Denver. I joined it near the northern end and ran it north for a few miles to its terminus. Then, after several days of running through the Rocky Mountains, the ADT joins the Colorado Trail again, only this time traveling south in the opposite direction. In short, the ADT makes a giant arc in the Denver area and adds many miles to the route.

Back at the airport, we found that her flight had been canceled. The entire weekend had been planned to the minute scheduling miles to run, getting the car, dropping it off, and appearing at a press conference the next day at 10 a.m. in Garden of the Gods. I had eight miles to run that night just to make the next morning's run feasible if I planned to arrive at the press conference on time. With a canceled flight, my planned late afternoon run was moved back to a night jaunt after Lydia finally was able to get on a plane.

I arrived back in Green Mountain Falls at 8 p.m. and immediately upon entering Dick's house, he asked, "Ready to run?"

"Absolutely!" We dashed out the door. As soon as I was shuttled back to Woodland Park and got on Highway 24, it began to rain. It was dark. Even worse, I was running on the edge of a busy highway with practically no shoulder. Dick was driving his Blazer behind me with his hazard lights flashing and headlights beaming, providing safety and light for me to see through the driving rain. Just as we turned off the highway to enter his town, a siren went off and lights started flashing behind Dick's vehicle. A state trooper had pulled us over.

I immediately congratulated the trooper on being Transcon Police Officer Number Four, which immediately brought the question, "What's going on here?"

Clad in my soaked nylon shorts and windbreaker, I responded, "Well, I'm running to California and this here is the Mayor of Green Mountain Falls hoping I enjoy my tour through his town!"

The trooper was taken aback and tried to cover for himself by explaining, "Well, no one called us about this, and we weren't prepared to handle this." He walked away in a huff and I continued my evening's assignment.

It had been a downhill run all evening, and I called it quits just past 9 p.m. A quick shower, a spaghetti dinner and I was in bed by 10 p.m. It had been quite a day but I was looking forward the coming press conference and sights of Garden of the Gods.

The next morning I had to run ten more miles, return the rental car, pick up my new pair of shoes and mail in Manitou Springs, take some pictures in Garden of the Gods, and arrive at my press conference by 10 a.m. Fortunately, things went smoothly. After picking up my batch of mail at the Manitou Springs Post Office, I arrived five minutes late to my press conference, planned for dramatic effect. There was a television crew waiting for me on the terrace of the Visitors Center. The cameraman framed me with the beautiful Garden of the Gods natural rock sculptures in the background and Pike's Peak behind that, and we conducted the interview on the balcony.

Garden of the Gods Park in Colorado Springs, Colorado gives visitors reason to keep moving.

Leaving the Garden of the Gods area, I ran on bike paths into and through Colorado Springs. A mechanic at a bike shop gave me directions on how to get onto the Air Force Academy's Santa Fe Trail, which is another paved bike path.

All afternoon student pilots were flying over me in training gliders. The instructor would pull them up in a small lead plane and then release a cable and let the students fly the gliders, learning the effects of the wind and performance of an aircraft. It was a pleasant diversion to watch as I ran.

It was to be a 32-mile day and, with 12 to go, I began to drag my feet. The traveling of the weekend, trying to make all the commitments on schedule and running 30-mile days had all taken their toll. I had arranged to meet Dick at a lake just north of the Air Force Academy at 4 p.m. but with 10 miles to go, I figured our meeting time was too optimistic. I finally arrived at 5:45 p.m., eager to be in a vehicle, done for the day, and looking forward to a home cooked meal at his girlfriend's home nearby.

Sue and Dick had invited several friends over to her house to join me for a lasagna dinner. Everyone had assembled on the back patio of the immaculate home. They were sipping wine and eating hors d'oeuvres. One couple had recently come back from a free trip to New Zealand and Australia, paid for with frequent flyer miles. The second couple was comically depressed. They had reunited when he came back from Saudi Arabia. He called her from the airport and asked if they could meet. When they did, she says he was thin and tan, and after she handed him a beer, he yelled, "Marry me!"

"And if he hadn't lived in Saudi Arabia, we wouldn't be married today!" So they moved back to Saudi Arabia and life, according to this couple, is much better in "Saudi." "Oh, it's so much better in Saudi. We'd love to move back to Saudi. We were so much happier in Saudi."

Finally at the conclusion of dinner, everyone got into a heated debate whether or not women should be allowed in the military. Interestingly enough, "Mrs. Arabia" insisted that they should not, as it detracted from the "masculine image of soldiers." Most everyone else in the room disagreed with her. Dick said that women can do many things just as well as men and many things even better.

I stayed up late and watched myself on the evening news well after everyone else had retired for the evening. It was a very short clip, as many of my news clips were. I found that I had become that "funny thing" the producers saved for the end of the show, that "feel good" story that makes you dream good thoughts after hearing about the telemarketing scams and the train crashes. I suppose just making people feel better before they go to bed was doing one good thing each day.

Running north towards Denver over several days, I began noticing that it would rain in a torrential downpour every day at 4:45 p.m. Once I came to expect the rain, I would scan the sky for its quick encroachment just before 5 p.m. I also learned to maneuver around these storms even on foot. Still not in the mountains, I could see the weather coming in from a good distance away. Any time I saw a hazy sky that continued to the ground, I knew a rainstorm was blowing across that area. By focusing on that storm, I could watch it and see which way it was progressing and the speed it was moving. If it was moving away slower than I was running, I would simply slow down and wait for it to pass ahead of me. Rarely did a storm ever come directly towards me, but if it did, I could tell early on and seek refuge before it hit. The short downpours in Colorado lasted no more than a few minutes, and the endless blue sky returned just as the last quarter-sized drop of rain hit the country road.

The day after leaving Colorado Springs, I followed a section of the ADT along side elaborate ranch homes with giant stone and iron gates, security cameras, and keypads allowing access only to owners and invited guests.

By the end of the day, I was now over an hour's drive from Sue's house, and it would be the last time I would be shuttled back to her home for the night. The next morning we got a very early start, leaving the house by 6 a.m. because, as I learned, every retired person in central Colorado plays badminton, and Dick couldn't afford to miss another competition and thus thwart his chances at state division team champion again.

Dick dropped me off just past 7 a.m. at the exact spot on the road I had called it quits the night before and I ran up to Indian Creek Campground, where I would join an approach trail that would take me to the Colorado Trail, heading north. Within a few miles of trail running I hit the C.T. and turned right to head north into Denver. Only a mile down the trail I met my first C.T. thru-hiker. He was an older man who had already section hiked all of the Appalachian Trail and the Pacific Crest Trail and now, this afternoon was beginning the C.T. A few miles beyond that, I passed the dam of the Chatfield Reservoir with a very scenic recreation path and rushing spillway. Hoards of lunch-hour business people were out expelling stress and getting their dose of exercise. Walkers, bikers, and even a healthy number of runners were swarming the road. One man came running uphill towards me at an astonishing clip.

"Hi!" he said as he passed me going uphill. A few minutes later, he had turned around and headed back downhill. When he caught up with me again he asked how far I was running with the pack around my waist.

"Oh, about 4,800 miles, give or take a hundred."

Hearing that he slowed down, and we had a nice chat as we ran downhill towards the city. His name was Sam, and he was a graphic designer who went for a daily run to "shake off the office" as he put it.

Dick had set up another press conference for me at the Chatfield Reservoir hoping to get some good press coverage in the Denver metro area. Dick had also invited staff from Runner's Roost, a running shoe store in Colorado and the West Coast. They had offered to help me out by bringing a few pairs of shoes to give me. To both Dick's and my surprise, there was no media at the building. When I entered the center, a ranger looked at me and asked, "Can I help you?"

I explained that I was there to meet some press and that some people should have been looking for me.

"Oh," he said. "You're the guy. We got a message about some runner guy at a press conference and we didn't know what was going on. We didn't know if it was a KKK rally or what."

I wasn't aware that the Klan was generating interest by having transcontinental runners solicit new members, as this ranger implied, but thought his skepticism was a bit strange. The staff from Runner's Roost did show up shortly, and they donated three pairs of running shoes, two running outfits, and several packets of energy drink mix. It was a very generous donation, but I looked down at my new pile of possessions and wondered, "What am I going to do with all of this stuff?" They offered to drive me to the post office in Littleton, Colorado where I mailed it all to Lydia with a brief note explaining that I would ask for it back in smaller shipments later on.

Looking for a hotel that night, I entered a brand new Best Western. In fact, it was so new that it wasn't even open yet. I went in the building anyway, hoping I could find a contractor who would get a kick out of my story and give me a free room for the night. I found no one. In fact, I walked through the entire four-story hotel and didn't see anyone. In many of the halls, the room doors were propped open and there were brand new beds, televisions, and even new pillows and sheets still in their packaging. I considered going in one room and closing the door for the night. It was Friday, however, and one of the few free items of my trip was long distance phone calls on Friday, so I decided to pay for a room with a working phone. Calling an editor at the *Denver Post* that night, I was finally able to get a few sentences about my run in the back of the Sports section on the first day of August.

The next morning I got back on my paved bike path and immediately was submerged in the heavy pedestrian traffic of Sunday morning suburbanites. It felt so good to see other people out exercising. In Kansas, I didn't see anyone out on the roads, mostly because I was on county roads and small highways much of the time. So whenever the rare occurrence arose of sharing the trail with others, I could not hold back from greeting them.

"Good Morning!" I'd say as I passed them.

"Hello…," a few said and looked at me in surprise as if to ask, "Why are you talking in my direction? We don't talk out here. We just stare straight ahead. If you are wearing sunglasses, you can sneak a peek at us but just to make sure we are not going to jump on you or anything. But please, don't talk."

Just as I was settling into a state of silence, I noticed a field full of small brown furry animals. A bicyclist started to pass me on a long hill and I instinctively turned to him and asked, "What are those brown varmints?"

" Prairie dogs."

"Huh," I said, "I've never seen those before."

"Never?" he asked, incredulously. "Where are you from?"

"Indiana."

"Wow, that's a long run," he said, jokingly.

"Yep, 'bout 5,000 miles," I said with a deadpan face.

At that point he slowed down and said, "Ok, I have to hear about this."

Soon after, we were trading information and working out how I could stay at his house that night. My new friend was a schoolteacher in the Evergreen area. He gave me his phone number and told me to call him at the end of the day.

Later in the afternoon, I stopped at a new city park with a small lake. I purchased a small lunch at the limited snack shop.

Sitting on the picnic table outside of the snack shop, I was joined by two other men. They were both sitting across from me, positioned to watch the young girls on the beach. They were making comments about one girl in particular. I was feeling quite at home, sitting at a picnic table with a couple of guys, looking at the women, and I even found myself chiming in with a chuckle or two at their comments. Just when I thought these guys had "checked out" as a regular couple of fellows, one said to the other, "Man, I wish we had to do community service more often. This ain't too bad!"

Two other older men were combing the beach with metal detectors. The girl in the snack shop told me the park had been open for less than a year, and here two men were hoping to find a wedding ring, lost treasure, or a stray Susan B. Anthony coin. As they finished canvassing the beach, I asked to see their loot. They said they always split whatever they found. Net combined earnings for that day: 27 cents and 57 metal construction slugs.

After my lunch, I finished the bike path and had to run on a highway with a very narrow shoulder. As I was running, I noticed a brand new bike path down a steep embankment to my left. This particular trail had a trademark iron bridge spanning a creek, something I had seen numerous times on other paths in the area. I figured this might be a recently completed trail I had heard about. I ran down the embankment stumbling and sliding on riprap the entire way down and jumped onto the trail with a "thud." A sign read, "Trail under construction. Please stay off." Looking back up the steep rocky slope, I decided against turning back and started down the new path. A quarter of a mile later it dead-ended.

At that time of day, I did not want to run back the way I had come and ascend the hillside I had slid down, so I continued. The trail under construction was fairly well underway at first but soon began to become less navigable. Not long after, I was bushwhacking over small hilltops and into narrow valleys. I was not really concerned with getting lost; I knew the main road could not be more than a mile to my right, so long as my compass was not lying.

As I turned to head back towards the road, I came across a single seven-point antler. It was very fresh, as smaller animals had taken out only a nibble. The antler was also quite heavy given its medium size. I took off my pack and tried to envision how I could carry it, my desire for mementos beating out any debate I had to leave it where I found it. The antler was formed with a nice curve and I was able to strap it to my pack with the attached elastic cord. I ended up carrying that antler for three days with one long point on it occasionally poking me in the back. A reminder, I figured, for the wrong choice I had made to remove it. Lydia received it in the mail in a large box and her reaction to me on the phone was, "Yeah, I got it all right."

I often wondered what she thought of the smelly shoes I would mail her, the old folded and dirty maps, the trail guides, pens from restaurants, and occasional shampoo containers from hotels.

At a payphone I spoke with my schoolteacher friend. He said that I was still more than welcome to come over to his house but that he doesn't really live in Evergreen, he lives in Lakewood, where I had started that morning. He would have also been happy to pick me up but he was having some friends over for cocktails and could not leave. If I was able to hitch a ride, I was welcome to come over.

Undeterred, I eventually got a ride in the back of a pick-up truck to Lakewood. I showered at his condominium and met his two female friends, both schoolteachers. We enjoyed Brie, wine, good fresh bread, and shrimp. After his friends left, we had some more shrimp and chocolate torts.

For an evening project, he suggested that we put together a computer desk in his basement. He said it had been sitting in the box for some time and that he was completely inept at putting things like that together.

While we worked on the pre-drilled particleboard office piece, he told me about his recent divorce after 26 years of marriage and three daughters. I told him that my parents had divorced after 28 years and three boys. He thought this was very interesting and asked me many questions about my parents. When I reciprocated with my own questions to hear how the tragedy happened to his family, he brushed off the conversation saying, "It's a long story."

He also kept passing gas, which I did not have a problem with except that he constantly reminded me that doing so was very good for you and that it was "unhealthy" to hold it in. Finally, as we were attaching the top on the desk, he began explaining his philosophy of life to me, in Latin. This might be a good time to point out that I do not speak a word of Latin.

"You see, Brian, my whole philosophy on life is…. (raised hand for gesture) Se kadre du milia." Then he would pause and wait for me to translate it, or perhaps to memorize it, or maybe to ask, "What does that mean?" So I paused for an attempted understanding, which never came.

"Sorry," I said. "What does that mean?"

"Well, 'Sa,' means 'life.' And 'Kadre' means, well, of course 'ka' – The Great. Right?" It was the kind of inflection that indicated I would sound incredibly stupid if I didn't agree.

"Oh, right, of course, 'Ka'." I said, as if I had just remembered from my Latin Books on Tape collection.

"And 'dre', means 'one,' or 'being'."

In the end I didn't get most of what he was talking about but I got the sense that he was an intelligent man who was proficient in cooking, farting, and Latin, but not computer desk assembly. I'm not even sure he finished his explanation of his philosophy on life, because he shifted the topic and began telling me why he chose to be a teacher.

"Well, 'Education', you know what that means, right?" Pause for contemplation.

"Umm."

He began again, "Ed', to think, right?" And on and on. Later, we sat on his balcony, eating a gooey chocolate dessert, and sipping hot tea.

As my host continued his multi-lingual life philosophies, I found myself speculating on why I was so fortunate to be taken into the homes of so many kind people. Countless times I would be running through a major city such as Washington D.C. or St. Louis and I would pass a number of homeless persons, never being helped, never being handed money or offered a home for the night, laundry, a bed, shower, and food. And yet, I received all of these things regularly. I completely understand the situation being different but my dumb luck almost seemed unnatural given the number of people who truly need help every day. The bizarreness of the regularity and the genuine kindness of everyone I met almost seemed choreographed.

The next morning the teacher drove me back to Evergreen. As I got out of his car to start the day, I noticed my back felt wet when I put on my new water pack. In only a few days of running, my CamelBak had sprung a leak. This was only the beginning of realizing that many hydration systems cannot stand up to the rigors of running, or perhaps my lesson that antlers and bladders don't go together. I thanked him for his generosity and took off down the road again.

In the afternoon Bill Stoehr, president of National Geographic Maps and past Colorado State Coordinator for the ADT picked me up. He and his wife travel the world, checking out places to make and market new maps. Just days before my arrival he had come back from a mapping expedition in Tanzania and two days after I left he took off again for several weeks in Nepal. He had not had time to compile maps for me before I arrived, so we did it together. Armed with only a one-page copy of a written description of the route across Colorado, Bill gathered eight different maps from his supply room and donated them, wishing me "Happy trails."

That night I got a cheap motel room in Idaho Springs. I was able to check a load of email messages at the library. One of which was all the way from Australia; "We're rooting for you! Cherrie O!"

In the morning I went to a bagel shop for breakfast. While munching on my sun dried tomato bagels, a man walked over to me and asked, "You're not traveling the American Discovery Trail, are you?"

"Yes, I am!" I said enthusiastically.

I joined him at his bike shop down the street. He had become involved with the ADT several years ago when the scouting team first came through. He was eager to make a donation to my efforts and handed me twenty expired banana flavored Power Bars. I told him about my water pack leak and he showed me his selection of the systems but none of them seemed to be the right size. I was looking for one that did not hang too low on my back to collide with my hip pack. I thanked him for the Power Bars and went across town to a camping store to purchase a Gregory Mirage Pack I had seen the day before. The pack held close to a gallon of water and was very short so seemed to work well in conjunction with my hip pack. The bladder for the Mirage pack is foil, however, which became an issue over the next several days.

A typical morning commute in the Rocky Mountains.

As I left Idaho Springs, I struggled up Spring Gulch Road, a very steep mountain pass that offers no respite to the foot traveler. Despite carrying nine pounds of water, several pounds of banana flavored energy bars, and a healthy supply of cheese crackers, I made an attempt to run up the mountain. Usually, armed with a load this heavy, I would walk such a long steep ascent, but on this particular morning I found myself running up the entire thing, perhaps for the novelty of it.

Along the way up the mountain I passed many abandoned mine shafts and my days at Camp beckoned me to explore their contents yet I pressed on. There were also numerous side roads and confusing junctions. Had the forest service not been diligent in placing carsonite posts at every junction with the roads marked in stickers, I would still be looking for the correct way to Georgetown.

Just as I came over the lip of the mountain pass, a young man in a Land Rover passed me. It had been raining off and on throughout the day and I tried to imagine his day trip from his driver's seat perspective, with his dodecahedral stereo system blaring rock music. His bouncing tour up the rutted rocky road would have been experienced from a heated dry chamber of foam, plastic, and glass. I could imagine him thinking to himself, "Wow, what a day...gray, raining. I'll bet there isn't a soul on that mountain over there. I think I'll get in my off-road vehicle to drive over the mountain and get in touch with nature. What's this, a guy running in the rain? Where's *his* Land Rover?"

Little did the driver know that I was safe and snug in my own vehicle of sorts. Warm and dry in my Gore-Tex running jacket, high tech mittens, and ball cap, I was glad that I was persevering through this rainy mountain range with nothing more than a few pounds tied to myself.

The pass down to Georgetown was described by the Foots in their guidebook as, "The Road From Hell." I soon found out why. On their bike trip, they had decided to bike this section in reverse. The pass up from Georgetown is considerably steeper with unforgiving switchbacks leading back and forth seemingly into forever. To try and imagine biking up that road with loaded bikes made me thankful for the few pounds I was carrying, and that I was running down this part instead.

Immediately at the bottom of the mountain and at edge of town, I proceeded directly to the local visitors center. Occasionally, these tourists' stops have led to free places to stay and, if nothing else, they gave me a good overview of the town. After checking out the cheapest place in town, I decided that I would rather pay $56 for a motel with a phone, television, and pool, rather than $19 for one without any of those.

My journal was generally lacking in entries and, if I had the will power, I likely could have saved a good deal of money by staying in the cheaper places and simply catching up on journal writing in the evenings rather than scanning the channels late into the night. I found, however, that even though I didn't write every night, my thoughts were my only occupation throughout the day. After 12 hours of talking to myself, the last thing I generally wanted to do was sit down and write it all down and have the conversation all over again. At least with a television or a telephone, I could have some form of company. I believe these comforts saved me mentally each evening that they were available.

The next morning I ascended Guanella Pass. Climbing for a dozen miles I finally reached the summit at 12,000 feet, much to the amazement of on-looking picnickers who had driven by me earlier in the morning, leaving me in their dusty aftermath.

Sitting on the edge of the parking lot, I ate a snack, chiseled off a chunk of banana Power Bar and let it soak in my mouth with the hopes that at some point later on in the day I would be able to chew part of it. A couple approached me and asked to look at my map.

They were considering hiking one of the nearby 14,000-foot mountains and upon seeing my map exclaimed, "Wow! Your map is much better than ours!" It seems that many people I met on my run were inadequately prepared for their treks into the backcountry.

After a break at the top, I readjusted my pack and started down the mountain, looking forward to a full afternoon of running downhill. The first eight miles of steep switchbacks were easy enough but soon after, a downhill weariness set in. All you can do on such a stretch of road is let the muscles go, lean forward a little to let gravity work with you and try and to hang on until you reach the bottom.

With only four miles to go to the next town, I came upon a couple in a car stopped in the middle of the road. Two very large male Big Horn Sheep were standing looking in the windows of the car. I hoped the couple wasn't feeding the Sheep. They were easily over seven feet tall and each must have weighed several hundred pounds. Hoping they would get off the road as I approached, I cautiously continued down the mountain. The Sheep took interest in me and turned, starting to walk my direction. In tourist areas, one has to be very careful because many animals have been domesticated and know that humans possess food. These sheep could have easily crushed my ribs with their gigantic antlers had they wanted to and then had their fill of stale banana-flavored Power Bars. Given my meager pantry, it would have likely been the last time they charged a runner for his food, however. Luckily, as I was standing in the road a dozen yards from the sheep, a couple in a Ford Explorer drove up from behind me and offered to give me a ride past the sheep. The couple drove me 50 yards down the hill where I got out and resumed my run, leaving the horned beasts behind.

The next town on the trail is Grant, population 25. Grant contains a bar, a post office, a country store, and a small automotive junkyard. Before my visit was over, I would visit all of them and then some. The store is not a separate building, but rather the living room of a woman's home. Interested shoppers need to ring a doorbell on the front of the house. The owner comes to the door, unlocks the store, and lets you purchase your supplies from an inventory containing blaze orange hunting vests, sodas, ground cloths, and beef jerky. After a sandwich at the bar, I casually asked how far it was to the nearest lodging.

"Ain't nothin' 'round here."

It was a usual response and I had heard it many times before. I knew there had to be something not too far away and eventually got an answer. There was a newly remodeled lodge five miles up the road. The price was $55 but the rooms did not have a television or phone. I was willing to pay for comforts, but if the amenities came down to basically camping in a room, I could do that anywhere. I decided to save some money and see if I couldn't work things out on my own.

Even trying something so simple as standing on the side of the road has its potential. I had eaten my dinner, had stocked up on crackers and chocolate, and now at dusk was standing on the side of a lonely highway looking for a miracle. He walked towards me. It was a man who had walked past me earlier, and I had greeted him with a warm "hello." This time, on his way home from the bar, I greeted him again and, using the most genuine tone possible asked, "Excuse me, sir, I'm running across the country and wondered if you knew who owns this closed motel behind me. You see I'm looking for a place to camp out for the night and thought I could maybe stay in one of those old rooms. It doesn't have to be nice or anything."

He looked at me, smiled and said, "Yeah, let me go ask the guy." A few minutes later he returned and said that the rooms were all full of storage but the owner had a truck camper for sale on blocks in his backyard, and I was welcome to sleep in it for the night. I thanked him and walked around to my new, free room for the night. There was a rushing cold stream a few feet away. The camper was secluded from the highway due to being behind the motel, and inside was a queen-sized bed, a small writing table, windows and a door. I couldn't have imagined a better arrangement. I stayed up for several hours writing in my journal, quietly satisfied that I had run 25 miles over a mountain, survived an encounter with sheep, and had just saved $50. To top it off, I was finally getting to sleep in a truck camper, something I had always wanted to do. In fact, I enjoyed the experience so much that it gave me the idea to get one of my own and live out of the back of it, repairing dilapidated structures across America for free.

The next morning was another big challenging day. The map showed it was 34 miles to Breckenridge over another big mountain and Kenosha Pass. I surveyed my provisions: three packs of cheese crackers, nine banana flavored Power Bars, and two chocolate bars. If I could stock up on water, I would be ready to head back into the mountains. Stopping at the local garage I walked though aisles and aisles of shelves filled to the ceiling with bushings, bell housings, catalytic converters and Polaroid pictures of girls clad in skimpy bikinis seductively modeling in front of highly polished Thunderbirds. The half-asleep mechanics let me fill my water bottles in their sink.

Ascending Kenosha Pass I stopped by a tunnel built in the 1950s that carries water to Denver. The tunnel goes through the mountain and is 24 miles long. If only I could have a water pipe that big for every time my bottle was empty. Soon after, I rejoined the Colorado Trail, this time heading southwest.

Chapter 23
A Rock and a Soft Place

I enjoyed passing the usual assortment of trail users on the Colorado Trail: a Boy Scout Troop out for a mountain bike ride, a young couple on a day hike, and finally, a pair of CT thru-hikers. The man had thru-hiked the Appalachian Trail but his girlfriend was a novice. He obviously wanted her to enjoy this new experience as much as possible. They were on their fourth day of the hike that usually takes people one to two months to complete. As the soles of her feet hadn't yet built up the thick pad of callous that long distance travelers pride themselves with, she was dealing with her "hot spots" and had already formed blisters. They both had taken off their boots and socks and were cooling their feet in a cold stream. Such a scenario is not unusual along hiking trails.

Often times, one person will have a great solo trail experience and will naturally want to share that experience with their significant other after being home for a year. Lydia and I have spoken of doing such a trip many times. But there is danger in bringing your loved one into the wilderness, particularly if it would be a new experience. Old hiking paces that were developed over thousands of miles creep back into motion. Daily routines become old hat once more for the hardened trail user, but if your feet are not used to the heat and pounding of a 16-mile day in heavy boots with a 40-pound pack, such a trip might not be a welcome introduction to the world of backpacking. Therefore, picking out such couples is usually an easy task. One person will be administering the blister kit, while comforting the other who is sitting on a rock, pack still on shoulders, leaning to one side with a dazed look in their eyes. That look is one of, "I really want to be able to enjoy this, but it hurts so much. When will the fun start?"

The partner realizes this is a rough introduction and so suggests frequent breaks, low mileage days, and constant checkups. They were taking their time, and I envied them for being able to share such a journey. After a brief chat I encouraged them to stick with it and trotted off.

Leaving the woods I entered a vast grassy meadow, which led me to the summit of Georgia Pass, elevation 11,800 ft. With a glorious day offering blue skies and warm sun coupled with a cool mountain breeze, I decided to take a short break at the summit. Eating my last pack of cheese crackers I enjoyed the expansive view all around, *this* was living. With a short afternoon of downhill running I would end up in Breckenridge, and the thought of that made me all the happier to sit and enjoy the scenery.

Arriving at a highway at the base of the mountain several miles later, the ADT turned right to go into Frisco, but I wanted to see Breckenridge, which lay five miles to the left. Tossing out my trusty thumb, I quickly secured a ride in the back of a pick-up truck.

The first thing I witnessed in town was the International Wood Carving Competition taking place in a shopping mall parking lot. Under a circus tent I perused the collection of sculptures of wooden mermaids, anchors, linked chains, and not yet recognizable objects being brought to the surface by a myriad of chainsaws, chisels, hammers, files, and knives. When several of the 20-odd artists were at work with their electric saws the parking lot sounded like a motor cross rally during the final lap.

My watch battery had recently died and the last time recorded had been illuminated for the past three days.

In such journeys as mine, people often romanticize getting rid of all that reminds them of home. Doing without computers, telephones, television, and especially timepieces seemed to epitomize breaking free of the daily mold most of us adhere to without thought. However, as I was almost always in need of a post office to send home fly swatters, beer cozies and old maps, I needed to keep track of time, not to mention meeting reporters on time and juggling the logistics of most of my trip alone. Even more than keeping appointments, my watch served as my odometer as well. So along with laundry, Internet chores and lodging, I also needed to find a watch repair shop.

With a new battery and a good dinner, I went about looking for a room for the night. After my expensive night with Lydia near the Rocky Mountain National Park, I knew finding affordable lodging in any resort town would be a challenge. Approaching a nice lodge, I began a conversation with the desk clerk, a young man in his early 20s. He told me that their cheapest room that night was listed at $70. I realized this was fair for the local market but still wanted to try and get the price down further. I noticed that he had a cast on his forearm which I learned came from a recent accident while mountain biking.

He went on to inform me that he was going to quit his job as soon as his arm healed. Now knowing this, I said that if he was going to quit anyway, then surely he wouldn't mind finding the lowest possible rate on his computer. Amazingly, he agreed and, by the time I signed the credit card slip, we had worked our way down to $35.

The next morning I decided to run the extra five miles to rejoin the ADT. It was along a beautiful heavily traveled bike path beside the highway. Upon leaving town I encountered an aggressive gaggle of geese. The whole family was milling about in a yard, and I simply wanted to run past them on the path, but the parents of the flock wouldn't hear of it. When I came within ten feet of them I was charged with wings fully outstretched and several of the larger ones hissing at me. A road construction crew was working nearby on a section of the highway and was having a good time at my expense. I was finally able to zip past the geese when they weren't watching.

After a late night of television in a motel I was awakened by the telephone at 5:30 am.

"Brian? This is Bill Foot. I'm surprised you're not gone yet!"

How does he keep finding me?

"I was just making my way out the door, Bill," I said as I rolled over under the covers. We caught up and he and Laurie gave me some tips for the upcoming section.

With the early wake-up call I was on the road with plenty of time to get to my destination. Camp Hale, 25 miles away, once a famous encampment for the Civilian Conservation Corps during the depression and now home to an elite mountain Army division. Crossing Copper Mountain Ski Resort, I could sense the over-priced real estate all around me. Oversized bleached blonde log cabins with bay windows and three-car garages dotted the hillsides in every direction. How many transcon runs could the cost of one of those houses fund? Later while eating some greasy pizza in a ski lodge, I enjoyed listening to a retired snowbird yell at a golf tournament on television.

"Oh, come on! How many times do you have to look at it? Just swing already!" I tried to imagine how many summer golf tournaments the bartender had to listen to this guy comment on before the ski crowd returned in the fall and the thought of it depressed me so I smiled as I walked out the door and headed for the woods.

Back on the trail I was eager to dive into the peaks and valleys to a place where money can't compare to a vast supply of wildflowers grass and ridgelines. Ascending a beautiful valley, on the CT, I was surrounded by tall prairie grass and thick pine stands on either side. Soon after at the top of Searle Pass, elevation 12,000, I met two mountain bikers. I commented that I couldn't imagine biking up this long pass with so many steep switchbacks. They said that they couldn't imagine running across the United States.

From Searle to Kokomo Pass the map showed the trail staying basically at a consistent 12,000-foot elevation. I decided to try and run the few mile stint between the peaks. The daily monsoon whould be headed my way soon, and I did not want to be high up during the lightening that was a familiar accompaniment with the monsoons.

This trail was a popular horse and bike trail and the numerous users had worn the tread down several inches below the surface. As I was running, I began noticing that my feet were veering to the left with every step and they kept hitting the left side of the small trench I was in. After a few meters of this, I said aloud, "Alright, enough! I'm going to run straight and not hit that bank again! ...only to hit the bank with both feet before I had concluded my oath.

I soon realized that I was suffering from mild altitude fatigue and was losing control over my functions. I've never been drunk but assume that this was close to the real thing. As I was laughing at my muddled mental state, I noticed the first bolts of lightening coming from the west and I stopped laughing.

I knew that if lightening came my way and I was exposed at altitude, to drop elevation and get into a depression. I found such a depression and watched the storm pass before me, counting the seconds between lightening and thunder, thus knowing when it was finally passing away from me. My brief break had also allowed me to recover, and my stumbling "drunkenness" was no longer a problem.

After arriving at Camp Hale, I was tired from my day at high elevation and decided that I would hitch into Leadville for the night. The next morning, I would hitch back to Camp Hale and run the portion I had missed. My driver this time was a nice man in his 30s. At first he was only going to take me into town, but upon arriving, he asked if I'd like to come to his house for some tea. It sounded nice so I agreed.

He had a full house. His wife was busy entertaining another friend of theirs who had just finished a bike tour, and the two of them were busy entertaining the three young children of the house. I was invited to stay for dinner, which I gratefully accepted. Then they asked if I'd like to take a shower while I waited to eat. I was happy to take them up on the offer.

After dinner they said, "Well, you may as well stay the night!"

I had a good time playing with the kids and hearing stories of life in the highest city in the United States.

The next morning I lucked out once again as I was treated to the Annual Boom Days Festival. That day's event was the Burro Race, where participants arrive from all over the country with their pack animal to run an 18-mile course with a burrow tied to their waist. Runners are allowed to load their burros down with food and water but they do not ride them. Some had even affixed the traditional pick-axes and shovels to their burros. There were separate races for men and women and given the temperament of the pack animals, some runners were having trouble even getting their partner to the starting line. Hundreds of spectators lined both sides of the streets.

Soon after, I was to meet another couple that had offered to take me in for the night in their home in Aspen. Dave and Janet had met my dad while on a sailing trip in the Caribbean. They had hit it off well and had told my dad to pass their names along to me when I got to their area. They had agreed to meet me in front of City Hall in Leadville but, as there were thousands of people in town, I had trouble finding the couple I'd never met.

"Brian Stark, please report to the judge's stand," blared over the public address system. They had paged me. They said that they had planned on fishing for the day and asked if I'd like to join them. It sounded like a great idea compared to hitching back to Camp Hale and running a section of road I'd already driven. So with another day off now planned, we got in their truck with boat in tow and proceeded to Twin Lakes. Each of us caught fish and Dave spoke of his other hobbies. He's into several extreme sports besides sailing and fishing. "Ultra-hang gliding" I was to learn involved going so high that you wear oxygen tanks to breathe. He's also into "Ultra fast snowmobiling," where the snowmobiles are so fast and small that if you stop, you risk sinking into the snow and getting stuck. If that happens, he explained, friends will hopefully notice you are missing and after finding you, will drive by in passes to pack down the snow so you can get out. (And I thought ultra-running was extreme.)

After fishing for a few hours we loaded up the boat and drove over Independence Pass to their home in Snowmass Village. First, however, we had to drive through Aspen. I'd never been to Aspen before and since Dave is a residential surveyor he was able to give me some quotes on houses on the market.

"Do you see that house over there, Brian?"

"Do you mean the one that looks like a converted one-car garage?" I asked.

"Yeah, 1.2 million," he said. I could run twelve laps around the entire world at that price.

We arrived at their beautiful home on a golf course with views of the ski slopes in the background and the snow-covered peaks beyond. That night, after dinner and while soaking in their hot tub, Dave told me about his job as a surveyor. He said that he has several employees who operate backhoes and heavy machinery. One day, one of his new employees didn't show up for work. He never received a call that day from the truant employee. The next day proved the same. A week went by during which Dave had to assume the burden of all the workload without his employee's help. Finally, after being gone more than a week, this worker showed up for work, without a word to Dave, his boss. Dave figured that the man had had some personal matters and decided to leave it at that without discussion. Several months later, this man approached Dave with an apology.

"I'm really sorry I had to leave like I did a while ago," he told Dave.

"Oh, well, everyone has problems to deal with," Dave replied.

"Yeah, well, I want to tell you what happened to explain my absence," he began. "You see, my sister married this guy who turned out to be a drunk and he started beating her. My brothers and I went up to him and told him that he'd better cut it out or we were going to kill him. He didn't stop beating her so we went over to his house, killed him, and threw his body into a mineshaft. Then we blew up the shaft." Dave said he was near speechless.

"Oh my gosh," trying to think of what to say, "do you need any help... with the police or anything?"

"No," the employee replied. "I got a cousin who's a sheriff and we told him what had happened and he said, "Alright."

And then Dave went on to say that this man said, "And you've been so good to me while I dealt with this, if you ever have any trouble, with anyone... just let me know." Upon hearing that, I thanked Dave for the use of his hot tub and offered to wash the dishes, do my own laundry, do his own laundry, and walk back to the trail...

The next morning both Dave and his wife were unable to return me to Leadville where they'd picked me up, so I was on my own to get over the pass and back onto the trail. Janet, Dave's wife said she had just enough time to take me to the start of the pass, outside of town.

Dropping me off on a scenic pullover, she wished me luck and drove off. I stuck out my thumb and was quickly met by a Colorado Department of Transportation truck being driven by a very nice woman. After hearing of my plight, she was extremely helpful and proceeded to get me a ride back into Leadville.

The road crew was working on the pass and as we approached the site, she saw who was assigned to hold the stop sign and said, "Oh, you don't want to try and work with him, he won't be of any help to you." Then she pulled over, took the sign from his hands and gave the man a lunch break, assuming the position herself. Since she now had the power to stop cars, she was going to use it to my advantage. At the first line of cars, and after asking me a few questions, she walked up to the second car in line and proceeded to give the nicest speech you'd ever want to hear about yourself. She said through the window, "Do you see that nice looking young man over there? He's a schoolteacher from Indiana and he's running all the way across the country and he needs a ride back into Leadville to get on his course. I gave him a ride here and he's just the nicest guy..."

The driver this woman had approached was a young woman just out of law school and she happily agreed to give me the ride. I thanked the construction woman for her help and the graduate took me all the way back to Camp Hale.

I was finally running the ADT into Leadville on my official arrival into town even though I'd already spent two days there by car. That night I checked into the Club Lead, one of the most famous hostels in the world for long-distance runners. The 100-mile Leadville Trail run was coming up in a few weeks and the hostel was nearly full with competitors acclimating to the altitude.

One of them, Robert, was 24 and was attempting to be the youngest person to ever run a "grand slam," which is four 100-mile trail runs in one year. Leadville was to be his second of the four. We sat and talked about running for several hours. Being in that hostel, surrounded by runners who were also going out and running 20-40 miles a day was an odd feeling. No longer was I the only novelty in the room. Some of the people there were preparing for their tenth running of the Leadville.

In the evening, a runner from Texas took me out and bought me a pizza dinner. Then, Robert drove me to a grocery store where he bought me a pint of ice cream. That night, I joined the others in one of the male bunkrooms. Beside each of their beds, I noticed an ammunition can covered with decals and filled with power gel, powder gunk, tape, foam, special cassettes of heart-pounding music, and all the other old dented smelly sentimental cargo that finds its way onto the racing circuit with its owner.

Hostels are great. The price is right and showers are usually included in a night's stay. There is typically a common area with a television and a few videos. I found on my run that the cheaper the hostel, the longer the lounging by permanent guests fulfilling a yearn for a "second home," or in some cases perhaps a "first home."

In these more affordable hostels, one can find the television quietly entertaining the guests from mid-morning till late at night. A rough crowd of five or so usually takes in a day's worth of reruns, talk shows, and another round of the same five videos available for viewing. "Prime movie time" is usually around 9 pm and it's typical for a crowd of varying socioeconomic backgrounds to gather on oddly stained, used college dorm couches to watch whatever the first person seated has selected for that night's feature film. In one night at another hostel I bore witness to, "Priscilla: Queen of the Desert", "Lethal Weapon 2", and "My Girl" in one sitting.

The kitchen of the hostel is a prime collection of blackened, stained, well-used pots, pans, and bent utensils. Some magical transformation takes place within you when you enter a hostel's kitchen: your standards decrease, you chalk everything up to international culture and budget accommodations, and you start noticing the free items. "Sure it's got yellow crud on it but hey, it's free! And hey! LOOK HERE! Free Paprika! I don't *care* if we're only making spaghetti, where else do you get free spices?"

The following morning in Club Lead, I was treated to a pancake breakfast served by Jay, the owner. With a free fine breakfast in my gas tank, I was powered up for a 38-mile day to Buena Vista, where I would pick up my next pair of shoes and batch of mail. Two miles after leaving Leadville, I noticed that my back was getting wet again, which by this point I knew could only mean one thing. Pulling off the road, I took off my second hydration pack to find that my gallon of water was slowly running down my back and into my hip pack. Upon inspecting the foil bladder, I found not one but three holes in the silvery material. Store salesmen reportedly fill these bags with water and stomp on them, to prove to customers that the bags can withstand lots of weight and pressure. The holes that formed in my water bag were very small and looked like they formed more from creases in the bag and pressure from the water sloshing inside rather than being punctured from some external force. Regardless of the reason, I was now losing my main supply of water with 36 miles to go. By inverting my water bag, I was able to control the leaking but now could no longer drink out of the tube as it was coming out of the top of the bag rather than the bottom. I decided to simply fill my water bottle from this bladder when I stopped for breaks.

Passing through the towns of Balltown and Granite, I got a lunch and three lemonades.

After eating, I passed a huge wooden structure, lashed together with cables, bolts, and rope. The massive tripod made of telephone poles was 75-

feet tall and had many ropes dangling off of it to climb on, rappel from, and swing on. There was a giant cargo net for climbing, and the entire structure made me stop and just admire the grandeur of it all. While standing there for a few minutes, a man came out of a building on the property of the tripod and yelled, "Hey, come over here!"

Waving me across the street, he had come out to talk to me. When I approached him, he said, "You looked interesting so I thought I'd ask what you were up to." We discussed my run for a few minutes and why he had built his huge tripod, a team building exercise for groups I came to find out. He was soon inviting me to come back with friends and play on his structure, handing me brochures and business cards. As I was leaving he invited me to run on his "private path."

An original stagecoach road went through his property and he had developed it into a mountain bike trail, equipped with suspension bridges and signposts. Thanking him for his invitation, I left the highway and joined the stagecoach road, a rutty lane now converted to an excellent trail along a gushing stream. It was a much more scenic route and more conducive to contemplative thought than where I had been earlier. On the earlier route my only train of thought was, "I wonder if that semi headed my way is going to veer off the shoulder and back into his lane before he hits me."

The rest of the afternoon was filled with great views. I passed a group of kayakers resting in eddies planning their next course through the coming rapids. I ran through a series of three tunnels, carved through rock and so close together that at one point, I could stand in front of the first and see all three tunnels in succession. I finally arrived in Buena Vista in mid-afternoon. Retrieving my mail, I was swarmed by the post office workers who were excited to finally meet the person responsible for having them look at a pile of packages for five weeks.

One of them commented that they had seen the article about me in the Pueblo Chieftain Newspaper and had expected me to come through town weeks ago. At first I couldn't understand how they had gotten a copy of that paper from 386 trail miles away. Looking at the map, I realized what had gone wrong. Colorado is the most circuitous state for the ADT. Though the state is only 380 miles wide, the trail winds it way along rivers and over mountains for an unbelievable 869 miles! While worming my way across the state on various trails and dirt roads, I had made a nearly perfect 400-mile loop from Pueblo up to Denver, and back down to Buena Vista. In doing so, I had re-entered the distribution area of the Pueblo Chieftain newspaper. Ever since then, I envisioned families looking out their living room picture windows as I ran by asking, "Say, isn't that the guy who was running through the area two weeks ago? What's he still doing here?"

With my new shoes, two boxes of snacks, and 12 letters picked up from the post office, I quickly checked into a motel to go through my goodies. Beth Mathers, my phone card-donating neighbor from home sent me several hundred more minutes of prepaid cards. She generously was continuing to be of great help in staying in touch with my friends and family.

The following day I passed through the small town of Mount Princeton Hot Springs for lunch. Pressing on, I arrived at the even smaller town of St. Elmo by evening. The only services in "town" were a small country store with trinkets, a limited grocery, and a small cabin for rent. I inquired about this cabin and was told that it was $40 per night with a minimum stay of two nights. The store was closing as I arrived but not before I was able to buy a dinner. Two pizzas, two burritos, two cokes, a bag of chips, and some candy did the trick. The management seemed to like my style and pretty soon, we'd worked out an arrangement for a good transcon price. Rather than the listed $80 fee, I got them to agree to $25 for one night only, provided that I didn't use any of the sheets or linens, and that they wouldn't be able to tell that I had been there the next morning so they wouldn't have to clean it again.

I micro waved my dinner and ate outside to keep the cabin clean. While eating, I watched a family sitting on a fallen log on the side of the road across from me. They had stopped in their car to visit the small town. Upon getting some snacks out of their car, a community of chipmunks came to pay them a visit. Here I witnessed a prime example of domestication by tourists. The chipmunks swarmed the young daughters, running over their laps, around their necks, and over their heads, leaping from one family member to the other. As the kids would feed them more snacks, the chipmunks would run around even more. Granted it looked cute, but seeing another community of wildlife become dependant on tourists was saddening.

After dinner, I retreated to my cabin and noticed for the first time that there was no bathroom in the small one-room structure. There was not even a toilet. Since I hadn't noticed this earlier, I had no idea where I was to use the facilities. I didn't mind walking into the woods when nature called, but it was hard to imagine a family on vacation paying the asking rate for two nights without proper facilities.

Lying down in my sleeping bag on the aluminum bunk bed that night I stared up at the underside of the top bunk. Affixed to the nylon-covered box frame was the consumer label: Made By Cosco Inc., State St.,

Columbus, IN 47201. I was sleeping on the only lodging available in St. Elmo, Colorado, deep in the Rocky Mountains, on a bed made three miles from my boyhood home in Indiana.

The next morning I swept the floor as best I could, wiped down the shower, rinsed out the cup I had used, and retrieved the manager to prove that the cabin was, indeed, still clean. He took one look at it and decided it was so.

Leaving St. Elmo the ADT joins an ATV trail and I shared the serene woods with a steady stream of four-wheel drive machines. Ridden by large couples, with coolers bungee-corded to the back, these hunks of plastic and metal announced their presence from over a mile away. By the time they finally passed me, it sounded as if they were actually *in* my eardrum. After they would go by, I would be forced to inhale long columns of their blueish-white exhaust for a quarter-mile. Ascending the summit of Tincup Pass, which is also the Continental Divide, a truck met me at the top and an older couple got out.

"Whew," the woman said, a bit shaken from their bouncy drive to the top, "I finally made it! This is some way to spend a 52nd wedding anniversary." I just laughed.

Descending the mountain, I arrived at Taylor Park Reservoir. There are cabins for rent in Taylor Park, and I learned that they had just rented out their last one before my arrival. With nowhere else to go, I decided to try and work things out on my own. I walked by the occupied cabins and tried for another miracle.

I came upon two guys hosing off their motorcycles next to their van.

"Excuse me guys," I began. "I'm running across the United States and wondered if you knew of a dry place I could sleep for the night, say, *in a van*, or *on a porch?*"

They said that they had an extra bed in their cabin and I was welcome to use it if I pitched in for the rent. I readily agreed and moved into my new lodging. After dinner, I learned that this motorcycle group meets regularly to ride some of America's best trails. One of the men is a professional remote controlled car driver. He gets flown all over the world to drive toy cars in television commercials.

The next morning, I awoke with the bikers at 6 a.m. as they were saddling up for a big day and I was going to go for the gold, trying to reach Crested Butte, which lay 43 miles and several summits away. With the early start, I was able to get in ten miles before my mind really woke up and realized what the rest of me was doing. Reaching the summit of Crystal Peak I passed some abandoned pioneer cabins. At one settlement, a couple was taking a break from their hike. When we exchanged plans for the day, this day-hiker laughed in disbelief of me.

"Crested Butte! HA! Well, you'll be getting there in the dark." Then he said, "Hell, I could get in my truck and drive there in an hour."

At that point I said, "Oh, was that your white Dodge truck I saw being towed away two hours ago?"

"That's okay," he tried to comeback, "it's insured and it's got a security alarm, too." I could see right through his counterfeited ambivalence. This guy would be stuck without his vehicle.

I was actually appreciative of this person for he gave me the drive to really want to make it to town now. Up and over Crystal Peak, I ran through the best wildflower display of the entire trip. Tiny fireworks of wildflowers all around my ankles swept past my feet while my eyes were drinking in the continuous panoramic views. Peak after uninterrupted peak for as far as the eye could see and everywhere I looked was green. The mountains may not have offered a touchable exactness like man-made monuments that I often craved, but the feeling of rich, unspoiled beauty in it's most perfect state was an entirely new memory burned into my conscious.

Ascending the mountain and within 15 miles of town, I encountered a rainstorm. Ducking underneath a pine tree to avoid the rain, I took a break and was eating a pack of crackers when a man hiked past me, unaware of my presence.

"Hello," I called to him. He looked but didn't see me. "Under here, under the tree."

We met and I asked if I could join him on his hike down the mountain. As we started crossing a field, it started lightening, and we decided to run across the field. We ran the fields and hiked through the trees, catching up on what we were doing in between. I learned that my new friend is a doctor in Crested Butte, and he volunteers to manage a winter cabin during the summer. He was just coming back from checking up on it when I met him.

The good doctor offered me a ride into town after arriving at his retrofitted mini-van with jacked up suspension and oversized tires.

"Thanks, but no thanks."

He then offered to put me up in his home for the night when I did arrive in town. In the heavy rain, I ran through a large Bureau of Land Management area with a free camping limit of 14 days. There were small communities of cars, with curtains in the windows, tents outside, and clothes on lines getting wet. I assumed the encampments belonged to the many teen-age drifters that frequent Crested Butte and its famed mountain biking trails. I finished my 43-mile day at 5 pm, *not* in the dark, as had been predicted by the pessimistic day-hiker I'd met earlier.

Upon calling my new acquaintance, he gave me directions to his house. Soon I was set up in an office on the third floor of his home, overlooking the town and surrounding mountains. After dark, I had an unhindered view of the stars through a large skylight. That evening, the family took me along to a dinner party.

The evening was great and everyone was very nice. We feasted on fresh grilled salmon, a huge salad, corn on the cob, and steamed vegetables. During dinner, they learned that I had just finished a big day of running and kept passing the food down my way. I learned that the party hosts actually lived in Point Reyes, California, where I would be finishing my run in a few months. They were renting a home in Crested Butte, and they gave me a cotton t-shirt that said, "Point Reyes," just to keep me going.

The following morning I went to the Post Office. After having called Gregory about their leaking water bladders, they agreed to send me two replacement bladders overnight to the Crested Butte Post Office. I picked those up, along with some Power Bars from Dick Bratton, and some homemade cookies from Sue, his girlfriend.

Leaving town with a very heavy pack, I began climbing up Schoffield Pass. My last taste of civilization was Mt. Crested Butte, a ski resort overlooking the town of Crested Butte below. Soon, I was past this community as well and the road turned to dirt, continuing upward.

Chapter 24
The Red Kayak

Finally at the summit of the pass, I was able to look down on "Devil's Punchbowl." This was one section that Reese Lukei had warned me about. He said it often was snow-covered year-round. He was right. There was snow here, but at this time of year it was less than 30 yards wide. The dirt road continues over the pass but the hill is banked just enough that snow on the road has caused many cars attempting to drive over it roll down the bank, crushing the occupants inside. Several dozen people have died trying to drive over this narrow patch of snow.

August snow crossing treacherous Schofield Pass near Mount Crested Butte, Colorado.

With this on my mind, I tiptoed over the slippery snow pass with caution. I was grateful to be on foot an not in a car but it would have meant a long slide down a hill had I lost my footing. Once on the other side, I began the long descent to the historic mining towns of Gothic, Crystal, Marble, and Redstone.

I approached a group of 20 young women taking a break on the side of the road. "Eureka! I've found it! The lost paradise," I thought. To my disappointment, they said nothing to me so I continued past them. Later, while passing a lake, a dog ran up to me and bit me on the hand. It was only the second dog bite I'd ever received and neither time did the owner apologize for his dog's actions. The owner assured me that the dog had received his shots.

The next town I came to was Crystal, which is home to the most picturesque mill I had ever seen. Over 100 years old, the vacant dilapidated structure hangs on precariously to the edge of a sheer 30-foot cliff as it has since it's bustling days when the mill was in operation. In front of the mill is a dramatic waterfall with a mountain stream flowing underneath the structure. Pushing on, I wanted to make it to the town of Marble, known for being home to the stone used in the "Tomb of the Unknown Soldier," as well as much of the stone used in the Washington Monument.

Between the two towns, I came to a line of parked cars in the middle of this remote stretch of road. It was an unlikely sight, seeing as how this was a mostly dead-end road, very narrow and extremely rough. People standing by their cars indicated something up ahead had been holding up traffic for some time. Many times I had run past construction while cars were forced to wait and I prided myself with being able to move faster than vehicles on occasion. Approaching the commotion at the top of a hill, I noticed an ambulance, stretcher, lots of paramedics, and a man on the ground. Deciding not to get in the way, I retreated to the line of cars where I later learned that a man had suffered a heart attack while hiking with a group of inner-city kids. When I learned that, I felt bad for trying to get past the "interruption in traffic," and waited an hour for them to clear the scene.

Once the road was re-opened, I continued down the pass now into sunset when I came to a bed and breakfast in Marble. Inquiring about rooms and rates, I asked if they offered the "transcon rate." Upon hearing my question, the woman exclaimed, "Oh, is your name Brian Stark? There's a note in town on a telephone pole for you!"

I thanked her, not having any idea what she was talking about. Dick Bratton, the media machine, had tried to secure me free lodging in a nice hotel in Redstone, a little further down the road. The desk clerk told him that they were booked solid but then the clerk began asking Dick what this was all about. The clerk and his friend, a co-worker, had taken a year off from college and were living in the mountains, working in the hotel to pay bills and enjoying a break from school. When this clerk heard that I was looking for a place to stay in the area, he generously invited me to stay in his rented cabin with his friend. I, of course, did not know this, and they had no way of contacting me. So they made a huge sign on a piece of poster board that read, "Brian Stark, come to the house with the red kayak."

When I got into town I saw the sign and, turning right, saw the house with the watercraft balanced against the roof. Knocking on the door of the home I still knew nothing about, the two guys greeted me saying, "Hi Brian, come on in!"

**Without any other means of contact,
the hosts posted a notice in town for free lodging.**

They explained how they had heard of me and offered to do my laundry. That night we had a great dinner and I told them tales from the road. During dinner, however, there was a knock at the door.

We heard a loud banging at the door with a young female's voice screaming, "Please open up. This is an emergency!"

Opening it, a young girl was in tears yelling, "Call 911, there's a huge fire across the street. Hurry quick!"

We reached for the phone, dialed the number and tried to describe where the fire was taking place. The fire station was not even three buildings down from the house we were in, so it shouldn't have been difficult for them to locate the fire.

Grabbing the small, disposable fire extinguisher off the wall, we ran over to the fire. Even from the front door of the house, we could clearly see the flames across the street in the campground. We figured it to be a motor home on fire. When we got to the campground, however, we learned the nature of the situation. No recreational vehicle was burning down and no people were in harm's way. There was simply a large campfire burning in a well-secured site. To make matters worse, the party responsible for the campfire was the local fire department and the operator who had answered our call was likely at the fire on a cordless phone the whole time. We stood there, out of breath, with the dinky extinguisher in hand, ready to fight nature's wrath. Apologizing, we slowly returned to the house, but not before meeting with some of the locals in attendance.

One of them, the storeowner, was very impressed with my trip and gave me a donation to help me out. We decided that our mystery girl must have been sent to our house by some overly concerned parents on their way through town. They hadn't stopped to make sure there was a legitimate fire out of control, but instead, told their daughter, who was in hysterics, to go to the nearest house by herself and summon help. It had made for an interesting evening.

The next morning I accompanied both of my hosts to their local church service, which, I was surprised to find, had a near-full congregation. My hosts stood up during "Prayers and Concerns" and introduced me to the congregation and asked people to pray for my safety during the remainder of my trip. Afterwards I got to meet much of the congregation outside while eating cookies and drinking lemonade.

After church, my hosts had to go to work and I still had to run to Redstone. It would be a full day of running so I planned to run to the hotel, take a quick swim in the pool, get a ride back to their cabin after their shift, and finally be returned to the hotel the next morning to resume my run.

It was a long gentle downhill the whole day into Redstone. That night, they threw a going away party at their home for a co-worker. These guys prided themselves on making really good food. During the party, I enjoyed trying to play my small harmonica while they chimed in with a guitar.

The next morning when they dropped me off in Redstone, I was to begin an 80-mile stretch of trail with no available food or lodging. I assumed I could find water either at ranches or treat it from streams. A local sheriff's deputy had heard that I would be coming through his area, and he offered to help me out. We agreed to meet mid-way into this 80-mile stretch, at the junction of two forest roads at 6 p.m. I would be running 38-miles over rough trails and jeep roads. In addition to his law enforcement duties, this man also served on the local search and rescue division. If I didn't show up at 6 he told me, he would call out his buddies with the dogs and helicopters and start looking for me. I usually didn't like such pressure but thanked him for helping me out and looked forward to meeting him that evening.

Leaving Redstone at 6 a.m., I immediately left civilization on a series of trails that I would be following for the next 12 hours. Three miles out of town the second water bladder began leaking. I was alarmed to realize that my only water for the next 80 miles was leaking down my back. I drank as much of it as I dared, topped off my bottles, and inverted the bladder once again to conserve my supply. Within six miles, I was losing the trail. My maps were adequate but the trails crossed so many cattle fences with no signs or markers that it made distinguishing hiking trails from cattle trails impossible. Using my compass, maps, and educated guesses, I chose a path and stuck to it.

Several miles later, I was bushwhacking up the side of a mountain. This was not good. I considered backtracking but knew that there were too many trails to keep picking a new one and taking it until it dead-ended.

Continuing ahead, I held my compass and tried to continue on a straight line, hoping to intersect the trail later in the day. After rounding the side of the mountain, I could plainly see three more summits ahead of me.

Bushwhacking through such pine forests is very difficult, even without a large backpack. Negotiating deep valleys with numerous fallen trees with branches still intact was like trying to pass through a tall cornfield with stalks made of jagged broomsticks. Growing in the places where a tree had not fallen were neck-high prickly weeds that snagged my legs and stuck to my socks. If I had fallen in this section, I knew there would have been no way anyone would have found me.

Shaking off the fear that this might literally be the end of my journey, I shifted to worrying about the logistics of my rendezvous. I knew I was losing precious time to meet my contact that evening and the last thing I wanted was a full-blown search for me before I needed it. Several miles down the valley I spied a paved road. Surely that could take me somewhere, I thought. After four hours of navigating this massive thicket, I reached the road only to learn that it was an access road to an abandoned mine. Traffic hadn't actively used this road in over 40 years!

Whenever you want to reach civilization, I was told always to keep going downhill and eventually you'll end up somewhere where there is help. I stuck to this and eventually came to a small settlement that belonged to the mining operation. Touring the now empty buildings, I searched for a pay phone, radio, or other means of calling out. The only hint of technology was the wiring, now leading to pointless destinations, their outlets having been stripped away years ago.

Continuing down the road, I was finally met by two older couples in a large truck. It was raining at this point, and I tried not to convey that I had just gone through a potentially life-threatening experience.

"Excuse me," I said as I flagged them down, "I'm running across the United States, and I'm supposed to be on a series of trails that will lead me to Grand Mesa. I'm lost and wondered if you could tell me where any established trails might be."

"We don't know, there isn't anything around here," the driver said, as he rolled up his window and continued to drive up the mountain, leaving me standing on the side of the jeep road.

I knew he had to have come from somewhere so I kept running downhill. Eight miles later, I arrived at the junction of this mining road and the highway, right in front of the entrance to the city of Redstone, precisely where I had started ten hours earlier. By abandoning my compass bearing to follow streams downhill and eventually this road, I had just completed a 25-mile loop. I now had an hour and a half to get 38 miles away before the military was called out to start a million dollar rescue that would be billed to me. What was I to do?

I stuck out my thumb. A man in a pick-up truck pulled over and asked where I was headed. I didn't even know how to get to this place by car, so to makes things easier, said that I was just going to the top of the mountain where the highway made a pass. At the top he asked if this was really where I had wanted to go and I explained that I really needed to go quite a bit further down a dirt road leading off the highway. He offered to drive me, "a little further."

We kept going until, after two hours of bouncing down a bumpy forest road, he had delivered me to my prearranged meeting spot with the officer. There was no one to be seen. The driver said he needed to be getting home. I thanked him over and over for taking me all that way and after he turned down my offer for gas money, he drove off. I looked at my watch. I was 45 minutes late for our meeting. Without seeing the sheriff, I assumed he had waited 30 minutes and decided to push the red button, make the call on the special phone, or whatever they do to start those massive search efforts.

After thirty seconds of standing on that small dirt road, I saw a vehicle approaching from the east. As it got closer, I could tell it was a sheriff's vehicle. The officer pulled up, got out of his car and said, "Sorry I'm late, I had to take a carjacker to the station. How was your day?"

He didn't even know I was late!

"Oh, fine," I said, "No problem," not able to form complete sentences in my tremendous relief that everything was now going to be okay.

"Great. Well, here's a chicken dinner I brought for you. I thought you might be a bit hungry after that big day. I also brought a Gore-Tex pup tent and a 60-degree below zero sleeping bag. I'd suggest you sleep in this horse corral, as there are mountain lions and bears in this area. Just stuff the gear under that cattle ramp in the morning, and I'll pick it up in a few days. Good luck, I gotta go!"

And he was off. I was standing in the middle of the dirt road, with chicken dinner in hand, pup tent and sleeping bag under one arm, and was watching this man drive off into the sunset. I couldn't believe the turn of events!

All night long as I lay in my tent catching up in my journal, chuckling, "Wow, that was crazy."

On television sets all across the country, as I snuggled in my winter bag inside a horse corral forty miles from anything, President Clinton was making his public confession about his affair with an intern. After 25 unofficial miles of bushwhacking, I also had to make my own confession that I had accepted a car ride on my run.

The next day was completely more successful. I didn't make a single wrong turn and reached Weir and Johnson Lakes where I met a friend of the ADT Society, Rick Spelanka. Rick and his son picked me up and drove me to their home in Cedar Edge, Colorado. That night I curbed my appetite with eight tacos and two rounds of ice cream.

The next morning Rick drove me back to the lake, and I continued west. The next night, the owner of Grand Mesa Lodge and Cabins offered to put me up for the night. I arrived there but not before experiencing the Crag Crest National Recreation Trail.

Though only six miles long on its upper half, the Crag Crest is one of the most stunning sections of trail I've seen. Running at 12,800 feet for much of the six miles, the Crag offers panoramic views of the surrounding pine forests with many lakes and the upcoming desert of Utah. The trail followed what is referred to as a "knife edge," where the land drops off on both sides of the trail with a sheer drop-off. One wrong step here and you're a goner for sure.

After checking into my cabin for the night, I was later interviewed by a local reporter. The next morning I ran to the edge of Grand Mesa and began the descent down Lands End Road. This road is a combination of pavement and dirt that winds its way downhill for 15 miles, switch-backing in wide half-mile lengths the entire way. Running one direction downhill for a half-mile, the road took a sharp bend to the left, where I ran the opposite direction for another half-mile. So it went for three hours down this hill. As the road had been sprinkled with light gravel, I would occasionally step on one solitary caramel-sized cube of rock and a pointy side of it would inevitably shoot straight up into the sole of my foot.

Once at the base of the hill, I hit the desert, which I would not leave until near Lake Tahoe some 800 miles later. As had been the case in Marble, Dick had been in action but I had no knowledge of the two hotels with free rooms, reporters, and local runners waiting for my arrival into Whitewater and Grand Junction.

The downhill with all its switchbacks had taken a lot out of me and at the first pay phone I called Judy. She was a trail volunteer in the area who informed me about the lodging arrangements and told me reporters were waiting to meet me. It was a very fast night with interviews, dinner, and bed.

The next morning Judy had arranged for a local runner to join me and show me the trails in the area. We had a good morning's run, and I began thinking about how I was going to handle the upcoming Kokopelli Trail which would take me into Utah. The Kokopelli Trail is 140-mile long mountain bike trail from Loma, Colorado to Moab, Utah. Along the way the trail roughly follows the Colorado River, but it is mostly inaccessible as the water lies over a half-mile down a steep canyon below the trail.

Judy arranged several free hotels for me, which I greatly appreciated. On one of my days off I even ran with a high school cross-country team for a workout!

Leaving Loma, Colorado, I went to a Post Office to pick up my small backpack that my friend Ricky had mailed me. Ricky sent me my small backpack, stove, water bag, and sleeping pad. I bought several days' worth of food at a local grocery store, and then went to a hardware store and filled my fuel bottle with white gas.

My next task was to fill my 2-½ gallon water bag. This last addition increased my pack weight by 20 pounds. My pack was only designed for light day hikes, yet here it was holding well over 40 pounds.

Finally, I had to come up with a plan for more water later on once I was on the trail. The amount I was carrying might take me a day or two, but not a week. I went into "Over the Edge" bike shop and asked if they knew how people got water while on the trail. They said that people usually arranged to have food and water dropped off at predetermined points along the trail. They then told me they were going to support some bikers who were out on the trail and that they'd be happy to drop off several gallons of water for me at two locations. They drew red x's on a map where the water would be waiting for me, and I walked out hoping everything would work out as well as it sounded.

By the time I had made all of the necessary arrangements, I didn't leave Loma until 11 am, nearing the hottest time of the day. The temperature was quickly approaching 100 degrees. After having been spoiled by the cooler temperatures of the Rocky Mountains, I was now suffering as I dealt with the hot arid desert as well as the extra adjustment of my new pack.

My first day on the Kokopelli was a harsh introduction. I only made it 12 miles to the first water stash left by the bike shop. I carried the 1½ gallons they had left me while still carrying over a gallon of water in my pack and proceeded up a steep hill for three miles. At the top I found a primitive campsite overlooking a train tunnel and the distant Interstate 80 to the far north. Seeing the steady stream of headlights was a comforting site. I knew that if things got bad, I could always flag down a car along the interstate for help.

The Kokopelli offered no shade larger than a waist-high shrub. By the second day I had already learned to abide by the rules of the sun. Starting at 5 am, I would speed hike until just past 2 pm when the heat would become unbearable. At that point I would start looking for a large boulder or bush to get under, or a dry streambed. In streambeds, I could sometimes find a rock outcropping where, if I leaned against the stream's bank, I could keep the outcropping just over my head and thus shade most of my body. There I would sit or haunch for three to four hours, until the sun started to set, then I would continue down the trail until 10 pm. It was a very draining experience, but the thought of Moab's many motels and eating establishments, as well as the lure of another state kept me going.

**Utah's Kokopelli Bike Trail offers little shade,
no water, and stunning desert for 140 miles.**

On day number two of the Kokopelli, I made 24 miles to my second, and last, water stash. I had now crossed into Utah but my celebratory feeling was cut short by concern about lack of water. I began devising ways I could get into Moab faster. Reading the Foot's Data book, I read that they had gotten off the Kokopelli Trail at Dewey Bridge and ridden their bikes on a highway into Moab, thus cutting the length of the Kokopelli in half. It seemed like a viable option, and I was certainly bound to have more access to water if I stayed on the highway.

When I arrived at Dewey Bridge I filled my water bottles at a house. After ten miles on the highway I decided to hitch into town for a day of rest. Then I would get another ride back to the spot where I was picked up so that I could run into town.

All of this sounded very good as I'd spent three hot days in the desert with loose sand, steep hills, and an overloaded uncomfortable pack. I quickly secured a ride in the back seat of a small pick-up truck. I was dropped off in Moab and was overcome by the noise, cars, and myriad of places to get smoothies, air-conditioned rooms, and camping gear. My fifth water bladder had sprung a leak on the Kokopelli, and I was determined to do something about the unending problem.

Speaking with Mike at Gearheads camping store in Moab, I explained my predicament. He understood the severity of the situation, especially as I was only just entering the deserts of Utah and Nevada at this point.

He offered to call his contact at Gregory and see if they would be willing to compensate him if he gave me a new pack. They were very nice on the telephone and agreed not only to replace the entire pack for me, but to upgrade me to a larger pack. This was part of Mike's plan to custom-design me a bombproof water pack.

With the larger Gregory pack now donated by the company, Mike took a MSR water bladder that has a thick nylon cover laminated to a thicker plastic lining. He then took some accessory tubing, an MSR shower adaptor kit, and a bite valve mouthpiece. By putting the MSR bladder in the Gregory pack, I now had a system that could hold six quarts of water and was nearly guaranteed to be leak-proof under any activity. Soon after, MSR came out with a very similar version of this system that Mike had pioneered for me.

I thanked him and the representative on the phone and left the store ready to tackle anything, after I had gotten a few days' rest and recovery in a most unlikely place.

Chapter 25
Honey, I'm Home!

The Kokopelli Trail had beaten me up. The combined heat, sun, and lack of food and water had drained me within a matter of days. When I jog-staggered into Moab, I knew it was time for a break. I checked into the Lazy Lizard Hostel on the far south side of town.

Looking at the map during dinner, I realized that Flagstaff, and Lydia for that matter, were only a five hour drive away! Ever since she surprised me in Indiana, I had wanted to get her back. Now was my chance. I checked into renting a car to no avail. My plan was that once I had made it to her house, I would rest up there and catch up in my journal for a few days. I also hoped she would be willing to drive me back to Moab to rejoin the trail. No rental car company would let me drop off a car in Flagstaff without a huge out of state penalty fee, so I decided to go it alone.

Calling a public radio station on my way out of town, I gave a short on-air interview. At the end they asked if there was anything else I'd like to add and I said, "Yes! Today, I am taking a break from my run and trying to get to my girlfriend in Flagstaff. If any of your listeners see a guy in running clothes holding a small sign that says "Flagstaff" on the side of the road, pick him up!"

They said that they would repeat the plug for me throughout the day. As I was hanging the phone up on the receiver outside a gas station, a windowless van pulled up to me. The driver got out and asked if I had just been on the radio.

"Yes! Are you going to Flagstaff?" He said no, but that he was going an hour down the road and would be happy to take me that far. I accepted.

Pete, my driver, was on a furniture shopping road trip with his wife and she had flown home early for work. They had traveled the west in search of new items for their house. Our conversation quickly turned to my trip and tales of other such endeavors. He tipped me off to a great book, "Into the Wild" by John Krackour. The book is the true story about a young college graduate who decided to become a minimalist and head into the woods of Alaska with only a sack of rice and a rifle. After taking up refuge in an abandoned school bus, his body was found by hunters. He had starved to death. Pete had a copy in his van and gave it to me upon dropping me off. Reading that book during my break, I strongly identified with the boy's zest to live without the comforts of civilization, although I believe he took it to an extreme, which eventually cost him his life. Granted, another key difference between him and me was that my sense of adventure on this trip was usually followed by an evening of television with a container of ice cream in hand.

With one ride down, and Flagstaff just four short hours away, I was hopeful for another lift. To satisfy the hole left in our dating during my run, Lydia and I would occasionally set up "phone dates," where we would call each other at a predetermined time. This night was a phone date night and I had agreed to call her at 8 pm wherever I was. My goal was to arrive at her house by 8 with a cell phone in hand and call her from her front porch. Then when she started getting sad at the end of the conversation, I could ask, "Why don't I just come over right now?"

"Okay," she'd say, playing along, whereupon I would surprise her by knocking on the door. That was the plan anyway. Meanwhile I was standing in the middle of Monticello, Utah, 270 miles from that becoming a possibility.

I was hopeful that I could catch a ride at a red light. I stood in the middle of town for an hour. A construction crew was working in the hot sun and one of the workers asked me if I would get her a drink of water. I knew a lot about thirst and was happy to be able to help someone else out for a change. Walking across the street to a pizza shop, I asked for a drink of ice water from behind the counter.

"We can't give that out, Hon'. We gotta charge 25 cents for the cup," the waitress told me.

"Ok, well, a construction worker is repairing the street in front of your shop and she's thirsty so I guess I'll pay you a quarter for that water," I replied.

"Well, aren't you a nice person," she said.

I took the water outside and, having delivered it to the road crew member, decided that perhaps the edge of town might offer better luck for thumbing a ride.

Walking to the south edge of town, I picked a spot with a wide shoulder and plenty of visibility for drivers to see me. In fact, I was standing right in front of a mileage sign. As cars would approach I would point up high to the word "Flagstaff." A small gray pick-up truck soon pulled over, and it turned out to be an Airborne Express delivery truck. There were packages and boxes all over the front seat. "Just go ahead and sit on down young man," the driver told me.

"Are you going to Flagstaff?" I asked.

"No, just about 15 miles further on deliveries, but I'll take you that far," she said.

The land between Moab and Flagstaff is mostly southwestern desert with very small and sporadic communities and the expansive Navajo Indian Reservation. I was nearing this reservation but needed another car ride, and stood on the side of the road.

My next ride also took nearly an hour to get and it was in the back of an open bed pick-up truck. In the cab was a Native American family on their way 60 miles to Mexican Water, Arizona. Now I was getting somewhere. When they dropped me off in town, however, I feared the worst. Few cars were going by this small outpost and it was now 4:30 in the afternoon. I still had 200 miles to go to get to Flagstaff. I would just make our phone date if I got a ride soon.

Panicking, I tried switching sides of the road for more visibility. I was in front of a great gravel parking lot with easy on and off access for anyone trying to pull over for me, but no one was stopping. After waiting an hour for a ride with a dozen cars going by, all with plenty of room inside, I started whining to myself.

"Well, it doesn't get any worse than this," would be one common quote I'd say aloud at this point. Just then, a new black Ford Explorer pulled over, screeching to a halt in the middle of the two-lane road. A young college guy with sport sunglasses rolled down his window.

"Are you going to Flagstaff?" I asked. I had asked the question so many times, it had now become like the kids' book, *Are you my mother?*

An enthusiastic, "yes" came the reply.

"EXCELLENT!" I shouted in the middle of the street as I climbed in. He took off and I began what might be the most interesting ride I've ever received. Derek was in school at Arizona State University but spent most of his free time at his parents' place in Crested Butte. He was on his way back to school from there when he picked me up. In addition to mountain biking and skiing, he has also taken up a few other hobbies. As we rolled down the road at 80 miles per hour, he began telling me of all the pills he had ever taken, which ones are the good ones, which ones are bad. He told me of the time some neighbors called the police on him and his roommates for drug possession and by flushing the toilet a few times, they had barely avoided real trouble.

As the conversation continued, I noticed that we would regularly swerve on the road. Later, I noticed that this swerving was synchronized with Derek's slapping his left arm.

"What do you have there, Derek?" I asked.

"Oh, yeah. I'm trying to quit smoking because it's bad for me. And my doctor hasn't written me a Nicotine Patch prescription yet, so I'm using my friend's old patch until mine comes through. It doesn't stick as well as it used to now though so I have to hit it to keep it against my skin."

As he would slap the patch, however, it seemed to be sending him a small rush of nicotine and that, I believed, was what was causing us to swerve off the road every 46 seconds.

We made really good time. We made it to Flagstaff with an hour to spare. I really wanted to try and find a cell phone for my plan to work, so I paid Derek some gas money and went to a pay phone. Lydia had lots of friends in Flagstaff and I hoped that I could borrow one of their cell phones for the prank. Unfortunately, no one I called was home. Taking a taxi to her cabin, I told the driver not to go right up to the house. I was five minutes early.

Standing in front of her cabin in a Ponderosa Pine forest on the edge of town, I couldn't believe I was actually there. It had been a wild and crazy day. Her car was in the driveway; the lights inside were on. I knew she was home. But now what?

Even without a cell phone I couldn't just knock on the door. After all I'd gone through to surprise her, I had to come up with something, but what? She is usually very good about keeping her doors and windows locked, but I decided to try the doorknob before resorting to knocking. To my astonishment it was unlocked.

"Okay," I thought, "I'll just open the door, and she'll be in the kitchen and see me come in. It'll be great."

Upon walking into the kitchen I did not see her and there was no indication that she had heard me enter from wherever she was.

"Okay, so she'll be in the living room reading. I'll just come around the corner and she'll see me."

She wasn't in the living room either. As I rounded the corner of the kitchen I saw her standing in the bathroom in her pajamas, taking her contacts out, and getting ready for bed. She liked to be ready for bed before our phone dates.

I was standing not five feet away from her and she had no idea that I was in the state of Arizona, in Flagstaff, in her house, within reach. I knew that I shouldn't jump at her or scare her in any way, and, to be truthful, I knew the shock was going to be pretty severe, so I tried to make it as subtle as possible.

I coughed. Not a loud hack, mind you, just a very quiet clearing of the throat. That was it. That's all it took. She shot upright from the sink, let out the wail of a dying animal, spun towards me and started backing up into the shower.

"Waaaaaaaaah. Oh, my gosh, no, No, NO, you're not real!"

At this point she was actually standing in the bathtub, having almost tripped over it on the way in. That would have put a damper on the surprise. It was, to be sure, a huge surprise.

She asked, "How did you get here?"

"Um, well..."

"Did you rent a car?" she continued.

"No. I hitchhiked."

She could not get over that. She was a little upset that I had hitchhiked so far but her happiness that I had arrived and was going to stay for a few days quickly squashed any ill will toward how I'd gotten there. I proceeded to have an excellent break.

Chapter 26
On the Road Again

After a week of visiting Lydia, seeing her family in Phoenix, catching up in my journal, doing laundry, and updating my website, it was time for Lydia to drive me back to Moab. From Moab to western Nevada, I had elected to follow an alternate route of the ADT established by Bill and Laurie on their bike ride a year earlier. The official ADT crosses these two states on very low volume four-wheel drive roads, some trails, and at times cross-country without much of a trail to follow at all. By following the Foot's route, I would be nearer services, and more importantly, would be accessible to the two vehicles helping me.

Both Lydia and my mother had promised me one week each of vehicle support and said that I could use them any time I wanted. I elected to use Lydia's help in western Utah and my mother's across central Nevada. Even though I was on an alternate route, I would still be required to run up to 110 miles between towns, so it by no means was going to be easy.

The alternate route began in Moab. Rather than heading out of town up a single-track trail between two mountains, I would be running down highway 191 towards Blanding. Since Lydia and I were driving this stretch to get back to Moab, we purchased several cases of spring water and left a bottle at every fifth mile marker, to be retrieved when I was running this stretch in a few days.

As we neared Moab I decided to get out and run a few miles north to Moab to take a small bite out of the 53-mile stretch it would take to get to my first services in Monticello. Upon entering Moab we checked in, once again, in the Lazy Lizard hostel, and planned the next few days.

219

An alternate route across Utah and Nevada provided basic services every 100 miles.

The following morning I ran from Moab to Hole 'N the Rock, a huge tourist trap that gives tours of a home that was actually carved into a massive red rock mountain by hollowing out rooms in a cave-like system.

To lessen pack weight, and since I had the convenience of Lydia's support car, I only carried a water bottle in a small holster around my waist. Being used to carrying everything, I felt particularly vulnerable with only a water bottle. Lydia would drive ahead in 10-mile increments and wait for me to catch up. I panicked that she would get tired of waiting for me and would simply drive back to Flagstaff leaving me with only 8 ounces of water and the shirt on my back. She never did, of course, and she was always waiting just up the road for my arrival, but it was interesting how much insecurity I began to feel when someone else was in control of my pack. I tried expressing my concern to Lydia but she laughed off the possibility that she was going anywhere but forward in five to ten mile increments. With that section of the road out of the way, we returned to Moab and went for a day hike in Arches National Park.

The next morning we went to a public radio station. I had talked to them earlier, just as I was getting into the windowless van on my way to Flagstaff. I promised I would come back so I was proving good on my word. The radio station, we found out, was perched on cinder blocks in a trailer at the far edge of town. Hundreds of quotes were scribbled on the ceiling tiles of the tiny DJ booth at one end of the trailer. We did a fun interview and as soon as it was over the telephone light started flashing. The "Star Diner" manager had called and wanted to offer me a free breakfast. After having a great meal, Lydia drove me back out to Hole 'N the Rock where I resumed my run. I would be seeing her again in a few weeks when she came for her "official" vehicle support segment.

But she wouldn't be heading home until she first drove 150 miles of my route, leaving a quart of spring water at every fifth mile marker. I was to find out that at each water bottle, she had also left me snacks sealed in Zip-Lock bags, and often times, a short note encouraging me to keep going. Every five miles for five days I was able to approach a mileage sign, see the footprints of my girlfriend imprinted in the sandy gravel on the shoulder of the road, read a note from her, and mix the Gatorade with the spring water for a refreshing break.

Running through Utah's dramatic Monument Valley.

We had put together a dinner box that she said she would leave for me at Natural Bridges National Monument. Neither of us knew at the time that the actual visitors center at the Monument lay three miles down a long driveway.

When I arrived at the Monument I got a ride from a nice older couple and met Emma, the ranger who had spoken with Lydia. When I met her she informed me that she had some good news and some bad news. The bad news was that the campground was full and that I couldn't camp there. The good news was that she had an extra bed and that I was welcome to stay with her and Ranger Duff, her roommate in a park trailer. More good news, she was just closing the visitor's center and she would be happy to take me on a tour of the Monument.

Driving the loop tour, we pulled over at each of the overlooks and she pointed out the different arches while the sun set on the horizon. That night several of the park employees were getting together at one of the houses for a dinner party and to watch old episodes of "The X Files" on video tape. Ranger Duff invited me to join them and I had a great evening with my new friends.

Ranger Duff spun tales of life as a park ranger. He told me of the time he came across a self-proclaimed group of Virgin Atheist Monks. I also learned of the dumb things people have done that have resulted in pet disasters in National Parks, stories of dogs falling to their death off cliffs and people deciding to go for a "short walk" in Death Valley, not realizing how far away things really are out there. I enjoyed being included in this closely-knit group of rangers and hearing their tales.

Leaving Natural Bridges I set my sights on Fry Canyon, a remote outpost offering simple rooms and a restaurant, miles from anywhere. Lydia had stopped in a week earlier and had arranged to get me a good discount. I arrived after having run a full day in the rain.

My next stop would be Hite, Utah. The best thing I found about highway running was the treasure hunting to be had on the shoulder. South of Moab I came across a mountain bike that had apparently fallen off the top of a vehicle, where it must have flipped many times on the pavement, then been run over by a battalion of semi-trucks as no piece of the bike remained more than three inches long. The entire thing was still wired together with its brake and derailleur cables into a tangled mess of spokes, metal, and shiny scratched tubing.

Leaving Fry Canyon and stopping at my next stash of water, I was staring down at the footprint my girlfriend had made almost a week earlier. Out of the corner of my eye I saw a film canister wedged inside the metal post of the mile marker. Picking it up, I opened the canister to inspect its contents. Inside, I found it half-filled with red sand and a small note written in pen on a scrap piece of paper that read, "5/10/96. All is well." It seemed like a very strange thing to leave at a mile marker in the desert and I wondered if it belonged to someone with a story like Chris McCandless, the boy of *Into the Wild*, who left indications of his whereabouts all across the country that were later pieced together after his body was found. Jotting down the mileage, contents of the canister, and date in my journal, I returned the canister where I found it and continued on, hopeful that someday the mystery might be solved.

I arrived in Hite at the marina to pick up my next pair of shoes. A girl came out from a phone booth asking if I was Brian Stark. Picking up my mail the girl invited me to stay in her trailer for the night along with her five male roommates. Housing was getting more interesting by the day! We cleared out a storage room in the trailer and then I joined them in their daily ritual of arrowhead hunting in the nearby area. We finally retreated to the trailer to watch free videos from the store. That evening after the two-day storm passed over, there was a spectacular double rainbow over the valley.

The next morning I left Hite again in the rain. It was a heavy rain and the accumulated water over the last several days had resulted in some massive desert flash flooding. All around me on both sides of the paved highway rivers of red chocolate water were flowing towards Lake Powell. Crossing the Hite Bridge, I was treated to an amazing view of the Colorado River a half-mile below.

As I left the Colorado River valley, I was running through a cut in the rock. On both sides of the road, so much water was spilling over the edge and into the road's gutters, that it was carrying large rocks and small boulders with it. These rocks would hit the gutters and actually bounce onto the road with alarming force. I was finally convinced to run in the middle of the highway to avoid being hit by boulders crashing in the waterfalls.

Later in the morning at Hog Springs Shelter, a roadside picnic area, my note from Lydia said, "Hog Springs Picnic Area: Under last railroad tie in parking lot." It was so much fun running in the middle of nowhere, being thirsty, and knowing that under the upcoming mileage sign was a cool drink of water with a bag of drink powder and perhaps a cookie waiting for me amidst the Ragweed, sand, and Juniper Trees.

I only had one more bottle past Hog Springs. It was 48 miles from Hite to the next town of Hanksville, Utah. I didn't want to try and make that in one day without regular meals and rest.

Ten miles past my last water bottle, I was running out of energy. I decided to hitch into town and come back out the next day, as I had done before. After trying to hitch for an hour, and being passed by hoards of boaters on their way back from the lake, I gave up and figured I'd better start the long walk.

A mile after I had given up getting a ride, a black Honda Accord pulled over. Two Hacky Sacks and a Frisbee flew out the window at me! Just as I was wondering what was going on, I figured out who was in the car. Uri Grubbs and Kevin Glenn, two of the most colorful people I know and friends from Camp, had just finished a summer season and, hearing that I might be in a remote section, decided to drive out from Indiana to try and find me somewhere in Utah. After two and a half days of driving, they had intercepted my route, at a time when I couldn't have needed them more.

Getting in their car, we drove to Hanksville and I got a room for the three of us at a motel. The next morning I made up the section we had skipped and they accompanied me for a week, meeting me throughout the day to bring me peanut butter and jelly sandwiches and water.

Throughout each day Uri and Kevin would drive off and sightsee while I kept making miles. During one of those days I came upon a Mexican-style woven purse on the side of the road. Inside, I found a driver's license of a woman from Fort Collins, Colorado, a Visa card and $145 in cash. It was quite a good find, especially when compared to my usual loot of random socket drives, scratched CDs, and single work gloves.

I called information from the next town and got the woman's number. Calling her, I spoke with her roommate who said that the woman wasn't in but that she had lost her purse while on a motorcycle trip with her boyfriend. I told her to relay the message not to worry and that I would me mailing it back the next day. To my surprise I never heard back from the owner. However, fate and karma have a way of surprising you when you least expect it.

A few nights later as Uri, Kevin and I were eating dinner in Otter Creek State Park, a man at another table in the restaurant started up a conversation with us. Upon hearing of my trip, he came up to me outside after the meal.

"Brian, I'd like to ask you a personal question, if you don't mind."

"Go right ahead," I said with a chuckle having no idea what he was about to ask.

"How are you funding this trip you're on?" I told him that I had saved money by living in a log cabin, teaching, and living on a modest budget.

He said, "That's great. I'd like to help you out with your cause," and he proceeded to press a $100 bill into my hand.

From our conversation during dinner I learned that he was a carpenter. He traveled around the country with a mobile home manufacturer. When the homes are delivered to the building site, he would go inside and tape the drywall of the two units together. I knew he wasn't wealthy, and I even tried to give him his money back, but he insisted.

Instances of generosity like that overwhelmed me. This man had asked for nothing in return. He had simply heard of my dream and wanted to help me make that dream a reality. It didn't take many instances like this one to realize that I was no longer doing this trip just for myself; I realized that many people were vicariously fulfilling some personal dreams of their own by supporting me.

While passing through the small towns of Loa and Bicknell, Uri and Kevin had made a friend at the local library. The librarian was very excited that I would be coming through town and suggested that I give a presentation to the local junior high school across the street. I readily agreed and, after she contacted the school, the principal came over to meet me. I suppose he wanted to check me out and make sure I didn't have an ulterior message other than to follow your dreams, get outside, and exercise. I gather our meeting went well because an hour later he had assembled the entire school in the gymnasium for an hour-long convocation on the benefits of cross-country running.

On another day I ran through the middle of Capitol Reef National Park. The park sits in a luscious valley fed by streams and sheltered by canyon walls. Inside the park historic fruit orchards are maintained by the park service but you can pick and pay for the fruit on the honor system. Inside each high-fenced orchard (to keep the deer out) you can pick what you want from apple, plum, peach, and apricot trees, weigh them on the scale and deposit your money into the metal box bolted to a table. We picked four pounds of apples, enjoying them throughout the week.

One of the pastimes my friends had been entertaining themselves with as I ran, I came to learn, was a game they made using a plastic gun and a single suction-cupped dart that shot out of it. The game was to shoot the other guy, retrieve the dart back and shoot him again. If the recipient of the dart was able to keep the dart, and then somehow get the gun as well, then he could shoot the other person. This might be a good time to point out that they played this game at all hours of the day, including the middle of the night as we typically shared a three-person dome tent, when other lodging was not available.

The toy gun game was appropriate for this section of trail because the next landmark in Reese's book came near Junction, Utah. Butch Cassidy's home lay just six miles south in the town of Circleville and we drove to see it. The large yellow welcome sign was no longer at the site like it was in the picture. We drove down the driveway towards the dilapidated cabin. I had expected the house to be a historical site with tours, furniture, and a docent answering questions about Butch's first suspension from school. What we found, however, was another letdown on my tour of interesting places to photograph. The cabin was still there, but the floor was missing. No trace of any life remained. The chinking had worn away. The roof leaked, and I don't even recall seeing a chimney or a stovepipe. We took a picture anyway, posing with the dart gun for historical representation.

My renegade road crew with cell phones and dart guns. Cassidy never had it so good.

The only thing that now lay between Beaver, Utah and us was Beaver Mountain and 39-miles of a narrow mountain road. I began the long ascent. Mid-way up the mountain I reached the milepost marking that I had run 3,800 miles and only had 1,000 miles to go. It was quite a great feeling to finally go from quadruple digits down to triple digits remaining in the run. "Only 999 to go," I thought.

Midway to Beaver I got in the support car and we drove to Beaver where we got a motel room for a last night with my friends. They had decided to head home the next day, as Lydia would be joining me soon.

The next morning Uri and Kevin drove me back up the mountain to resume the run into Beaver. I said goodbye to them and thanked them for making the long drive. I told them that I didn't feel I would have been able to make it that far without them. They said that they had enjoyed their time out west, and they would tell everyone at home hello for me. Closing the car door, they drove down the bumpy mountain road one last time, headed for home.

Chapter 27
Viva Las Vegas

After entering Beaver for the second time, I checked into a motel by myself and went about looking for a birthday present for Lydia. She would be arriving the next day and I felt bad for not having planned a better gift for her than whatever lay in Beaver. I had assumed that the town would offer the usual assortment of department stores, shops and perhaps a mall. (This was my first experience in the west, and my assumptions were a bit naive.)

My choices became obviously few. With some creativity I found a string of sunflower lights in a variety store, since she grew up collecting them. Then at an electronics store I purchased a car stereo for her because she only had a radio and out in the remote desert, there were bound to be very few stations. I even found all the tools required to install the stereo at a flea market. On my way back to the hotel I stopped at a florist and had an arrangement made for the room. Prepared at last, I said to myself.

The next day Lydia showed up, and I went to meet her at her car. On the dash, I noticed that the faceplate on her existing radio looked different from the one I bought and realized that my gift was not going to fit in her car. I told her about my mistake and she said she understood and that she loved the flowers and sunflower lights, but I felt I had bombed the whole event.

After running to Milford where we celebrated her birthday dinner at a local Chinese restaurant, I covered 35 miles entering the long series of mountains and valleys that I would become accustomed to as I made my way across the remainder of Utah and Nevada.

Finding a nice camping site in the saddle of a mountain, Lydia parked her car, got her bike out and rode back to bicycle alongside me. An hour later, we met up in the middle of a 30-mile wide valley.

We continued traveling and camping and meeting each other in valleys for the next several days. Each day people slowed down in their cars to ask me what I was doing or if I needed help. In between the curious passersby and meeting Lydia, I was able to take in the active but subtle desert life out in this vast land where I could see so much.

The low foliage allowed me to see anything taller than a few feet, and the stillness of the place allowed me to notice small movements even very far away. I was able to spot antelope, coyote, eagles, hawks, lizards, rattlesnakes, and perhaps a mountain lion though it was only a glimpse.

Lydia continued to scout out secluded places for us to camp between the towns that were now 80 miles apart. One day after leaving me to search out that night's camping spot, she came back two hours later, frustrated that she hadn't been able to find a good spot close to the road but protected from view. When camping next to a highway with traffic at all hours, it's hard to feel secluded when the highest object in the desert is lower than your kneecap.

So after a 32-mile day, we arrived at the car, found a dirt road and drove down it for ten miles, until we were sure we were far enough away from the highway. Setting up camp on the side of this primitive lane, we quickly cleaned up, prepared dinner, and went to bed.

"Camp Lydia" somewhere along Highway 50 in Nevada.

The next morning, while getting out of bed, I heard Lydia outside getting very excited.

"Ooh, Brian! Come here!" As I was dealing with the usual stiffness in my legs, I could only imagine what was so exciting that I had to dash out of the tent to see at that moment. Upon inspecting our campsite for any foul play in the night, Lydia discovered that a coyote had visited our site as we slept and had defecated on an area where she had earlier gone to the bathroom. She told me that she had read somewhere that this meant the coyote was sending us a message that it accepted us. Lydia said that she felt this showed our connection with nature. I took a less "Pocahontas" point of view and figured it was a sign to get off someone's turf.

Perhaps it was a sign for me that this would be a very noteworthy day of my run. Over the course of the day I ran my 4,000th mile of the trip; I crossed into Nevada, my 12th state; and I celebrated my 200th day on the trail. All this I would get to share with my partner. I was really excited. But since Lydia had not suffered through all of the long hot miles, cold nights, and meager meals of crackers, she was not as enthusiastic about the special mile mark and merely watched me take pictures of myself at each major landmark throughout the day. At one point during a rest stop, I got into the car and sat quietly in the passenger seat sipping Gatorade.

"What's the matter?" Lydia asked me, sensing something was bothering me.

"Oh nothing, I just ran my 4000th mile and you didn't even get out of the car to take a picture of me." It would have been hard for anyone to have been able to share what I was feeling at that moment, but the realization that I really was alone to deal with the emotional challenge of this trip became clear as even she failed to realize the power of such seemingly trivial statistics. She apologized but gave me a little dose of reality as well, reminding me that she had taken a week off of work to drive across the desert in five-mile increments in a non-air-conditioned radio-only car and that if that didn't show committed support, I could cross the desert alone. She had made a good point.

Feeling proud to finally be in Nevada and to have survived Utah, we entered Garrison, the first town in Nevada on Highway 50. At a country store I met a man who had just run in the Wasatch 100-mile trail run near Salt Lake City. As I ran away from the store, he slowed down beside me in his truck and handed me a Power Gel pack, saying, "Keep truckin'!" I would be running along the shoulder of Highway 50 for 350 miles, billed by Life Magazine as "The Loneliest Road In America," so I hoped I would be trucking to make the miles go quickly.

Most people are unaware that Nevada has more mountains than any other state in the nation. All of these mountains are aligned into chains that generally run north south. By crossing the state east west, you are guaranteed to cross each of them. In between each of these mountain chains lie valleys varying in length from 15 to 35 miles. During these long stretches of road you can see your destination the entire day. The road is a narrow ribbon stretching straight ahead and ascending the mountain before you. When a car approaches, you can see it coming from four miles away and watch it grow bigger since it takes over five minutes to finally pass you.

The entire time I could imagine the driver staring at me bobbing on the side of the road, wondering what I was as I neared him. Was I an animal? Surely I would run off the road at any moment. Why wasn't I running away yet? Then, when they noticed I was a human, they likely became even more curious. I had many cars just slow down next to me, driving along side me for minutes at a time. When you pass less than one car every 20 minutes, there's not too much traffic to watch out for.

"Hey there!" they might say to me.

"Hi."

"Where you headed?"

"California."

"Wow, where'd you start?"

"Delaware." With that, most decided that I had been enough of this valley's entertainment and resumed their 65 miles per hour pace across the desert, but not before leaving me with some salutation like, "Better you than me!"

Later during the day's run, I passed a pair of bicycle riders. Behind them I saw four more, then three more after that. Eventually there was a steady stream of about 100 riders in all. I later found out they were riding across Nevada. Even though they seemed surprised to pass a man running on the highway in Nevada, none of them stopped to talk to me. Instead, they just each asked a question or made a comment as they went by.

Rather than trying to explain my whole trip to them as they flew by in the opposite direction, I tried to vary my answers so that later that night while they were sitting around the dinner table talking about, "that guy," they could put together my trip from the different responses.

"He told me he is from Indiana," one might say.

"I heard he's running 5000 miles!" would come from another.

"He told John he's been gone for eight months!"

The final rider in the line said to me as she passed, "There goes the loneliest runner on the loneliest road in America."

After a day of running, we retreated to Great Basin National Park and camped at one of the pine-forested campsites at a chilly 10,000 feet. Great Basin makes the unique claim to being host to Nevada's only glacier. We took a tour of Lehman Caves in the park the following morning and our tour guide enjoyed hamming up the historical recreation, speaking with a false-Scottish accent and pretending we were all tourists who'd made long carriage rides to the park from far off places.

Taking her Mag-Lite flashlight off her long cotton dress and pointing it onto me she said, assuming I was the typical vacation tourist, "And you sir, how long did it take you to get to Lehman Caves?"

I was dying to say, "200 days on the dot, but you can't really count six of those days because I was recovering in Flagstaff after coming across the Utah desert," but it is unfair to steal the show of a two hour tour within the first five minutes, especially when the guide was having such fun with her character portrayal. So Lydia and I just stood there giggling in response.

The next night we made it to Ely, Nevada and stayed at the very inexpensive and historic Hotel Nevada. Still trying to make up for her birthday gift gone awry, I visited a Radio Shack where I was able to buy her a tape player that plugged into her cigarette lighter.

Our plan all week had been to camp as much as possible. Then at the end of the week when my mom was going to fly out to take Lydia's place, we would drive to Las Vegas to meet her at the airport. We accomplished this goal and arrived a night early to take in the city.

A word of caution to those considering a trip to Vegas: Even though I'd heard of the thousands of rooms in town, DON'T go there on a weekend without reservations! To reward ourselves after so much camping and eating out of a cooler, we decided to stay in one of the bigger hotels. We tried the Luxor. They only had smoking rooms for $130. The MGM Grand with 5005 rooms: booked solid. Caesar's Palace: Sorry. We finally found a "deal" at the Holiday Inn Boardwalk for $100.

The next morning we drove to the airport to meet my mother. She was very glad to see me and gave me a long hug. It was sad saying goodbye to Lydia but we both knew it would only be a few weeks before we would see each other again on the beach of the Pacific Ocean. After lunch we picked up my mother's rental car and said our final goodbye to Lydia. My mom and I then made the four-hour drive back to Ely and a hotel for the night. I could feel big miles ahead!

Chapter 28
Hail Mom!

The first morning with my mother, we left Ely and she drove me out of town to mile marker 51 on Highway 50 where I had stopped running with Lydia. After dropping me off, my mother said she was going to go back to Ely to buy a few provisions for the week. We agreed to find each other in three hours or so.

It was always easy finding me on US Highway 50, since there's no place I could go unless she happened to drive by while I was off the road at a pit stop.

Mom had taken longer than expected and when she found me, I had already completed 20 miles without a single break. I had come quite a long way from the first days of my trip where I could only run for 15 minutes at a time. Pulling off the road at my mom's parked Olds 88 rental Town Car, I snacked on Pringles, some more of Grandmother's cookies sent by special delivery, a banana, and some Gatorade. While I ate, my mom showed me some of the other provisions she had acquired in town.

From the back seat she produced two folding lawn-chairs. The best was yet to come. In addition to the lawn chairs she also purchased a nylon sun umbrella with a plastic c-clamp that affixed to the armrest of the lawn chair. It was a novelty and looked pretty silly, especially on the shoulder of Highway 50, but I agreed that it might be nice to sit under some shade on my breaks and thanked her for it. She had also brought me a Big Mac from McDonald's, but the two slabs of beef spread with special sauce didn't look inviting in the middle of a hot day of running.

After my snack and short break, I still felt surprisingly fresh and told her that I'd like to do at least 10 more miles and that I would see her that far up the road. Packing up the lawn chairs, she told me to be careful and drove off. After the quick ten miles and a snack I still felt good. Perhaps it was the excitement of switching support crews, or letting my mother experience what I had been doing all summer, but after another break, I decided to go another ten, making for a 40-mile day.

My mom was astonished at the amount of ground that I was able to cover and afterwards we drove west to Eureka, Nevada, which has billed itself as, "The Loneliest Town on the Loneliest Road in America." There was definitely a lonely theme going on out there.

We stayed in Eureka for the first of two nights as we base-camped from the town. The first hotel we checked into had hair on the pillow and my mom promptly decided that we could not stay there. Driving across the street we got a much nicer room at a brand-new Best Western for twice the price, but with a giant hot tub and a very nice continental breakfast.

Driving east I was dropped off 15 miles outside of town where I had stopped the day before. Life is so much easier on the road with support. You only carry a water bottle, versus a 10-20 pound pack, snacks come at regular intervals and in any desired quantity, and there is no stress to worry about where you will end up each day because with a car, you can always drive anywhere you want. The only downside to a support vehicle is that little guy in your consciousness who keeps reminding you whenever you get tired that you can pause the game and get into the car, calling it quits at any time. I had tried this once with Lydia.

I had been running greater miles than normal and even though I was not carrying the large pack, the accumulated miles over several days in a row began to take their toll. On the next to last day with Lydia, I was very tired and, although I never considered quitting the entire run, on this day, as with several others, I decided to cut it short. Getting into the car at a rest break and not leaving, Lydia looked at me and asked, "What's going on?"

"Well, I'm really tired, and I think I'll stop here for today and pick up the rest tomorrow."

"No, you're not," came her reply. "I'm here to support you in your run, now get out there and do it!"

I suppose I loved her for that, although at the same time I was a bit upset. How could she know what I was feeling? Maybe I really was tired and needed a break. 4000 miles is a long way to run! After all, shouldn't I be able to listen to my body at this point? I did get out and squeak out another eight miles before she let me stop. It had been another good day of running.

My mom, however, was a different story. Mothers are assigned to watch out for their children's best interests and, while she wholly supported me on this run, she was always making sure I wasn't hurting myself or running beyond my means. My scheduled progress across Nevada with my mother was a serious undertaking. With her help and lots of luck, I would just barely make it to the other side of the state before she had to return to work. If I got injured or sick during the week, it would mean having to go across the most remote part of the desert alone.

Mom gives me a shoulder to rest on.

After running into Eureka and having my picture taken in front of various "Loneliest" signs, I was back out into the open desert. My second day with my mother ended up being 37 miles. I had fantasized about running 40 miles a day for a week with her, making for a 280-mile week. I found, however, that as the week wore on, I was slowly breaking down over the accumulated mileage. The third day was 35 miles. At the end of that day we drove ahead again, this time 45 miles to Austin for the night. We based out of Austin for three nights while I ran 32-mile days. Now I was really feeling the mileage, and each day I was slower to get out of bed.

The high school in Austin had Internet access, and I offered to speak to the students and hopefully check my e-mail. The elementary school heard I was in town and asked if I could come speak to them before I went to the high school. I was happy to do this and they assembled the entire school from kindergarten through fifth grade into their common area. Total enrollment: 36 students.

They also had very good questions.

"Mr. Stark, what happens if you break your leg?" a second grader asked.

"Well, hopefully I'll be near a house or a passing car where I can get help."

"What about sunscreen?" a third grader surprised me with.

"Oh, yes, I forgot to pull that out. Thank you!"

After the elementary school my mom drove me to the high school for my second presentation. The high school was a much larger facility. Every student except the senior class had been assembled into one social studies room. Total attendance: 42. The students were a good audience but surprisingly, I spent most of the presentation simply trying to convince them that I was actually running across the United States. The idea was too far out for some of them to comprehend.

Austin, Nevada: One of the many school presentations along the way.

With a late start to the day, I had to get in 30 miles by nightfall, and I just barely finished before the sun set and my reserves ran dry. We retreated to our last night in Austin.

The next morning I was dreading having to go out on the road again. If my declining mileage was any indication of my abilities, I was in for a sub 30-mile day for sure. I felt pretty good for the first 15 miles and upon meeting my mom sitting on the shoulder in her lawn chair reading her novel and waving to honking truckers, I told her to push ahead eight more miles. Starting down the shoulder with only a water bottle, I watched her drive away, where I would meet her at the Hickison Petroglyph site later in the morning.

As soon as she was out of sight, black clouds rolled in overhead. A cold wind picked up and a chilly rain began to fall. As the wind picked up the rain turned to hail! If I had been wearing my hip pack, the storm would have been welcomed because I had braved the cold before with my meager wardrobe. But the only supply around my waist was my water bottle.

When the first large piece of hail hit my arm I shouted, "Ouch! That hurt!" Then another one pelted me, "OW! Stop that!" The hail's intensity increased, "Ouch!" Soon, the sky was so heavy and thick with ice that I was being pelted mercilessly and couldn't take it any more. I had to find cover, but where to find such things in a 30-mile desolate valley?

Jumping off the roadbed and down the embankment I found, by pure luck, a cement box culvert under the roadway. Squatting, I was able to crouch inside. On either end of the culvert a solid white sheet of hail now pelted the earth. A strong icy cold wind billowed through the giant cement coffin I had found. Within minutes the storm blew over and in its aftermath I discovered five inches of ice covering the desert floor.

"That was so crazy!" I thought. Crawling out of the other end of the box culvert I stepped onto the crunchy, icy snow. Everything in sight had turned to a solid white. Walking out of that culvert was like waking up to snow on Christmas morning. As I turned around to scramble up the steep embankment of the highway, I was taken aback to discover that a car, unbeknownst to me, had slid off the road during the short storm and was hanging off the road over the culvert above me. Four other cars had pulled over to help this stranded family.

When I had retreated off the road, there had been no one else in sight. This time when I emerged, there was suddenly a parking lot of cars and people. Ascending the embankment I noticed the faces of three young kids in the back seat of one of these cars looking out the car window at me. The fearful look on their faces as saw me emerge, they likely cried out , "Daddy, what's that creature coming out of the desert?!"

With only my dingy t-shirt, blue nylon shorts, and well-tanned body, I must have made a great contrast to the pure white background. Not to mention having seen me crawl out of a pipe under the road and heading their way. I gave them a little wave but their startled expression was frozen.

Assuming the other four cars had things under control, I decided to continue running, now on the ice-covered road.

Soon, passing cars started slowing down behind me and asking, "Hey, was that your car that went off the road?"

"No," I'd reply. That caught them off guard and forced the next question.

"Well, where's *your* car?"

"I don't have a car," I'd reply.

Finally, not being able to make sense of anything, they'd ask, "What in the world are you doing in the middle of Nevada without a car?"

"Running to California," I'd say with a chuckle.

In the meantime my mother had been taking the walking tour of the nearby petroglyphs when she noticed a car coming from my direction, covered in snow.

"Hmm, that's funny. I wonder where that car came from?" she said aloud. Then looking off to her east she could see a massive black cloud moving across the horizon and feared the worst. Jumping in her car she raced back to find me running on the shoulder, but this time in thick puddles of slush. Semi-trucks were very nice to me, slowing down and switching lanes so as to not splash me with a wave of gray ice water.

Go figure…skating. An October ice storm in Nevada.

The remainder of the day my mom kept close tabs on me in case another surprise desert storm blew our way.

At the close of the day when the pavement was nearly dry, I was pulled over by two sheriff's deputies. After handing them my transcontinental runner business card, I congratulated them on being law enforcement officers number seven and eight who had "pulled me over" on my run. They were very nice. When parting after our visit, they said that they would keep an eye out for me, which my mom particularly thanked them for.

Officers number seven and eight to ask (more or less), "Can I help you?"

The final day with my mom proved to be the one I was most worried about. By this point in the week, my right tendon was very sore from the high miles and constant pounding on the pavement. The only way I was going to make the final 32 miles across the desert was if I took it extremely slowly and took my time to get to town. My mom agreed, and I set out for my final day with her. All went well as I started out with near 12-minute miles. By mid-day, I was feeling my old self again and knew the end was in sight. I stopped at one break with my mom at Sand Mountain National Recreation Area. Driving up to the giant sand dune, we came before a 300-foot tall pile of sand. It was so pure in color and so alien to all of the other mountains around, it looked as if a giant truck had just delivered a gigantic load, creating a massive sandbox.

As we drove closer down the approach road, we could see small ants moving around all over it. These turned out to be ATV users zipping around all sides at breakneck speeds. At the base of the massive pile was a sprawling tent city of F-350 trucks, pop-up campers, dune buggies, and workshops on wheels. Some of the machines looked as though a small family fortune had been put into their design and maintenance.

Back on the road, I was now feeling the tingling sensation of being so close to done with the mighty desert. The final stretch to Fallon offered some surprises. Highway 50 runs straight across dry Carson Lake and its expansive salt flats. All along the highway passing pedestrians and the occasional driver have pulled over and left an environmentally friendly mark that they were there. Most of these are in the form of dark volcanic rocks, gathered from across the fields, and formed into written messages along the highway.

"Debbie Loves Arnie," was one. "Bike USA," was another. "William J. Donnell," and hundreds others.

Throughout the day, when I wasn't reading the messages written in stone, I was watching the spectacular air show going on overhead. The Fallon Naval Air Station was nearby and missions were flying over the highway every few minutes. The 12 miles across the salt flats had offered much more than I would have thought.

By day's end, overjoyed, I reached Fallon, the end of the emptiness. I had just completed a 238-mile week. Nearly every major accomplishment in life has some early indication of pending success. For instance, you might not have graduated yet, but you just wrote your last paper for class. Although I still had an entire other state to run across, reaching Fallon, Nevada was my early indication. Barring some horrible injury, my feet were getting ready to touch an ocean and I knew it when I reached Fallon. The feeling was incredible.

From here on out, I would be in good shape. I thanked my mom for all her work to get me across Nevada, and we celebrated with a nice dinner and then watched "Antz" at the local cinema.

I had four days of running to get to Carson City where my last traveling companion would be meeting me. The end was at last in sight.

Chapter 29
Four Feet

My mom took off early in the morning and told me to sleep in to rest and recover from the week. I slept a few more hours but got up to prepare for a newspaper interview I had later that morning. After the interview I still hadn't packed up my things and had to mail coolers and gear back to Lydia. The reporter gave me a ride to the Post Office. I didn't end up leaving town until well into the afternoon.

My goal for the day was to get to Fort Churchill State Park where I would finish the alternate route and rejoin the official route of the ADT. That park was 28 miles away. It hadn't dawned on me until I left that afternoon that when I resumed my run, it would be the first time I had been alone in three weeks, as well as the first time I had to carry all of my possessions since then.

Leaving Fallon that afternoon, it was already hot outside. My body was beat up from the personal record breaking week I had just come off. Rather than subjecting myself to further pain and suffering, I elected to cut the day short. Even so it took all of my will power to keep going.

By late afternoon, and only having covered a handful of miles, I decided it was time to buckle down and do some running. Turning off every inner urge I had to throw my pack off the nearest guardrail and lie down in a ditch, I slowly found my second wind, finally arriving at a casino and restaurant in Silver Creek for dinner after a painfully short 19 miles.

I was in luck. This diner had a Monday night special, They were offering a two-for-one spaghetti dinner. Upon ordering that, however, I learned that they have a policy against serving two plates of food to one person. I considered offering to pay one of the slot players three nickels if she would sit with me so I could double my servings but decided against it, preferring the company of my maps and journal to that of a smoking slot player.

During dinner and while wondering where I was going to sleep for the night, I learned that the casino had hotel rooms in the back of the building. I got the last room for $37. It had a television, a bathroom, and plastic brick paneling lining the walls, but no phone. In my current state, it was a haven. Using a pay phone in the parking lot I called my friend Robert and firmed up our plans to meet in Carson City.

Robert Webster was my college roommate. Bert, as we call him, was a bit of an outsider like me in school. We were a perfect pair as we enjoyed finding alternative forms of entertainment in school to the traditional fraternity house parties. Over the course of four years with many late night "missions" as we called them, we found ourselves in curious places throughout southern Indiana: atop water towers, in the belly of an abandoned nuclear power plant, camping in secret overlooks in the Ohio Valley, and inside many locked buildings just to see if we could get in. Our missions included everything from building elaborate forts in the woods to simply sitting in trees over campus sidewalks on weekend nights, seeing how low on the branches we could get before people started noticing us. We usually got within inches of their heads.

It seemed natural then, that upon graduation, we both decided to hike the AT. Starting a few weeks later than me, Bert eventually caught up to me in Massachusetts, where we hiked together off and on for the remaining 1,500 miles.

It was a welcome surprise to me when Bert sent me a postcard during my run. "Hey Brian, I've got a deal for you," he began. "If you can make it all the way across the country to the Nevada-California border, I'll run across the last state with you."

At first I considered whether having his company would ruin the solitude I had come to embrace as life on the road, but then decided that by that point, I was sure to enjoy sharing this trip with a fellow runner and friend for several days, especially someone like Bert who had much the same yearning for adventure. It was set. He was going to take a Greyhound Bus from his home in Eugene, Oregon to Carson City, Nevada and we would contact each other through his wife, Gwyn at home.

Arriving at Fort Churchill I met two couples who travel the west every summer, gathering artifacts on their hikes. One of the women said that she has created a homemade version of a Power Bar, and she gave me a few. They also treated me to a sack of trail mix, some carrots, and a juice box! I love those little encounters.

From that point on it was obvious that I was once again on the ADT for I followed a dusty, winding, narrow road for 25 miles heading uphill to Virginia City. I finally arrived in town and was very relieved to be at the top of the hill I had climbed all day. After a pizza with every topping, I went out to find a room for the night.

I had heard so much about Virginia City but never expected it to have become so touristy. Being a Nevada town gambling is a very popular activity for the visitors, and nearly every building has placed the one-arm bandits in corners and hallways.

I only had one more day of running alone on my trip, and I woke up to run it over a small pass to Carson City where I would be meeting Bert the next morning. Taking a city aqueduct road, I worked my way along a series of dirt roads and soon had the sprawling Carson City in my sights below. Dale Ryan, the Nevada ADT Coordinator, was out of town on business when I arrived, but his wife, Bonnie, offered to pick me up and drive me to a motel. She had brought along her 80-year old mother who is very sharp. We all ate a dinner at Sizzler where I put down four large plates of food.

Packing up in my motel room on the big day of Bert's arrival, I heard a fake bird call that could only come from one person. While on the AT, when either of us finally approached a shelter at the end of the day, we had a special birdcall greeting taken from the musical, *West Side Story*. I returned the greeting, and we had a great time catching up on how the trip was going, how we were going to handle the final state, and planning the day. We called Bonnie who came and gave us a very interesting two-hour tour of town. Part of our tour included the city's industrial park.

"Now this is the industrial park. I'm not sure what they do here, but my sister Jane could tell you. She lives in Ohio." Then we went by the state prison.

"That's the prison there, and on that fence right there is where they shot a man who was trying to escape. They left him hanging on the wall for three days." We were glad we hadn't received the same treatment for our adventures in college!

Our tour concluded with views of the city, and she finally dropped us off back at the hotel. That night we planned for the next day when we would head out of town and onto the remote Tahoe Rim Trail and Western States Trail into California.

California, at long last.

The next morning Bonnie came and picked us up one last time to drive us to the trailhead on the western edge of Carson City. The trail leaves the city limits in a little obscure subdivision.   The trail immediately ascends a steep mountain for several miles. This was quite an introduction to welcome Bert to the trail! I was taking frequent walking breaks and Bert was a bit jumpy, wanting to run more. I told him that he would get all the chances in the world to run during the next three weeks, but right now I needed to take it easy going up this mountain.

Over the summit and back down the other side, we decided to head into Incline Village. When we came to a road, we studied our map and realized that the town lay several miles away, off the route, so we got a ride and our driver took us to the Fleet Feet Running store. From there the manager called Laura, a PBS volunteer and firefighter. She came and picked us up and drove us to the local PBS station, located in a garage. After setting up camera equipment, she interviewed me for a segment that they would run during a special outdoor program.

After the interview she offered to put us up in her home, to which we agreed. We had a great night in her house enjoying the expansive views of Lake Tahoe and the Tahoe Rim forest.

The next morning Laura said that she was headed out of town for a few days and that we had better take the food in her kitchen so it wouldn't go bad.

"Here," she said, "take these cookies. They won't be any good when I get back."

She also made us some sandwiches and drove us back to the trail.

All day long we had expansive views of the deep blue Tahoe Lake while running at 8,000 feet. Later on in the afternoon we got lost. At one point we came upon a sign that said, "Leaving Baker State Park."

"There is NO WAY we could be all the way down there," Bert said, looking at our map at an area miles from where we should have been and thought we were.

It turned out that we were completely off course, and we came out in Tahoe City, California, south of our trail. After a snack at a gas station, we got a ride back to the trail in Squaw Valley, home of the 1960 Winter Olympics. Laura had arranged lodging for us in a firehouse in town.

The fire station didn't have extra beds at the time but there was a large weight lifting room. This exercise room was in an open-air loft above the fleet of garaged fire engines. Should a call come in during the night, we would know about it!

The next morning we needed to purchase some food to get us through the difficult stretch over the Sierra Nevada which now lay directly before us. Hitch-hiking back into Tahoe City, we went to a grocery store and bought light, high-energy provisions. Bert had also shipped ahead many small packages to Post Offices care of general delivery, and he had hoped to save money by having his wife send him food rather than having to buy it along the way.

With provisions bought, mail collected and a ride from a chef, we headed back to the ski resort, ready for the mountains.

The ADT climbs up the steep ski slope on a trail gaining several thousand feet of elevation within a few miles. Travelers have the option to take the gondola to the top, thereby saving the long uphill climb and offering great views to boot.

We arrived at the top within minutes of leaving the main station far below. I was relieved to have saved one massive climb, though I had already run many others, even doubling back on wrong turns many times. I knew the purity of my run would be tainted by a gondola ride, but the hundreds of extra miles run during wrong turns throughout the trip more than made up for a two-mile hill in my opinion.

At the top of the mountain we found our trail and joined the Pacific Crest Trail for a few miles. It was also at this time that we came across the headwaters of the American River that we would be following all the way into Sacramento, California. We knew our nights camping out in the mountains would be chilly ones.

Neither of us had a tent, but we both had ground cloths. Stopping in the late afternoon we began piling up pine needles, which we used to cover our sleeping bags once we were nestled inside. We found that the needles were excellent insulators and were in abundant supply given our location.

**Staying warm in the Sierra Nevada.
One dirty runner + sleeping bag, sheet, and pine needles = human burrito.**

The next day we were running on the Western States Trail. The Western States is home to two famous races each year. The 100-mile trail run is legendary for its elevation changes and challenges. Stories of racers with various hallucinations after 80 miles are abundant. One person mistakenly tried to swim in a parking lot that he thought was a lake. Participants in other races have claimed to see talking gnomes, dragons, and parked airplanes in the forest.

The other famous race on the same trail involves horses. (There are no reports for hallucinations that endurance horses experience, however.) When we were running the trail, the signage was written for both types of users. Crossing one footbridge, the sign read, "Weight limit: 5 runners or 3 horses."

College Pal Bert joins me for the final state as we run the Western States 100 Trail.

During the day, Bert began complaining that the mileage was affecting his knees, and he started wrapping one of them with an Ace bandage. Throughout the day we would fill my bombproof water bladder with spring water, treat it with a few drops of bleach, and slowly work our way closer to sea level.

The second night we came across an abandoned mining camp, as much of this area had been mined and some of it was still actively so. Camping in the yard of an old home we again piled up needles and had great views as we stared up at 200-foot tall pine trees towering above us on the forest floor.

When I awoke the next morning and started to put on my shoes, I found that a slug had made its home on the side of my running shoe. Apparently in love with the salty sweat in the fabric, he had made slime tracks all over the material throughout the night. I nudged him off my shoe. No passengers allowed on this trip!

Throughout the afternoon we tackled the final and most challenging piece of this section: three valleys with 2,000-feet of elevation gain in each. At the conclusion of that long day, now quite dirty, smelly, tired, and famished for anything to eat other than smooshed and bleeding peanut butter and jelly sandwiches, we entered Foresthill, California, the first sign of civilization after coming off the Western States Trail.

Getting a room in a newly opened Inn, we took long showers, cleaned our shoes, and went across the street to a restaurant. The place was so proud of the amount of meat they serve, even their menus are made of full-grain leather. Bert, being a vegetarian, ordered a salad with no bacon bits.

The next day we treated ourselves to a light 16-mile run to Auburn. A bit more rested now, we covered a 29-mile day to Granite Bay State Park. That night we camped out on the grass under some trees. The area was becoming more developed the closer we got to the ocean, and I could sense the end was very near.

Arriving in Discovery Park in Sacramento, I called a contact I had from 1,500 miles earlier. While in McPherson, Kansas Jane, one of the bikers I had met going cross-country, had told me to call her when in the Sacramento area.

She was elated to hear that I was still going and said she would meet us that evening. She took us out for a great dinner and insisted on paying for our hotel room for the night. We thanked her over and over and had a great time hearing more about her bike trip and answering her many questions about the run. Though we had only met once before, it felt like old friends catching up.

The next section of the ADT is a trip back in time to another world. Passing through the old Chinese communities of Locke, Isleton, and Walnut Grove, we got a taste of what life must have been like in central California during the 1940s. This part of the state relied heavily on farming, and the many canals prevented all but the major roads from continuing in a straight direction. While pausing to take in the authentic but dilapidated Chinese architecture in the town of Locke, a man walked up to us and asked if we were in the mood for a good steak.

"Always in the mood for a good steak," I said as I played along with a wink to Bert.

"Well, you're in luck, because right down the street there you can get the best damn steaks in the whole world, man." Then he held up both hands to show the girth of a single serving. "I'm not kidding man, those damn things are THIS DAMN HUGE!"

We laughed and thanked him for his recommendation. The restaurant was called "Al the Wops" and after I'd seen the sign, I remembered that the Foots had also recommended the establishment. After checking the prices of the food, we decided to save the visit for another time and press on.

A few nights later we were standing at a shopping mall trying to figure out how to get five miles down the road to the nearest motel. We had been doing a good job of camping out and saving money for the most part, and this was a day when we decided to sleep in beds. After calling a cab company that never showed up, we stood around hoping to meet someone who could take us to the motel.

An older man walked up and asked where we were headed with our packs. After talking to us for 15 minutes, his wife finally came out of the store, and he offered us a ride to the motel. He even waited for us to make sure they had a room available before driving off.

That night while eating in the restaurant across the street from our hotel, I thought I overheard two men behind us mention "Columbus." There are many towns named Columbus in the country, and I figured it was not very likely that they were speaking of Columbus, Indiana.

The more I heard, however, the more convinced I became that they were speaking of my hometown. Turning around in my booth and overcoming the guilt I felt for eavesdropping I said, "Excuse me. I don't mean to interrupt, but were you just talking about Columbus, Indiana?" They were in fact and, once we introduced ourselves, I learned that they were good friends of my mother's and even belonged to the same Rotary Club. It is a small world indeed.

The next day we arrived at Berkeley and enjoyed running down Telegraph Hill and along College Avenue to Jack London Square to take the ferry across the bay. The ferry ride would be my fourth and final segment of the trail on which I would have to use public transportation to cross the country.

Once on the other side of the bay, we stood at Fisherman's Wharf, in the heart of San Francisco and marveled that we had made it. Less than 55 miles now lay between me, the finish line, and a surprise that would last a lifetime.

Chapter 30
The Price Is Right

Call me greedy, but I was in need of an incentive. While crossing Missouri and Kansas I decided that despite the finish line of this whole endeavor, I needed something additional to look forward to in order to keep me propelled towards California. By some crazy notion, I decided that, having been a *Price Is Right* game show fan all my life, even scheduling college classes around it when possible, I would try to get on the show at the conclusion of my run.

When I left my cabin in Indiana, my former housemate Ricky agreed to cabin sit for me while I ran. I periodically called him from the road and checked in with how it was going and to retrieve messages. One particular day while calling home, I said I was toying with the idea of going to *The Price Is Right* at the conclusion of my run. Ricky thought it was a surprising but great idea and offered to come out and join me. He agreed to acquire tickets and get any necessary information.

Three months and 2,000 miles after that daydream I had crossed California with Robert and Project Game Show was still in effect. To up our chances of getting on stage, Ricky had made special t-shirts for us to wear to the show. His and Robert's said, "Friend of Runner" and had a large arrow pointing towards me so they could sit on either side of me in the audience and frame my shirt. My shirt said, "Hey Bob, I ran 4,800 miles to hear Rod Roddy say, "Brian Stark, Come On Down." On the back of the shirt he had printed, "And I had my cat neutered," an homage to Mr. Barker's life mission to help control the pet population.

Once in San Francisco, Robert and I met Ricky at the airport and, renting a car, drove eight hours to Los Angeles. We stayed at a youth hostel

229

in Santa Monica. Sunday, the night before the show, Ricky and Robert were discussing what I would wear to the show. I assumed I would wear my running shoes and nylon shorts, for authenticity. Neither of them thought wearing a 2,000-mile old pair of faded smelly nylon shorts was a good idea for an appearance on network television. Seeing their point we made a trip to the local Banana Republic's sale rack and purchased a network-friendly pair of cotton khaki shorts.

At 6 the next morning we left the hostel headed for the long wait outside Television City.

We arrived at 6:30 a.m. for the 1:30 p.m. show and I was already number 113 in line. Although very early, everyone was excited about the upcoming show. It was as if all our neighbors had finally met up again after a time away. Audience members had video cameras taping everything going on.

At least half of the audience had special t-shirts made up in hopes of getting them called down to contestants' row. A band of young blonde girls wore identical shirts that said, "Future Barker Beauties." Another group of older adults had written, "I got a car, I got a job, but I don't care, I'm here with Bob." One of my favorites was a large older man with the shirt, "Neutered and ready for play." Others were somewhat desperate, "Dear Rod, first time, NOTHIN, second time, NOTHIN, third time, PLEASE BOB." Apparently this woman was going to attend until she won, a practice that is looked down on by the show's producers.

Two of the husbands, a large man resembling "the Skipper" from Gilligan's Island, and an apparent new best friend of his, a bar-handle mustached man with a large gold belt-buckle with huge letters spelling, "STRAP," were rousing the crowd. They were pretending to be Rod Roddy, the announcer. They would ask strangers their names, then scream, "JANE THOMAS, COME ON DOWN," at which point Jane would come running through the crowd screaming and giving multiple high fives.

I had heard a rumor that CBS sends undercover agents into the audience in the morning to scout out who has a nice personality. Even though none of us really believed this, we were trying to be nice to everyone just in case. Perhaps it was Strap and his skipper buddy. Just to be safe I asked Strap to call my name, and I went running through the audience.

After an hour of waiting, a page came out of a door and the crowd went wild. He handed out numbers. People cheered. We then had an hour break to leave before we had to come back and sit in the order on the benches outside.

Another hour after sitting on the benches and being told precise instructions over a public address system about how to fill out the cards that were going to be issued to us, we started what they repeatedly referred to as "Processing."

A card was given to each of us. We were to fill out our social security number, name, address, if we had ever been a contestant on this or any other game show, and if we were currently running for public office. Then a long explanation was given warning us to use our legal given name instead of any nicknames. In order to be awarded prizes you must use your legal given name, otherwise, you forfeit any winnings. Ricky got very upset at this rule and planned to say something to someone about it.

Next, two pages came through the audience and were writing each person's name on the large yellow price tag name cards. Ricky is a cartoonist, and we were assuming that the pages must have been hired specifically for this purpose and therefore must have impeccable penmanship. Such was not the case, however. Ricky's given name is Charles and after the page took a lengthy consideration to just how the angled tip of his Sharpie pen should be best utilized for maximum artistic effect, he proceeded to write in a jagged hieroglyphic that we only hoped wasn't supposed to be English. The size of the letters started decently enough but by the time he got to "LES," the letters were so large they were running off the edge of the tag. Later, we coerced the second page into rewriting Ricky's and Robert's tags, a request that was to be repeated by the next 20 people sitting near us. I chose to keep my original tag, assuming that, perhaps in doing so, fate would work with me.

At this time we were told we would be standing up and filed past the producers in what they call "the interview" stage. All morning the atmosphere had been happy, exciting, and casual. This was when all of that changed.

As soon as we left our benches, network pages were standing erect holding white signs with bold red letters saying, "Absolute Silence!" Other pages, who weren't lucky enough to have their own red sign had to resort to the "Shush!" finger-over-mouth gesture. Two producers were sitting in director's chairs just outside the studio doors. The audience filed past the producers at a rate of one person about every eight seconds. We were standing on the road, about ten steps below the producers. They read each nametag and asked very basic questions of each contestant such as, "Hi, Jim, tell me about yourself?"

Jim would say, "Well, I'm retired. Worked for 48 years and hoping to win some prizes."

The producer would respond, "Ok, good luck to you." A woman sitting next to him had a large red clipboard and was making notes on what the contestants said. Mostly, she was looking for an interesting personality, a good story, or a network friendly pair of tan khaki shorts. Finally, it was our turn. Ricky was first.

The producer said, "OK, Charles, tell me about yourself."

Ricky, in true form, responded, "Well, first of all, my name is not Charles, it's 'Ricky,' but they said I had to use this name because it's my legal name."

He was having a meltdown and all I could do was watch. I couldn't believe he was doing this. Here we were in the key moment of selection for a chance to win fabulous prizes and Ricky was complaining about the rules! He then made up for it, however, with, "And I wouldn't mind getting on stage, but I'm not the guy you want." All of Television City could hear the producer thinking, "Oh, really?"

"This," pointing to me, "is the guy you want, and he's going to tell you about himself in just a minute, but I'm not the guy you want."

With heightened interest the producer turned to me and asked, "OK, Brian, tell me about *yourself*." All I said was, "Well, I ran 5,000 miles to meet Bob Barker."

"Why?" he asked, a bit of shock and curiosity in his voice.

"I wanted to run across the country to see America and I figured going to *The Price Is Right* would be a fun finish."

At this point I noticed the female producer writing something down on her red clipboard, which I took to be a good sign. During Robert's interview, he basically said that he had run across California with me and hoped I got on stage.

As we continued the slow procession now past the focal point of the shushing, we eavesdropped on what the other audience members were saying.

"I have worked at a factory for 18 years, and I'm here to win a car!"

On at least two occasions the producer asked audience members, "And did you run here as well?" We thought that we had made a good impression when we heard that.

The last stage of processing is to sit on a third set of benches just outside the studio. Moments later and eight hours after our arrival, we entered the studio.

Upon entering, the first impression a person has who has watched the show all his life is that the actual studio is very small. The studio seating holds about 350 people but it looked as if only 100 could fit into it. Where was the expansive stage that they drive the cars onto? Where were the enormous aisles that had been trod by thousands of lucky audience members since 1972? I saw the three doors that hid fabulous prizes but saw no room for the large set of the game "Plinko," the giant cliff of

"Mountain Climber," or the enormous bank vault for, "Safe Cracker." In time, I would see just how all these illusions came to reality in the magic of Hollywood.

Second impression that hits one upon entrance is the frigid cold temperature in the studio. The air-conditioner is running on high to keep the equipment and lights cool for the taping. Our next surprise came when we suddenly noticed that the whole studio was decorated for Christmas on October 26. Our seats were just to the left of a large artificial Christmas tree sitting in the middle of the audience.

Once seated, we started to examine the décor and theorize just how it was all going to work. We saw contestants' row at the front of the stage. We could see the shiny silver and glass tray perched high above contestants' row that gets lowered down on wires to display watches and jewelry items. The only object we could not figure the purpose for was a large yellow box with a black square on the side and lights all around it.

Minutes later, Rod Roddy, the announcer, came onto stage and gave the audience a preview of what would happen and how to act as an audience. For instance, he told us when to clap, when to yell, and what to do if you get called down. With an average of two tapings a day, Rod looked like he had gone through the routine before. Despite this, he used a surprisingly large volume of body English as he instructed us on the show. With that said, he got behind his booth on the right side of the stage. On television, it always looks like Rod is in a balcony, perched high over the audience. Rod is actually just standing behind a podium on the stage never more than 15 feet from Bob and the contestants.

A crew of five cameramen walked onto the stage, lights turned on, and Rod announced the taping of show Number 0954k to air on December 24, 1998. We noticed a camera focused on the big mysterious yellow box and the small light bulbs around it started flashing. Another camera was panning the audience. We then learned how the opening shot for the show was performed. The image from the first camera is taken by focusing on the flashing lights, then a second camera super-imposes the panning shot of the audience in the box. It was neat seeing all of these inside Hollywood tricks first-hand despite how simple they really were. While they were panning the audience, Rod was announcing the first four contestants to "come on down." With everyone screaming and clapping, elated that something was finally happening after eight hours of waiting, we found it impossible to hear anyone's name actually being called, and the producers held up poster board with the names of the first four contestants so that in case you missed hearing your name, you could see it on stage and proceed to go crazy. This particular episode was to air on Christmas Eve and, because of the holiday,

Bob Barker came walking down the aisle for his appearance, an entrance he rarely makes.

The show was going well, although very fast. Even during taping an episode they only stop for commercial breaks. I suppose this is so the show can tape continuously and station affiliates do not have to stop and start the tape.

After the first three contestants had been on stage, and they had spun the *Big Wheel* in the *Showcase Showdown*, I was starting to worry that I would not get called down. After all, you're never told that you will or won't get called down, but if you have an interesting story and wear network friendly khaki shorts, you might have a good chance.

During the commercial breaks Bob would answer questions from the audience, such as his age and what his favorite game is. One woman invited Bob and Rod to a church picnic in her hometown in Texas.

The producers came back from a commercial break and Bob asked, "Rod, for whom doth the bell toll?"

Rod replied, "The bell tolleth for Brian! BRIAN STARK! COME ON DOWN, YOU'RE THE NEXT CONTESTANT ON THE PRICE IS RIGHT!"

I remember Robert just started laughing. Ricky and I stood up and gave each other high fives. Robert was still laughing. I worked my way to the aisle and took baby steps down the isle, running the whole way. I wanted to make it seem like it took me a long time to get down there, symbolic of my run, but since it was only eight feet anyway, even baby steps didn't do the trick.

Bob asked us to look at the first item up for bids. It was a roll-top desk. Just as the camera was turning to Bob to ask me for my quote on the desk he said, "Hang on a second. I have to get the answer to this. I was looking at Brian's shirt, and it says, 'Hey Bob, I ran 4,800 miles to hear Rod Roddy say, "Brian Stark, Come On Down.' Do you mean you ran here?"

"Yes," I said. "I ran here from Delaware."

"You mean you actually ran all the way?"

"Allll the way, Bob." Bob was at a loss for words.

"Where did you run? Did you run on interstates?"

"Back roads and trails, the whole way."

"Well, Brian, I'm proud of you. By the way, what do you bid on that prize." By the time our initial discussion was over, the prize had already been taken away, and I almost didn't remember what it was. I stupidly bid $2,800. The audience groaned at me. I had overbid.

During the next commercial break Ricky yelled to me, "Brian, listen to me next time."

The audience laughed in agreement.

"Okay!" I yelled back.

After the commercial break another contestant was called down, and we were to bid on a wood-burning stove. Bob started the bidding with the new contestant. When he came to me, he paused and had to ask another question.

"Now hold it a second, I was doing some thinking during the last commercial break and I have another question for Brian. Brian, you said that you ran 4800 miles to get here."

"Yes," I replied.

"Delaware is only about 3,000 miles away. How did you manage to run and extra 1,800 miles?"

"I ran a lot of extra mileage," was my response.

"You have a bad sense of direction," Bob said without missing a beat.

Trying to stay focused on the game, I turned to Ricky who was telling me to bid $1,300 on the stove and I did. That was too low of a bid.

During the next commercial Ricky shouted to me again, "Brian, don't listen to me anymore." The audience cheered. We came back from commercial and there was only one more chance to get on stage. The item up for bid was a collection of eleven stuffed Russ Collectors Teddy Bears. I thought they could be expensive but so did the other contestants. I had the advantage this time being the last bidder. The others bid $800, $999, and $650. I knew they would be expensive bears but those bids sounded a little high. I went for the classic bid reserved for just such an occasion - the $1 bid. The object is to come as close as possible to the actual retail price without going over. With such high bids from the others and each so close together, my odds of having the only bid under the price were pretty good. The "actual retail price" was $521, and I was on the stage!

Bob walked ahead of me to the third set of doors and said, "Brian, you ran 4,800 miles to win what?"

As the giant doors were opening, Rod said, "A fabulous trip to Canada and a romantic trip to Hawaii." There were two billboards with "Canada" and "Hawaii" written on them. I played the 50/50 chance game of "One Right Price."

One of the models, was holding up a price of $2,819. I had to decide if that price was the cost of the trip to Canada or the trip to Hawaii. Each was a six-night stay in a world-class resort with coach airline tickets from Los Angeles. If I chose correctly which trip went with the price I would win both trips.

I had only been to Canada twice to visit Niagara Falls, and we had driven both times. That seemed like a lot of money just to go to Canada.

However, the woman sitting behind Robert and Ricky in the audience had just been to Canada and told Ricky that the price shown seemed like the right amount. I turned to him and even though I couldn't hear him over the yelling and screaming, he was holding up his left hand in a "C" shape, what we since refer to as him giving me the "High C." I went against my better judgment and told Bob I believed the price should go with the trip to Canada. The Barker Beauties flipped over the price tags and Ricky had been correct. I won both trips!

Since I had been the last contestant to get on stage, the next segment was the second *Showcase Showdown*. During the commercial break, they pushed the *Big Wheel* onto the stage again and the previous two contestants joined me on stage where the producer explained to us in a huddle how the big wheel worked. The person closest to a dollar in one spin or a combination of two spins would get into the showcase at the end of the show. If your spins total a dollar, you win $1,000 and get a bonus spin. During your bonus spin if the wheel stops on either of the two green sections you win $5,000 dollars more. If you land on a dollar in your bonus spin you win an extra $10,000. He asked if there were any questions.

I asked him what the wheel was made of. He said it was a steel bar held by a natural fibrous material, rather than saying leather out of respect for Bob, who is a vegetarian. He also said that on occasion they oil the axle to keep it spinning smoothly and can tighten the wheel to adjust spin.

Just as we were coming back from the commercial, the three of us were lined up at the wheel. Since I was the top winner in the second half of the showcase, I had the advantage of spinning last. Bob asked me where I was from. I told him Indiana and how I had been a fan of his show since it started 26 years ago. That set him off again, and when we came back on air, he was still laughing and told the audience that I had been watching The Price Is Right since I was six months old and could remember watching it in my playpen. He turned to Rod and asked, "I don't think they start any younger than that, do they? And remember it, anyway, that's great, Brian. I love it. And if he wins on the big wheel, he is going to buy a car, he doesn't want to have to run all the way home. I love it." Apparently, Mr. Barker and I had hit it off.

The first two contestants spun the wheel and tied at 70 cents. They chose to have a spin-off unless I could beat them both and automatically be in the showcase. My chances were again pretty good. Before the show Robert said that if I got on stage, he wanted to see me spin the wheel off its axis. I really gave it a yank and paid the price for it. The wheel stopped on 15 cents. One more "plink" to the next number and I would have had 80 cents and been in the showcase. One less "plink" and I would have hit one dollar for a thousand dollars and a chance for ten more. With 15 cents, I spun again and landed on 25. The wheel was slowing down on 70 cents, which would have given me 85 cents, but it went on and my time was up on the show. It would have been nice to get into the showcase. There was a computer, a camper, a motorcycle, and an electric guitar, all of which I would have enjoyed. I cannot complain, however. In 15 minutes of stage work, I won $7,286.

A fun (and successful) day on the set of The Price is Right.

After the show, the contestants were escorted into a small room at the back of the studio sectioned off by curtains. There were nine chairs lining the walls, one for each of us. We each had to sign several documents verifying our social security number and address. Then we were free to go. The whole process took about two minutes. I reunited with Robert and Ricky and we walked back to the car, dazed from what had just taken place.

As I was getting into the car, two women saw me and started screaming, "Liar! You said you RAN here! You didn't run here, LIAR!" I was still in too much shock from winning to respond. I just laughed.

We returned to the hostel all the while saying, "Wow, that was crazy." I made some phone calls and told my family that I had won which was fun. Lydia posted my news on the Internet on my web site.

The next morning I had a message from a family friend who lived in Los Angeles but was originally from my home area. He had wanted to meet me and offered to buy me breakfast. He worked in the stock market and since the stock exchange is in New York, his workday starts at 3 a.m. on the West Coast. He was willing to meet us "later" in the morning at 6:30. We walked into the lobby five minutes early. He was already there reading a book. We had a nice breakfast at a nearby restaurant and talked of the Appalachian Trail, a hike the three of us had in common. He then offered us a tour of Beverly Hills, which we gladly accepted.

He first drove us down Sunset Boulevard, then for a quick tour of his nice home, and finally to the "test course." He drove us to O.J. Simpson's old home, told us to start our stopwatches, and proceeded across town on the impossible journey Simpson's lawyers said couldn't be driven in less than 15 minutes in the best traffic. We made it to his girlfriend's home in 7 minutes and 20 seconds without even speeding. Our excellent tour was over, and, having accomplished our mission in LA, we needed to get back to San Francisco to finish the remaining 50 miles of the run. We'd had fun on our getaway vacation, but the best part of the trip was yet to come.

Chapter 31
End

The drive back north to San Francisco went quickly. We retreated to Avi's house, a friend from the Appalachian Trail. The next day I tried to coerce media to attend the finish of my run. Limantour Beach, the western terminus of the ADT, is a very beautiful ending point, however, the remote beauty is also what keeps many people from driving up there for an afternoon. From downtown San Francisco, the terminus of the ADT is only 50 miles away, yet it takes two and a half hours to drive there. There is not a stretch of straight road for more than 30 feet the whole time. I was having difficulty getting any reporters interested in attending my finish.

For eight months I had envisioned all of the media that would be at the finale of my run. I dreamed of anchormen, camera crews, helicopters, and spots on evening national news shows that would air at the end of a broadcast and put a nation to bed with happy thoughts. Having spent four frustrating hours on the phone, I decided I had tried my best.

Robert and I took a bus to Fisherman's Wharf to rejoin the trail where we'd left off. Avi joined us on his bike. We ran along the wharf, through Marina Green and Chrissy Field, up the stairs to the Golden Gate Bridge. This was the next to last picture in Reese's book. It was a shot of John Fazel, the ADT California State Coordinator finishing his own run across California.

I had looked at that photograph many times and tried to imagine what I would feel when I finally got to cross that historic trestle. Would I be able to sum up eight months of my most intense life experiences into one emotion as I ran across the Bay? The bridge is over a mile long, but that wasn't nearly long enough. The entire time Robert and I were running across it, I just kept saying, "Wow."

Alcatraz and Angel Islands were off to my right, the Pacific Ocean was off to my left, and only 44 miles of trail now awaited me before this trip would be over. I could have stayed on that bridge for weeks trying to sum up how I felt. We didn't have weeks, however. Robert had already dipped into meager savings to join me across California, and in three days I would have a small group of friends and family waiting for my arrival on the beach. At least with each foot-strike on the bridge, I was connecting with the exactness of the location, grateful for this last opportunity to know where I was.

The Golden Gate Bridge means 48 miles to go and time for a side trip.

We kept running and, once across the bridge, turned west and ran along trails on the east side of Mount Tamalpias. We ran all day through unforgettable grassy fields with the tall grains blowing in the wind, reminding me of Kansas. The dry, blonde grass underfoot meeting the endless blue sky and oceanic horizon made for a palate of beauty.

By day's end we arrived at the Point Reyes Visitors Center where we were to meet my mother who was flying out for my finish. She rented a car and met us at dusk. Gwyn, Robert's wife, also planned to meet us, and we awaited her arrival. People not accustomed to the road conditions in that part of the country might be shocked as to just how slow going it can be. Gwyn had been given horrible directions as well which likely didn't help. When it got dark, my mother left to stay in a nearby bed and breakfast.

Gwyn finally showed up at 10 pm, having had a near mental breakdown during her ordeal. We tried to comfort her and proceeded to our reserved campsite at Wildcat Campground overlooking the ocean and the bluffs of Point Reyes. This campsite was a "hike-in" type, meaning you had to park your car and walk a few hundred yards to your spot. The extra effort it took to get to the campsite prevented most from choosing that spot and we enjoyed the quiet solitude.

It is safe to say that Wildcat is the most beautiful campground location I have ever seen. We were perched on a grassy knoll, high atop the soothing Pacific waves. Mingled in and amongst our campsite were occasional giant boulders offering shade from the sun and shelter from the wind. Having just been in the bustling microcosm of San Francisco only two days earlier, arriving at this campsite on foot was a welcome respite for the end of my run. The next morning would start the last full day of running.

We paused occasionally for dramatic photographs, to try and absorb as much of the remainder of the trip as possible, and to savor each step of this beautiful sanctuary.

"It's all going downhill now." Ten miles to the end.

At day's end, Robert, Gwyn, and I drove to Samuel Taylor State Park and dropped off our gear. I then took Gwyn's car and drove back into the city to pick up Lydia who was flying in for the weekend. With only ten miles left to go, it felt a little distracting to be driving around the city in a car.

After picking up Lydia, we drove back to the state park and camped with Robert and Gwyn. The next day was Halloween, my predicted finish date for the past month.

"It's finally here," I thought as I rolled out of the tent.

Gwyn drove Robert and me back to the trail as Lydia slept in. My friend and I began running the last of the ten miles.

While crossing Kansas in search of mental conversation, I thought back to the day in Indiana in that small town where the candy bars were sold over the couch in the man's living room. I thought back to how I sat in the rain for three hours waiting for my mom to drive up, and remembered how surprised and glad I was to see Lydia in the passenger seat. Ever since then besides my grand surprise to her in Flagstaff, I had always wanted to truly show her how much she meant to me and if it could be wrapped up in another surprise, then all the better.

Throughout my run, I began devising a plan of how I could propose marriage to Lydia at the end of my run. We've all heard the stories before.

"Man swims across Atlantic Ocean, proposes to girlfriend on beach."

"Man parachutes to girlfriend at base camp, proposes in front of drill sergeant. Both assigned to push-ups and peeling potatoes."

I wanted to be that guy, so that when people asked how we got married, there would be a great story to tell. I also felt that if I proposed to her at the end of my run, assuming she said, "yes," I would be able to give her everything I had at that moment. Everything that I had worked for to get from one ocean to the other would, in effect, be given to her in that proposal. So, naively, I began the master plan of all plans to carry out this mission.

I knew Lydia was not a traditional "engagement ring" type of person. We had casually discussed at one point that exchanging bracelets might be one acceptable way to handle the initial step to marriage. I wanted to give her something that she liked and preferably something she had picked out. Having grown up visiting the Hopi Indian Reservation with her father who was a museum curator, I knew she had a love for Hopi jewelry. One particular store on the reservation was where she always found her favorite items. Earlier, I had learned that she was headed up there on an invitation to visit some friends.

Calling information, I asked for the number of Joe Day at the Hopi Reservation. That number did not readily come up. My operator was a trail angel, however, and after ten minutes of searching, we finally found that the number I needed was in a village called, and more importantly, *spelled*, "Shongopovi." With that knowledge in hand I was given the correct number and made the call. I explained my situation and told them that Lydia would be coming into their shop in a few days and if she noticed anything, or picked anything out, to please make a note of it.

A week later I called back and, sure enough, she had found a bracelet she really liked. I paid for it over the phone, and they arranged to transport it to Flagstaff for me. Next I had to get it sized properly. Shopping for bracelets on Indian Reservations and measuring my girlfriend's wrist were not easy things to do from 900 miles away while running across Kansas and Colorado.

Luckily while talking with Lydia on the phone, she told me a friend of hers was coming to visit her in Flagstaff and would be staying with her for a week.

"Now's my chance," I thought.

One day, while Lydia was at work, I called her house to talk to her friend. I explained what I was trying to do and asked if she could get one of Lydia's bracelets out of her jewelry box and trace the shape of it onto a piece of paper. Then I asked her to tack that piece of paper to the underside of Lydia's front porch where I would have a jeweler come retrieve it and size the bracelet to Lydia's wrist.

Her friend came through beautifully and the traced bracelet was found without a problem. The jeweler then sized the new bracelet and mailed it to me to my last general delivery address in California. Everything went as planned, but I had still not popped the question.

Robert and I sat at the Coast Campsite with two miles to go. As the ADT winds through Point Reyes, it stays on the bluffs and mountain trails for much of the way. At the Coast Campsite, it finally joins the Coast Trail and follows the water's edge on the beach for the final two miles. I had the bracelet in hand. Robert and I were sitting at a picnic table contemplating what was about to take place. In less than a half-hour, I would end my run across America, jump into the ocean, and propose to my girlfriend.

We reviewed the plan. The bracelet would be in the small nylon pocket of my shorts. When I crossed the finish line, I would drop my pack, turn left and jump into the ocean. While underwater, I would carefully remove the bracelet and hide it in my hand. Still standing in the surf, I would then call unsuspecting Lydia into the water, get on my knees and propose to her. It was to be a memorable morning.

As we were getting up from the table, a wilderness school van pulled up and one of the leaders asked us where we were headed.

"To Limantour Beach... from Delaware," I said.

"Yeah, right. Delaware," came the sarcastic reply. I didn't care anymore. We started the final run.

The sand was loose high up on the beach, so for better traction, we ran close to the water. A half-mile down the beach, still over a mile away, I could make out the form of several small groups of people up ahead. Some of them were surely just out for a Sunday on the beach. One of the groups, I knew, was waiting for Robert and me.

When we got within one mile, I could make out the outline of a banner. A half-mile away from the finish, I could clearly see the group. There were about eight of them, and an ADT banner had been erected. They were all waving, clapping, and cheering us on.

With 50 yards to go Robert broke off and let me finish alone. I ran under the banner with my arms in the air. Dropping my pack in the sand as planned, I turned towards the crashing surf and jumped into the frigid cold water.

Fears of losing the bracelet underwater had been discussed, but I was very careful to have a firm grasp of it the entire time. With the silver in hand, I pointed towards Lydia who thought I only wanted to get her wet. She played along and somewhat reluctantly came forward, having no idea of what was to come.

After she joined me in knee-deep water, I got down on my knees and looked up at her smiling. For a brief second she cocked her head in wonder as to what I was doing. Then a split-second later she realized what was about to happen and a look of shock, horror, and surprise came over her. I confessed my love, presented the bracelet to her, and asked for her hand in marriage.

Let me just say right now, as long as I have your attention: THIS IS A STUPID THING TO DO! DON'T try this at home. Don't do what I did. And don't think this is a happy ending.

She *did* say yes, but I was to later learn over the next two years that her "yes" was more precisely the beginning of her sentence to respond to my question.

"Yes-terday would have been a much better day to propose to me. There wouldn't have been a crowd of on-lookers waiting for me to accept. We could have talked it over, and shared something really special. But instead you just assumed that the way you did it was the way that I would have wanted to do it."

Obviously, I didn't wait for that version. As soon as I heard the, "yes," part, I hugged and kissed her and we went back to the group. As far as I knew, I had just proposed to my girlfriend, she said, "yes," and we were now engaged. Different thoughts were going through my fiancé's head, however. Later in the day, I would hear the version I had not waited for in the water. But unknowing of the situation at the time, we proceeded to the celebration on the beach.

Having crossed a continent, having proposed, having food.

We retreated from the frothy water to join our friends. There was wine, cookies, sodas, vegetables, gifts, and letters from fans back home. I noticed that there wasn't a single reporter. Trying to keep my spirits up, I shrugged it off thinking that no one had shown up to watch the Wright Brothers' first flight, either.

Coach Weinheimer's class had written me dozens of letters congratulating me on my finish. Beth Mathers had found a miniature antique banjo that she requested my mom bring to the beach and give to me. There were lots of photographs taken, a little inquiry from the Sunday beach-goers as to what was taking place, and then it was over.

We carpooled back to the hotel, had a very nice dinner in town, and the next morning everyone flew home.

As Bob Barker predicted, I didn't want to have to run home. With the free car having fallen through from his show, a friend of mine from junior high school left me a message that he had bought me a first-class plane ticket home. I sat in my luxury leather seat, with my running pack safely stowed overhead, no checked baggage, and hoped to strike up a conversation with the person next to me, or perhaps have my name read over the loudspeaker, but no one paid attention to me.

It was an amazingly quick flight home. Within 15 minutes of takeoff we were over the Sierra Nevada, which I had spent four long days crossing with Robert. Now they were covered in a thick blanket of snow. I had crossed my last obstacle within eight days of the first snowfall. It was just one of a thousand good fortunes I had on a trip that changed my life forever.

Post Script
I'm happy to report that Lydia eventually agreed to marry me, and we were wed in a beautifully intimate ceremony in a friend's garden in Tucson.

The Athens Messenger

Monday, April 13, 1998
Vol. 93 No. 119
A daily part of your life
Athens, Ohio • 592-6612
35 Cents

Running down a dream

Promoting Discovery Trail is Indiana man's inspiration

By LEEANNA POTTS
Messenger staff writer

What would make a man want to run through 12 states covering some 4,678 miles?

The desire to inform others of the American Discovery Trail — the first of its kind — a public trail that goes through towns and scenic areas.

Brian Stark, 26, from Nashville, Ind., is that man, made a stop in Athens last week.

Stark wanted to see the country and get a thorough perspective, but admitted even after this he will have only seen past "a sliver" of America. He has been a runner since his junior high school days.

A graduate of Hanover College in Indiana, Stark met up with a friend of his in Athens, who had transferred from Hanover to Ohio University. His friend helped organize his trip to Athens.

He is running through Ohio on the south leg of the Buckeye Trail, which is part of the American Discovery Trail. Stark said the Discovery Trail has a total of 407 miles in Ohio and 300 of those miles are on the Buckeye Trail.

The American Discovery Trail runs through Delaware, Maryland, West Virginia, Ohio, Indiana, Illinois, Missouri, Kansas, Colorado, Utah, Nevada and California, according to Stark. He didn't include Kentucky, even though it has some 5 miles of trail.

The American Discovery Trail was organized by a man and woman in 1989 who loved the outdoors and hiking and began connecting parts of previous hiking trails to others to create the trail spanning from Delaware to California. They were sponsored by Backpacker Magazine and American Hiking Society Magazine. Stark was on his fourth state and had covered 700 miles with less than 4,000 miles to go when he arrived in Athens.

Upon reaching California, he will be the first person to travel the entire trail on foot. Stark figures after he completes the trip he will have run the distance around the world — which is 24,000 miles — during his running career.

Before he began the Discovery Trail, Stark was working as a substitute teacher, summer camp director and youth fellowship leader in Indiana. To get in condition for this trip, Stark said he would run to work, about 10 miles per day.

"I've lost 11 pounds, since the start (of his trip) on March 8," Stark said. "Right now, I'm a week ahead of schedule and to a point of slowing down."

Those who wish to make contributions to the American Hiking Society National Trails Endowment, may send them to: AHS National Trails Endowment, 1422 Fenwick Lane, Silver Spring, Md. 20910. To learn more, call 888-766-HIKE.

— *Messenger photo by John Halley*
AMERICAN DISCOVERY — Brian Stark, 26, of Nashville, Ind., is running the American Discovery Trail which has some 407 miles of trail in Ohio.

Article and photograph reprinted courtesy of *The Athens Messenger*.

Discovering America on foot

Trails promoter Brian Stark is running coast to coast; 'I just kept going'

BY JOE MCFARLAND
AMERICAN NEWS SERVICE

ALTO PASS

First there was the local media hoopla with the big send-off from family and friends, and then Brian Stark, who had announced he was running all the way across America, was finally on his own.

Exactly 4,678 miles of good, old USA lay ahead of him as he trotted away from the Atlantic Ocean on March 8.

Nothing but back roads and trails awaited this 26-year-old Indiana native who'd promised everyone he would hoof his way between Cape Henlopen, Del. and Pt. Reyes, Calif.

"I knew all of my life that I wanted to run across the country," he explained.

Unfortunately, he felt like quitting.

And for good reason: The Discovery Trail itself had been more than expected.

"I wanted to meet the people in the towns and back roads," Stark says of his original plan to see outdoor America via this passage across the country which links local trails to connect the Atlantic and Pacific oceans.

"I've been so surprised. I can't begin to tell you how great the people have been I've met," he says.

America, Stark says, is an incredible place to see one step at a time — the people, the landscape, every small town and grazing cow have all kept him going. One step at a time. Three pairs of shoes so far. All of it one, huge trip.

"Anybody who says America is in trouble hasn't seen what I've seen," Stark says enthusiastically. "It's hard to describe how many good people are out there; and I've met the gamut of people."

He was approached by a prisoner.

A Brian Stark at Alto Pass in Union County, part of his 4,678-mile running trip across America. The Indiana native is following the American Discovery Trail to promote trail awareness throughout the U.S., a journey which will take eight months.

O'Dell says trail use is growing strong in Illinois — and is a major recreation of the future. Unfortunately, this state isn't moving quickly enough to accommodate trail users, he says.

"Illinois is just about the lowest state in the nation for number of miles of trails for recreational use," he explains with some frustration.

According to the Department of Natural Resources, there are 1,500 miles of trails statewide, with 600 additional miles in the works. But O'Dell says, with so many trails lovers, we're not keeping pace with competition.

Article and photograph reprinted courtesy of *American News Service*.

248

Mile Post 4800

June 20-21, 1998

Transcontinental trek tests runner

By Frank Haight Jr.
The Examiner

Sleeping in an outhouse in West Virginia, nearly being struck by lightning and assisting lost and injured animals along the road are just a few of the experiences that Brian Stark is logging in his journal as he tries to become the first person to walk the American Discovery Trail.

A transcontinental runner from Nashville, Ind., Stark arrived in Independence Thursday morning — 103 days after leaving Cape Henlopen, Del., and almost halfway to Point Reyes, Calif., at the far end of the 4,673-mile trail.

The 26-year-old runner says he is trying to be the first person to run the American Discovery Trail — the nation's only east-west transcontinental recreational trail. He also is promoting the American Hiking Society's national trails endowment that gives grants to local trail clubs to build and maintain local trails.

Stark will reach the halfway point of his transcontinental run

Brian Stark
. . . approaching half-way mark

in about 10 days "somewhere in Kansas." If there are no glitches, he will arrive in Point Reyes in early November.

Stark isn't a novice when it

Please see TRAIL, Page 7A

From Page 1A

comes to long distances. Three years ago he traversed the entire 2,150-mile Appalachian Trail from Maine to Georgia.

While trekking that rugged north-south trail would have been the ultimate challenge for most athletes, Stark was the exception. Wanting a greater challenge, he decided to tackle the American Discovery Trail.

The nine-year-old trail is "everything you can imagine — except interstates," he said during an interview Thursday afternoon.

"I have been on abandoned railroad beds, gravel roads, dirt roads, oil roads, through back yards, and I have traveled down streams, through farm fields, climbed over fences and walked along highways."

The trail is co-aligned with pre-existiting trails.

"When I am not on those trails," he explained, "I am on back roads that connect the trails together."

In St. Charles, Mo., Stark says he got on the Katy Trail and took it to Boonville, Mo. There he picked up the Santa Fe Trail, which brought him to Independence along U.S. 24.

With no one to talk to on his cross-country trek, Stark whiles away the hours computing mileage, writing songs, talking to cows and horses, and apologizing to all the dead animals.

"Two days ago, I came across a racoon that had been hit by a car — but was still alive. I gave him some water and pulled him off the road."

Wednesday, Stark did a good deed for a stray kitten. Picking up the lost animal along the highway, he carried it two miles to a farmhouse. There a "a woman identified the kitten as hers."

Traveling 20 to 35 miles a day, Stark packs lightly, with a nine-pound hip pack strapped around his trim waist. It contains a water bottle, camera, sleeping bag, longsleeve shirt, maps, a journal and a couple of snacks — but not a change of clothing. Every even-

ing, he rinses out the clothes he is wearing: a white T-shirt and black running shorts.

During the day, Stark's biggest concern is staying hydrated.

"I only carry a 20-ounce water bottle and when I run out of water, I go to the nearest house, knock on the door and ask for water."

During the evenings, finding somewhere to eat and a dry place to sleep is his biggest concern. However, he's never gone to bed hungry or wet.

"I usually find dry shelter somewhere," he said, recalling he has taken refuge in churches, barns, fire stations, abandoned schools, underneath a handicapped wheelchair ramp, as well as in an outhouse. He also has slept on picnic tables under shelter houses.

And it was under a shelter house in an open field that Stark experienced one of his biggest scares. During an electricial storm, lightning struck and split a nearby tree.

"I wondered if I was next," he said with a smile.

Before embarking on his trip, Stark purchased 12 pairs of shoes, leaving 11 pairs at home with his mother. Every 400 miles — or two weeks — Stark receives a new pair of shoes, along with film, maps and other personal items from his mother and friends.

The welcomed supplies and letters are sent to pre-selected post offices along the route.

"At my last post office, I got 13 letters and five big boxes of food," he said. "I couldn't even carry them."

Is there another transcontinential trip in Stark's plans?

The substitue schoolteacher and summer camp director, who took off eight months to make the trip, doesn't see such a trip on the horizon.

"There are other adventures to pursue," he said, noting he will be leaving the Kansas City area Monday for Council Grove, Kan., his next stopover.

Trail: He wants to be first to finish

Article and photograph reprinted courtesy of *The Examiner.*

TUESDAY
JULY 21, 1998

Chieftain photo by Chris McLean
Brian Stark during Pueblo stop: "People have been wonderful."

Runner makes stop in Pueblo (with a long way to go)

By DAVE MCKINSEY
The Pueblo Chieftain

He's on his fifth pair of shoes, traveled 2,000 miles and is on his way to the coast of California — on foot.

While not inspired by the movie "Forest Gump," Brian Stark, 26, is the first to run across the nation on the American Discovery Trail.

The route, created and designated by the American Hiking Society, begins in Cape Henlopen, Del., and follows the original trails blazed by settlers more than a century ago. One of Stark's hundreds of stops was in Pueblo on Monday.

Stark, an Indiana native and substitute teacher, said he was inspired to run the trail because he will be the first to ever do so.

He began on last March 8, and, he said, that at the pace of about 30 miles a day, he will reach the California Coast on Nov. 1.

Receiving no substantive financial support beyond his own means, the 6-foot, 170 pound runner is equipped only with a nine-pound bag, that contains supplies such as a sleeping bag, maps, camera and film, two water bottles, candy bars and a harmonica.

Stark is an experienced in long-distance running. He also has run the nation from top to bottom, from the Appalachians to Florida.

In his four months-plus afoot, Stark said, he has had no negative experiences but has been pleasantly surprised at the general kindness of people he has encountered.

"People have been wonderful. They have invited me in, fed me, done my laundry and given me money," Stark said, noting that he never asks for donations.

So far, a daily average of three cars a day stop to offer him a ride. Stark declines, of course, but said he is impressed with their generosity.

Stark said that he has found some interesting sleeping arrangements. He has slept in churches, barns, picnic tables and even an outhouse in West Virginia.

Because the American Discovery Trail follows those made by the early settlers, it is not "a straight shot, he said. Instead it crosses rivers, mud and "people's backyards."

While Stark faces several challenges along the trail, loneliness is not one of them.

Besides his encounters with several kind people, Stark's girlfriend — who lives in Arizona — occasionally drops by somewhere along the trail and Stark's mother insists that he call her every two days.

Food for the trip rarely varies: French toast for breakfast, cheese and crackers for lunch, and a dinner of salad and pasta.

Water, of course, is most important and Stark consumes two to three gallons daily.

When asked if he'd run the trail again, Stark laughed and said no. He said he probably will move closer to his girlfriend when his run is through.

In the future, he said, Stark anticipates writing a book about his experience. And he may someday hike across Europe.

Until then, Stark is simply looking forward to reaching Point Reyes on the California Coast where, he said, the first thing he will do is take a nap.

Lyons, KS
Mon July 6, '98

Business as unusual
Trail runner second guest

The Hotel Ly-Kan opened the second floor to overnight guests Friday night, and it was a full house. Owner and manager Shane Schneider said the second room was rented to coast to coast American Discovery Trail runner Brian Stark, who ran from McPherson to claim the room.

Schneider said he and his wife, Terri, had the room in reserve in case any problems arose, but when the runner came in hot and tired, they couldn't turn him down. (Story Page 5.)

It was a really good weekend," Schneider said. "People were pleased."

Guests from Washington state, Indiana and Wyoming registered. Some were here for a family reunion, others to visit.

The next project for the Schneiders, who reopened the hotel restaurant a year and a half ago, is to ready the third floor for occupancy.

Article and photograph reprinted courtesy of *The Pueblo Chieftain.*

Back Home Again

4,800-mile jaunt over for Stark

'Price Is Right' visit sidetrip for runner

By Leslie Saunders
The Republic

NASHVILLE — With his Oct. 31 finish in Point Reyes, Calif., Brian Stark became the first person to run the coast-to-coast American Discovery Trail, a trip of nearly 4,800 miles.

Stark, a 26-year-old Hanover graduate and a former Nashville substitute teacher, spent 238 days on the trail, passing through 12 states.

For the most part, Stark ran alone and tried to make 35 miles a day. His longest day was 48 miles.

To pass time, he said he often made up songs about sights he passed.

"Or I'd make up songs about the idiot who told me it was only going to be three miles to the next town when it was really 13," Stark said, laughing.

But for the most part, Stark's best memories are of the people he met.

"So many people were just openly friendly, without question," he said.

He received cash, rides into towns off the trail, and offers of places to stay.

Stark would offer to speak at schools he passed about his trip in exchange for use of their facilities and a place to sleep.

"I hope that I inspired kids to do some of the things they want to do," Stark said.

He contrasted these school visits by speaking with adults he met.

"Often they'd get this far-off look and say they'd always wished they'd done this or that," Stark said.

His best advice is to make time for these dreams, saying he quit five jobs to have the time for his run.

When Stark could, he left those he met with a goodwill gift. The idea for these gifts came from a book about a runner who stuck to highways and noticed how many good tools he passed.

"I always thought, 'Why would you just leave them?'" Stark said. So he collected items of value he found. Those he could not send home he gave away.

Besides the items he picked up along the way and would either mail or give away after one day's run, Stark tried to keep his gear light.

His 10-pound pack typically included a down sleeping bag, ground cloth, small flashlight, camera and tripod, 20-ounce water bottle, journal, maps, candy bars or cheese crackers, long-sleeved shirt, pair of tights and a light-weight wind-

Friday

THE REPUBLIC

November 13, 1998, Columbus, Indiana

For The Republic
Brian Stark runs along the Nevada stretch of U.S. 50, called the "Loneliest Highway in America" by Life Magazine.

Article and photograph reprinted courtesy of *The Republic*.

A run across America would be little more than a treadmill workout if it weren't for the people I encountered. Below is a list of some of those who helped make it a good journey. To you, I say thank you for taking part in the story. Success was also possible because no one beat me up along the way. To you, I also say thank you for *not* taking part in this story.

Thanks to:

America By Bicycle; American Discovery Trail Society; American Hiking Society; Appalachian Trail Conference; Friends of Arrow Rock, Missouri; Bruce & Beth Archibald; An Arizona State University Student on his way to Tempe; Bob Aurich; Bhaskar Banerji; Bob Barker and staff of *The Price is Right*; Bob Barrett; Frank & Roenna Bates; Avi Benjamini; Blenderhasset Hotel, Parkersburg, West Virginia; Vickie Binnie; Mike Blaney; Jim Boeger; Mike & Cathy Bovaird; Becky Boyer; Jim Brackett; Mayor Dick Bratton, Green Mountain Falls, Colorado; Robert Breunig & Karen Enyedy; Lydia Breunig; Bryan Brown; Boonville Chamber of Commerce; Buckeye Trail Association; Eunice Buening; Juanita Bushman; Candlewyck Inn, Keyser, West Virginia; Canyonlands National Park Service Rangers; Chesapeake & Ohio Canal National Historic Park; Club Lead, Leadville, Colorado; Colorado Trail Association; Columbus North Cross Country Team, Columbus, Indiana; Tim Cooney, Advantage One Color Lab, Columbus, Indiana; Jim Coplen; Cottage House, Council Grove, Kansas; Council Grove Republican; Sheldon Crook; Harry Cyphers; DHL Moab Route Driver; Paul Daniel, OH ADT State Coordinator; Todd & Jan Davis & Family; Davis West Virginia Nature Center; Jim Dougan; Tessa Drake; Coach Ron Drozd; Ted & Melissa Eden; Mike Engeman; Rick Ervin; Jean Esarey; Mike Esarey; Jose Fajardo; Muriel Farrell; John Fazel, CA ADT State Coordinator; Mike Felkins; Dan Ferguson; Fire Station of Lexington, Missouri; First Presbyterian Church of Columbus, Indiana; Marvin Fisher; Shirley & Stan Fite; Brian Fitzpatrick; Albert Flamm; Bill & Laurie Foot; Parker & Dania Foy; Greg & Doug at Gearheads Camping Supply, Moab, Utah; Kevin "KGB" Glenn; Nancy Goldsberry; Jim, Lou, & Caryn Gostlin; Andrew Bresnin & Andy Grace; Richard Gragg; Grand Mesa Lodge and Cabins; The Grove Family; Uri Grubbs; Frank Haight; Kathy Hearne & Family; Tom Heil; Butch Henley; Mayor Darwin Hindman, Columbia, Missouri; Fred & Delores Houston; C. Huckabay; Jim Ippolito; Alberta Johnson; Gary & Diane Johnson; Judy Jones; Jan Kennedy; Dave & Judy Kennedy; John Kevin B&B; David King; Jeanne Kline; Rick Langenberg; Noah Larson; Laura Levaas; Dennis Lierd; Lucky's Marina & RV in Hasty, Colorado; Lou's Country Store & Bakery; Reese Lukei Jr.; Krystyna & Stanley Lupinski; Marti, Mike & Nick Manthey; Victor Marshall; Mason Dixon Council Boy Scouts of

America; Beth Mathers & Family; Ronnie & Bev Mayle; Dave McKinsey; Jane Mengel; Bill & Kay Miller; Mineral Tribune Newspaper of Keyser, West Virginia, Carletta Misselhorn; Dan & Kenna Myers; David Myers; A Navajo Family; Sue Nawojski; Mike & Syd Nickels; North Bend State Park Lodge in Cairo, West Virginia; John & Marilee O'Dell; Osage City Baptist Temple; The Parsons House of Defiance, Missouri; Postmaster, Hendricks, West Virginia; Postmaster, North Bend, Ohio; Postmaster, Boonville, Indiana; Postmaster, Chester, Illinois; Postmaster, Council Grove, Kansas; Postmaster, Manitou Springs, Colorado; Postmaster, Hite, Utah; Postmaster, Sacramento, California; Troy Rarick & Rondo Buecheler; Rawleigh House Bed & Breakfast; Debra Ray; Andrea Renick-Bell & Adair Cabin State Historic Site of Osawotomie, Kansas; Harley & Evaline Rhodehamel; Steve Rider; Mrs. J. Kirby Risk; Walt Root; Runner's Roost Running Store in Denver, Colorado; Dale & Bonnie Ryan, NV ADT State Coordinator; Salem-Teichyo University; Saucony Hyde Athletic Company; Sue & Bob Sauer; Lu & Midge Schrader, WV ADT State Coordinator; Dr. Roger Sherman & friends; Jerry Siegel; Sally & Lloyd Simmons; Ken & Connie Simpson; Elsie Smith; Gordon & Carol Smith & Family; Connie & Mike Snyder; Kent Spellman; Craig & Heather Spinner; Rick Spelanka; Ricky Sprague; Chris & Ann Stark; Eric Stark & Jon Smith; Jim & Michele Stark; Marian Stark; Richard & Vicki Stark; Sherry Stark; Steedman's Only Bar, Steedman, Missouri; Bill Stoehr; T.H.E. Restaurant, Fort Ashby, West Virginia; Michael Terry & Dennis Lowe; Tiller & Toiler Newspaper, Larned, Kansas; Trails Illustrated; Michael Tobin; Dr. Stanley Totten; Doris Towne; Julie Turner; Una Pizza, Boonville, Indiana; The Unger Family; Cathy & Gary Vaal & Family; Doug Wasmuth; Dr. Dan & Nita Webster; Gwyn Hamilton & Robert Webster; Coach Rick Weinheimer; Wigwam Mills Sock Company; Mr. & Mrs. John Winkler; Doug Wright; Michelle Wycoff; and Tom & Barb Yokum, and all the other wavers, honkers, and smilers along the way.

About The Author

Brian Stark attributes his success as a distance runner to his parents who drove 300 miles away from a pit stop on a family vacation before they realized that he had gotten out of the van. Brian was nine years old. He started running after the van and hasn't stopped.

Since completing his 10,000th mile in high school, he has crossed 26 states on foot, including one solo-5000-mile trail run across America. With a fair amount of endurance, uncanny luck, and the assistance of hundreds of strangers, learn how America is really doing, from one who crossed its forgotten byways at six miles per hour.

Printed in the United States
85453LV00006B/4-6/A